The Smithsonian Guides to Natural America

NORTHERN NEW ENGLAND

WA
The
Pacific
Northwest
OR

MT
The
Northern
Rockies
ID
WY

ND
The
Northern
Plains
SD

NV
The
Far
West
CA

UT
The
Southern
Rockies
CO

NE

KS

AZ
The
Southwest
NM

OK

TX

HI

The
Pacific

AK

Northern
New England

Maine

Vermont · New Hampshire

The Mid-Atlantic States

NY

MA
CT RI

Southern
New
England

MN

WI

MI

The
Great
Lakes

IA

OH

PA

NJ
MD DE

The
Heartland

IL

IN

MO

WV

VA

The
Atlantic
Coast

Appalachia

KY

TN

NC

SC

The
South
Central
States

AR

MS

AL

GA

The
Southeast

LA

FL

NORTHERN NEW ENGLAND
VERMONT – NEW HAMPSHIRE
MAINE

THE SMITHSONIAN GUIDES TO NATURAL AMERICA

NORTHERN NEW ENGLAND

VERMONT, NEW HAMPSHIRE, AND MAINE

TEXT
W. D. Wetherell

PHOTOGRAPHY
Len Jenshel and Diane Cook

PREFACE
Thomas E. Lovejoy

SMITHSONIAN BOOKS • WASHINGTON, D.C.
RANDOM HOUSE • NEW YORK, N.Y.

Copyright © 1995 by Smithsonian Institution
Maps are by Allan Cartography. Raven Maps & Images bases are used by permission.
Cover design by Andy Carpenter
Permission credits to reproduce previously published photos appear on page 288.

Front cover: Little Niagara Falls, Baxter State Park, Maine
Half-title page: Moose cow feeding at Baxter State Park, Maine
Frontispiece: Mount Kearsarge summit, Winslow State Park, New Hampshire
Back cover: Coyote in heavy snow; maple tree in fall foliage; common loon on nest

Library of Congress Cataloging-in-Publication Data
Wetherell, W. D.
      The Smithsonian guides to natural America. Northern New England—
   Vermont, New Hampshire, and Maine/text by Walter David Wetherell;
   photography by Len Jenshel.
      p.   cm.
   Includes bibliographical references and index.
   ISBN 0-679-76153-5 (pbk.)
      1. Natural history—Vermont—Guidebooks. 2. Natural history—New
   Hampshire—Guidebooks. 3. Natural history—Maine—Guidebooks.
   4. Vermont—Guidebooks. 5. New Hampshire—Guidebooks. 6. Maine—
   Guidebooks. I. Jenshel, Len. II. Title.
   QH105.V7W48 1995   94-32174
   508.74—dc20   CIP

Manufactured in the United States of America
98765432

HOW TO USE THIS BOOK

The Smithsonian Guides to Natural America explore and celebrate the preserved and protected natural areas of this country that are open for the public to use and enjoy. From world-famous national parks to tiny local preserves, the places featured in these guides offer a splendid panoply of this nation's natural wonders.

Divided by state and region, this book offers suggested itineraries for travelers and briefly describes the high points of each preserve, refuge, park, or wilderness area along the way. Each site was chosen for a specific reason: Some are noted for their botanical, zoological, or geological significance, others simply for their exceptional scenic beauty.

Information pertaining to the area as a whole can be found in the introductory sections to the book and to each chapter. In addition, specialized maps at the beginning of the book and each chapter highlight an area's geography and geological features as well as pinpoint the specific locales that the author describes.

For quick reference, places of interest are set in **boldface** type; those set in **boldface** followed by the symbol ❖ are listed in the Site Guide at the back of the book. (This feature begins on page 263, just before the index.) Here noteworthy sites are listed alphabetically by state, and each entry provides practical information that visitors need: telephone numbers, mailing addresses, and specific services available.

Addresses and telephone numbers of national, state, and local agencies and organizations are also listed. Also in appendices are a glossary of pertinent scientific terms and designations used to describe natural areas; the author's recommendations for further reading (both nonfiction and fiction); and a list of sources that can aid travelers planning a guided visit.

The words and images of these guides are meant to help both the active naturalist and the armchair traveler to appreciate more fully the environmental diversity and natural splendor of this country. To ensure a successful visit, always contact a site in advance to obtain detailed maps, updated information on hours and fees, and current weather conditions. Many areas maintain a fragile ecological balance. Remember that their continued vitality depends in part on responsible visitors who tread the land lightly.

C O N T E N T S

PREFACE

Northern New England brings to most minds images of rocky coasts and the blazing kaleidoscope of autumnal forests, but to me, in my youth, it was the place where I had the first opportunity to explore a summer's worth of nature. The grandeur of New Hampshire's White Mountains was not lost on me, but here, too, was the chance to watch chattering red squirrels, to marvel at the splashes of silver paint on the wings of fritillary butterflies, to find the primitive plants called horsetails, to watch the blur and stop of testy ruby-throated hummingbirds, or to have patience rewarded by the sight of the pinwheel proboscis of the star-nosed mole as it emerged above ground.

Despite the advent of acid rain and its ill effects on red pines (first noted in Vermont) and many a lake, Maine, New Hampshire, and Vermont, the three states of northern New England, still offer a vibrant opportunity to explore natural America. They also present landscapes that speak of change. The grinding forces of nature molded much of these three states, leaving behind great boulders and scrapes and gouges on tough granite, as well as innumerable crystal lakes. Glaciers ground the region's jagged notches and precipitous cliffs, the "Great Stone Face," and other mountains of modest height but grand appearance.

The highest of these mountains, at 6,288 feet (1,917 meters), is named appropriately for George Washington. Whether ascended by the cog railway, by car, or on foot, Mount Washington is a commanding place—and one best visited in summer. There, on a cold

---

PRECEDING PAGES: *Near Vermont's Harriman Reservoir, the autumn sun illuminates a classic mix of gloriously colored northern hardwoods.*

spring day in 1934, the oldest mountaintop weather station in the country experienced the highest wind gust ever recorded on earth—an awesome 231 miles per hour (370 kilometers per hour).

The landscapes of northern New England speak of changes other than those wrought by ice. Here, colonial deforestation laid bare much of the land, but as better farmland was found to the west, much of northern New England's acreage was allowed to return to forest. As if taking to heart Robert Frost's "Something there is that doesn't love a wall," the forest has drawn on the seed bank in the soil and the fragments of forests that were left and has once again spread across the land. Today, anomalous stone walls course through woods instead of between farmers' fields.

The melting of the great glaciers raised the level of the sea, flooding river mouths and producing the 3,478 miles of rugged coastline we see today. The rocky coast brings back to me memories of the flat accent of a great uncle, "the Professor" (he taught at Maine's Bowdoin College), who lived well into his nineties without losing his characteristic Down East intonation. This is also Rachel Carson country, the inspiration for her *The Edge of the Sea*, which introduced America to tidal pools, periwinkles, and limpets, both through the printed page and on the silver screen. The seawater itself is ohmigod cold, but the sea life, from harbor seals to seabirds, is bounteous, and every tidal pool is a treasure chest of marine life.

The northeastern edge of natural America is also Wyeth country, where the mind's eye frames scenes reminiscent of Wyeth family paintings. Other artists, too, have found inspiration in this coast, including Childe Hassam and Winslow Homer. The haunting sound of the foghorn stays with one for a lifetime. No wonder the artists were attracted.

As one proceeds west to Vermont, the landscapes soften, culminating in impressive Lake Champlain. Here, Ethan Allen's Revolutionary War Green Mountain Boys mimicked the calls of wild turkeys and other animals to outwit the British. Today, almost all the species of those days can still be heard, but no sound

is more memorable than the cry of the loon on a summer evening. Such wonderful vignettes of nature have been preserved in great part through prescient private and public local action.

Two of the region's important features run north and south. The Connecticut River separates Vermont and New Hampshire before flowing through Massachusetts and Connecticut on its way to Long Island Sound. And in Maine the Appalachian Trail begins its ambitious meander southward toward Georgia. It is testimony to our affinity for and romance with natural America: How else can one explain the trail's creation just before it was too late?

Northern New England has only one national park, Acadia on Maine's coast. Although the White Mountain National Forest covers 11 percent of New Hampshire, most of the region's land is in private hands. Thus it is both remarkable and a grand challenge that so much forest remains, particularly in Maine. Here stands a veritable wilderness, vulnerable to economic pressure, valuable beyond the ability of the public purse to acquire.

It is incredibly important that we maintain this wilderness, for without it we can never comprehend the ways we have affected the land, and never, in much the same sense, fully comprehend the history of our nation. We now know that the first European colonists did not encounter pristine wilderness. The Native Americans were sophisticated in the manipulation of the land and its denizens. Nonetheless, the modern wilderness is similar enough to that first encountered by the Europeans that to lose it would be to lose our perspective forever.

—Thomas E. Lovejoy
Counselor to the Secretary for Biodiversity
and Environmental Affairs
SMITHSONIAN INSTITUTION

LEFT: *The largest body of freshwater in Maine, Moosehead Lake is surrounded by isolated mountain peaks and extensive bogs.*

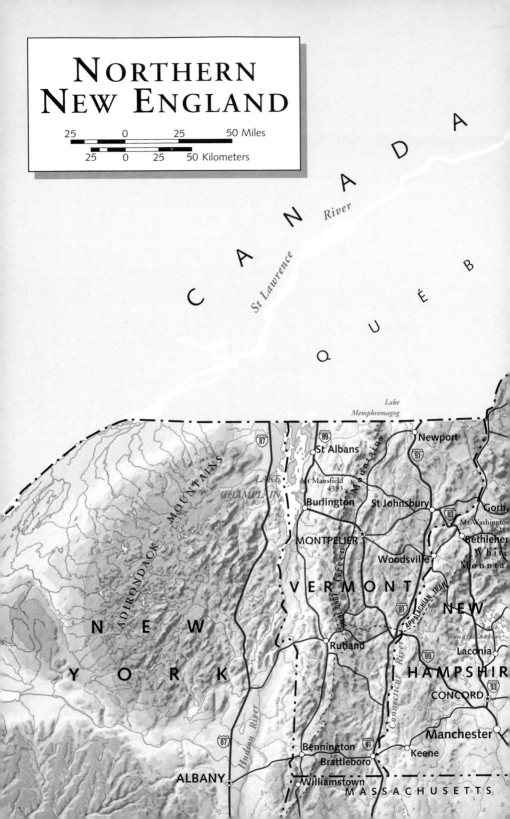

NORTHERN NEW ENGLAND

25   0   25   50 Miles

25   0   25   50 Kilometers

CANADA

C A N A D A

St Lawrence River

Q U É B

Lake Memphremagog

Newport

St Albans

Mt Mansfield 4393

Burlington

St Johnsbury

Gorh

Mt Washington 628

Bethlehem

White Mounta

MONTPELIER

Woodsville

VERMONT

NEW

Green Mountains

Long Trail

APPALACHIAN TRAIL

Lake Winnipesaukee

Rutland

Laconia

ADIRONDACK MOUNTAINS

LAKE CHAMPLAIN

N E W

Y O R K

Connecticut River

HAMPSHIR

CONCORD

Hudson River

Manchester

Bennington

Brattleboro

Keene

ALBANY

Williamstown

MASSACHUSETTS

INTRODUCTION

INTRODUCTION:
NORTHERN NEW ENGLAND

On a United States map, draw a line straight down through Lake Champlain, slant it over to the Massachusetts border near the little village of Pownal, Vermont, and then run it due east to the Atlantic. The area within the line is northern New England, the country's beautiful northeastern wedge. Roughly the size of Illinois, the land is mostly forested, its deep green canopy broken by lighter-colored pastures in the western portions. Hills distribute themselves fairly evenly over the region, bunching toward the center into mountains that curve northeastward like an irregular spine. Towns checker the landscape in the south but become fewer and farther apart to the north; in the east, forests, fields, and villages end abruptly in the brilliant blue of the ocean. Covering some 52,115 square miles, Vermont, New Hampshire, and Maine stubbornly pride themselves on their differences, yet display as much consanguinity in terrain and temperament as any other three states in the country.

Flying over northern New England in November, after the overarching green covering of leaves is gone but before the first snow, one sees mile after mile of dark, suturelike lines. They run every which way over the landscape, along the outskirts of towns and up across all but the highest hills, disappearing only in the far northwestern reaches of Maine. These are the stone walls built by settlers who cleared the land two centuries ago, their legacy still visible even though their fields have grown to woods and their labor has largely been forgotten. Like sutures, the rough walls bind the states together with historical and natural ties as strong and enduring as the hard granite hills that characterize this region.

Rugged Vermont, flinty New Hampshire, rockbound Maine: The states share a common history from their earliest occupation by Native Americans. The landscape, the winters, the rocky soil, and the Puritan inheritance of the first Europeans who settled here give the region a somewhat spartan image in the minds of casual visitors, who envision a beautiful area with a personality that is somewhat—how to say it?—icy

---

PRECEDING PAGES: *A sure-footed hiker climbs above Upper South Branch Pond in one of the many remote areas encompassed by heavily wooded Baxter State Park, part of New England's great northern forest.*

4

and aloof. And the picture is true enough: In March or April there cannot be many other places on earth as uniformly bleak.

But that image is only half the story in northern New England. Visitors arriving when the apple trees are in blossom, the wildflowers bright with color, the meadows waving in the lush green exuberance before the first haying could just as easily see it all as a pastoral Eden, a land of softness and ease. In this contrast between moods—the constant, almost bewildering fluctuation of light and dark, hard and soft, warm and cold—lies the key to appreciating northern New England on its own terms.

To understand this region's personality and its temporal and geographic contexts, one must start literally at its foundation—the bedrock. Some of the oldest rocks in New England date back more than a billion years. Most of these ancient mountains have eroded away, although worn nubs are still exposed here and there—Pico and Killington peaks, for example, in central Vermont. Over the eons eroded rock remnants—gravel, sand, and silt—from these mountains worked their way down to the coastal waters of an earlier Atlantic Ocean. There the sediments became part of new mountain ranges formed as slowly but inexorably the American, Eurasian, and African continental plates collided and the seafloor buckled, producing mountains, volcanoes, and earthquakes. The Taconic and Green mountains of Vermont date from this time, half a billion years ago, and particularly in the Champlain Valley, rocks still reveal evidence of their ancient marine lineage.

For the last 200 million years, the continents have continued to move away from each other, an inch or two per year. Northern New England now sits about 6,000 miles northwest of its former equatorial location next to Africa and Europe, and the Atlantic Ocean has filled the growing chasm in between. As the plates began to pull away from each other, a bit of Europe became attached to North America. This land mass is now the states of Maine and New Hampshire.

During this same geological period, active crustal movements in northern New England fractured already formed rock, allowing molten volcanic material to rise just below the surface. These igneous intrusions, varying from narrow ribbons to enormous plutons, eventually cooled and solidified. Some of the largest formed the famous granite deposits near Barre in central Vermont. Nearer the surface and younger (only 180 million years old) were the deposits that became the White Mountains of western Maine, New Hampshire, and northern Vermont,

which emerged as the softer rock around them wore away.

The combination of different crustal origin (Eurasian-African versus North American) and predominant rock type (igneous versus metamorphic) may well explain why, as many nongeologists have casually observed, New Hampshire and Maine appear different from Vermont in some undefinable way. The massive mountain building caused by the collision of continents over unfathomable stretches of time has also left an indelible north-south imprint upon the land, an ancient orientation that has profoundly influenced all that followed: the mile-thick glaciers that crept down from the north, the climates of different epochs, the plants and animals that flourished here, and the lives of the peoples who have inhabited northern New England for more than 10,000 years.

At least four times within the past two to three million years—in geologic terms, the Pleistocene epoch—massive ice sheets, responding to significant climate changes, descended upon and then retreated from North America. Their weight and movement reshaped the land. The most recent episode, called the Wisconsin glaciation, occurred between 20,000 and 10,000 years ago. Covering even the highest peaks, a deep sea of ice obliterated in its coming and going, its grinding and melting, virtually all evidence of previous glaciers and left behind many distinctive features clearly visible today.

At its maximum reach some 20,000 years ago, the Laurentian ice sheet formed a huge swath from the Arctic south to present-day New York City and west to the Rocky Mountains. In New England, the glacier bulldozed the land as it advanced, scouring the bedrock and carrying away great quantities of material, from giant boulders to fine sand and silt. The tremendous weight of the ice, which was between one and two miles thick, crushed the land below it, compressing it by as much as 700 feet. Inching its way over mountains, the ice smoothed north-facing slopes and summits but plucked rocks from leeward slopes, leaving them steep and jagged. Like a giant rasp, the ice rounded the sides and excavated the depths of river valleys and lake basins.

After about 2,000 years, the climate slowly warmed and the glacier began to retreat, leaving huge mounds of rubble as visible testament to

LEFT: *Among dense stands of gray birch and striped and sugar maple, huge Ice Age boulders known as glacial erratics dot the forest floor on the Mount Pisgah Trail near Vermont's Lake Willoughby.*

its farthest southern reach. These so-called terminal moraines are most visible as the arc of islands sweeping southwest from Cape Cod to New York: Nantucket, Martha's Vineyard, Block Island, and Long Island. By 13,000 years ago, ice remained only in northern Maine and on the northern borders of New Hampshire and Vermont. Water pouring in torrents and braided sheets from the melting glacier covered the landscape with lakes, ponds, and rivers of all configurations. Lake Vermont, a larger predecessor of modern Lake Champlain, lapped at the foothills of the Green Mountains, its exit to the Saint Lawrence and the ocean beyond blocked by the wall of ice.

While vast volumes of melting glacial water swelled seas worldwide, the land too started rebounding as the pressures of glacial ice disappeared. Thus began a seesawing process, with the land rebounding and the oceans rising at differing rates. By about 7,000 years ago, seas had reached modern-day levels. In Maine the incursive sea inundated eastern portions of major river valleys—such as the Penobscot, Sheepscot, Androscoggin, and Kennebec—and created the intricate series of long, narrow embayments that characterize the coastline today. In northern Vermont, the ice retreated, opening the Saint Lawrence and allowing the rising Atlantic to extend a shallow saltwater arm into Lake Vermont. Eventually the rebounding land barred the invading sea. As the marine environment slowly changed back to freshwater, modern Lake Champlain was born.

Today the distinctive landscape of northern New England—hills and forests that divide the sky into intimate patches and bowl-shaped openings—is its Ice Age legacy. The roughly smoothed peaks and U-shaped valleys, bowl-shaped gulfs and broad, cradling river valleys, rock-infested soil (the bane of every farmer) and ubiquitous lakes, ponds, bogs, and wetlands are all ancient creations. Nearly everywhere, the horizon appears close, usually curved and scalloped into interesting lines. Nowhere else, it seems, is there such a splendid, ever-changing mix, the hills swelling now this way, now that, rolling like a sideways S here, an upside-down U there, sharpening into inverted Vs for variety's sake. Even in flatter areas, mountains impose definite bounds. In Vermont's Champlain Valley, for example, the Adirondacks flank the horizon on one side, the Green Mountains on the other. On the Maine coast, where by right the ocean vista should stretch forever, the view is often broken by a neighboring headland jutting out to sea or a lumpy offshore island. A horizon so intimate and close poses the danger of parochialism—the temptation to think one's own small valley is the center of the world. But

ABOVE: *Early European settlers, like the horseman in Thomas Cole's romantic* Notch of the White Mountains (1839), *cleared vast tracts of virgin New England forest. Today much of the land they worked is forest again.*

this limited horizon can also focus the vision so deeply inward that even a delicate wildflower or small salamander is treasured, imbued with a significance that might be lost in a vaster place.

If hills are half of this region's story, then water is certainly the other half. Visitors from more arid regions quickly learn the source of all this greenery. Toward the top of nearly every hill or mountain is a pond; down the side of each hill flows a stream; along the bottom of each valley flows a river; the rivers swerve in and out of lakes; the lakes end only at the sea. Maine alone has more than 6,000 lakes and 5,000 miles of rivers; its coast, when all the wiggles are straightened out, is more than 3,000 miles long.

Just as the rivers flow one into another, smaller into larger to the sea,

OVERLEAF: *The last light lingers along the far shore of Lees Mill Pond in Moltenborough, New Hampshire. Formed during the Ice Age about 10,000 years ago, many New England lakes were filled by glacial meltwater.*

9

so the flow of time is an underlying current binding the region's history and landscape together so tightly that it is impossible to discuss one without the other. Into the terrestrial and aquatic places vacated by the waning and disappearance of the Laurentian ice sheet, for instance, soon came invaders—plants, animals, and people.

Earliest to colonize the tundralike landscape left by the retreating glacier were hardy species of willows, sedges, and mosses, as well as animals that could survive in arctic conditions: caribou, elk, wolves, even the extinct mammoth (whose bones were discovered in 1848 in western Vermont). During this period northern New England's earliest people migrated from the south and west. Called Paleo-Indians by archaeologists, they were hunter-gatherers who followed the big-game herds.

Over the next 6,000 years the climate warmed and the tundra was largely displaced by forest, which gradually assumed its present appearance, predominantly a mixture of softwoods (spruce, fir, white pine, eastern hemlock) and northern hardwoods (sugar maple, yellow birch, beech). During a short interval of climate warming, trees of more southerly origin moved in—oaks, hickories, American chestnuts, tulip poplars, and black gums. Today some of these species survive as oddities in the mildest, most protected coastal stretches and in the Lake Champlain and Connecticut River valleys. The tundra now sits atop only the highest peaks like Katahdin in Maine, New Hampshire's Presidential Range, and Mount Mansfield and Camels Hump in Vermont.

Through centuries of prehistory the Native Americans gradually shifted away from territorial hunting and gathering toward settlements and social orders. During the so-called Woodland Period, the native peoples divided more distinctly into five regional language groups; the Eastern Algonquian dominated the northern New England region.

The land that welcomed the first white explorers and trappers in the early 1600s, although rich and beautiful in its natural splendor, must have been somewhat daunting in its untamed landscapes, deep forests, and trackless mountains. Within this huge and unbroken wilderness lived trees hundreds of years old and animals that still illuminate our legends: mountain lions, timber wolves, wolverines, even caribou and elk. Passenger pigeons, now extinct, were once the most abundant bird species on earth, and their flocks saturated the woods and sky. One early ornithologist described a migration, estimated in the billions of birds, that was a mile wide and 240 miles long. Bald eagles nested along the coasts and countless lakes; wild turkeys grew fat on acorns and chestnuts. And the indigenous peoples lived in basic harmony with their environment, if not always with one another.

The appearance of the land soon changed. Forests fell in waves to the axes of European settlers who needed land to use for crops and pastures, wood to burn for warmth, sun to light shaded recesses, and open spaces to provide a margin of safety from wild animals and native peoples. Big trees were cut indiscriminately for ships' masts and lumber and later for the vast quantities of hardwoods needed to stoke railroad steam engines. Within 150 years sections of the northern lands went from virtually 100 percent forest to almost none. Today's residents are shocked to discover in 1840s and 1850s daguerreotypes that fields, walls, and houses extended far up the mountainsides and barren landscapes, appearing where they now see only forests.

Beginning about the middle of the nineteenth century, the population began to drain from northern New England, drawn by the lure of free western homesteads and deep, rich prairie soils. Men who marched off to Civil War battlefields never returned; women moved on to higher-paying industrial jobs in the burgeoning cities. On scores of abandoned farms, shrubs and tree seedlings grew thick in fallow fields, and soon new forests replaced hard-won open land.

As the century wore on, large-scale timber operations moved into the vast northern coniferous forests—some 26 million acres across three states—harvesting huge quantities of spruce and pine. During spring log drives such major rivers as the Connecticut, Piscataqua, Kennebec, and Penobscot were clogged from bank to bank for miles as logs floated to mills downstream. Within 50 years the wild north woods, once seemingly so limitless that they swallowed all traces of human activity, went from wilderness to logged-over land, a vivid testimonial to how quickly and pervasively humans can alter a landscape, even with primitive hand tools. By the turn of the century, almost all the big trees were gone. Today woodlands again blanket the region, seemingly similar in composition, acreage, and outward appearance to those that flourished four centuries ago. In fact, only tiny pockets, preserved as old-growth natural areas, of the once-magnificent ancient woodlands have survived.

One of the many ironies of this land is that large parts of it once contained more people than they do today. Southwest of Stratton Mountain, in the near wilderness of Grout Job, Vermont—once a thriving community but now known only to hikers on the Long Trail or an occasional adventurous motorist—stands a monument commemorating the spot where Daniel Webster addressed a crowd said to number

ABOVE: *A harsh environment for all but the hardiest species, the rocky coast of Maine does support thriving clumps of intensely fragrant rugosa roses, which have naturalized freely along the shore.*

15,000 in the presidential campaign of 1840. Hikers find the sense of *temps perdu* almost tangible when they discover telltale signs of the land's earlier settlers: the apple tree, ancient and gnarled, its limbs unpruned for more than a century; the old lilac, hardly more than a black stump now, but once someone's brave attempt at ornamentation; the cellar hole with its neat stonework deep in the underbrush, an ancient birch growing out of its center.

By the beginning of the twentieth century rural New England was considered a backwater, and jokes about its inbreeding and primitiveness abounded. This is the land Robert Frost described—the fields reverting to forest; the people clinging to life in increasing isolation and stubbornly refusing to give up. The farmers who stayed worked out a rough-and-ready symbiosis with the land, and the mix of open pasture and shaded woodland that they created has become the quintessential New England landscape. The classic village with its neat church, small white school, and weathered houses around a central common remained the model of habitation—one of the few areas where humanity's creations have enhanced the beauty of the landscape rather than spoiled it.

The attractions of the White Mountains had already been discovered by the 1840s, and for much of that century they remained one of America's most popular holiday destinations. With the introduction of the paid vacation and the first automobiles, northern New England became a favorite vacation spot for the urban Northeast. It remains so today, when its stock of clear air, undeveloped land, and unpolluted water has become literally priceless. Through a mix of isolation, luck, and design, northern New England retains the unspoiled landscape that so much of America has lost.

At least in the north, logging, farming, and tourism remain the land-use trinity around which the environment revolves, a difficult balancing act between what the land can provide and what humankind demands of it. Recreational pressure, suburban sprawl, second-home and condominium development, subdivision into ever-smaller parcels, boom-and-bust economic cycles, damage caused by acid rain, and the decline of the dairy farm are all problems. On the other hand, more and more people are beginning to recognize that only extraordinary measures will preserve what remains, and efforts have accelerated to protect land through the purchase of development rights, private easements, and land trusts.

Conservationists' concern now centers on the intense debate surrounding the future of the northern forest of Maine, New Hampshire, Vermont, and New York. This predominantly coniferous forest, nearly continuous for tens of millions of acres, has been largely owned by the timber industry for a century and a half. Even with logging, the area is the nearest thing to wild lands left in the heavily populated Northeast. Its integrity, however, is no longer assured. Global economic pressures are impinging on the forest industry, as are the skyrocketing costs of forest management and increasing demands on forest resources. In 1988 one timber company was forced to sell millions of acres, an event that served as a wake-up call for many environmentalists. A blue-ribbon panel, the Northern Forest Lands Council, was established in 1990 to study the situation. In early 1994, the council recommended that states change the way forest properties are taxed to encourage owners to keep control of large tracts of land, rather than forcing them to sell small parcels to developers. Although it concluded that individual states should try to acquire particularly valuable areas and protect species in the forest, it did not recommend the establishment of extensive natural preserves or profound changes in forestry practices. In the end, the council's conclusion, that long-term economic pressures threaten "to damage both the forest and

the people who live there," surprised no one.
The themes of landscape and land use that link the three states of northern New England also display distinct variations. Vermont is the most pastoral, with more of its land given over to dairy farming and the checkerboard pattern of field and forest. Its mountains, the Greens, where only five peaks top 4,000 feet, are relatively low compared with those of Maine and New Hampshire. ("The Vermont mountains stretch extended straight," Frost wrote; "New Hampshire mountains curl up in a coil.") New Hampshire, its neighbor and near twin in total area, is distinctly different in atmosphere. It has fewer farms, higher mountains, and in the crowded southeastern third, northern New England's closest approximation to megalopolis. Maine differs from both, not only in its vastness (its 33,215 square miles comprise just under half of *all* New England), but also in its wealth of wild land (more than either Vermont or New Hampshire) and in its seascape, with a history and environment all its own.

It would be hard to pack a wider variety of flora and fauna, landform and seascape, into an area this size. The region includes the exposed remains of an ancient coral reef on Lake Champlain; alpine flowers more common in Labrador than New Hampshire; beech-hickory forests that seem transplanted from Pennsylvania; islands as thick with breeding waterfowl as those in the Canadian maritime provinces; moose so common in some areas that viewing them has become a favorite after-dinner pastime; huge, virtually unexplored bogs; and potato fields and blueberry barrens that extend for miles in a region of otherwise small farms. The infamous variety of weather, from hurricanes to blizzards, combines with seasonal changes of color—the gold of autumn, the white of winter, the rainbow hues of spring, the exuberant green of summer—to stage an ever-changing spectacle that delights visitor and longtime resident alike.

Variety is the theme of the sites listed in this guide. Almost all display examples of regionwide characteristics, as well as some variation that makes a special visit worthwhile. A flower found nowhere else, a last stand of virgin pine, a nesting osprey visible through binoculars, a boulder of world-class dimensions—to those interested in the natural world and its miracles, northern New England offers singular treasures.

RIGHT: *Low tide reveals periwinkles, rockweed, and a variety of intertidal species at Rachel Carson Salt Pond Preserve in New Harbor, Maine. The author researched her 1955 book* The Edge of the Sea *here.*

VERMONT

WESTERN VERMONT:
THE CHAMPLAIN VALLEY
AND THE TACONICS

T he only New England state without a seacoast, Vermont received a remarkable consolation prize in Lake Champlain. Running 109 miles along the state's western border with New York, the lake is the largest body of fresh water in the United States outside the Great Lakes. Its valley is like no other spot in New England. Offering expansive views toward flanking mountains, rivers that meander rather than rush, a climate that is relatively clement compared with weather elsewhere in the state, billowy clouds that seem to take up half the sky, and the sparkling, ever changing surface of the lake in all its moods, this is pastoral Vermont at its best. Caught on the right summer day, the valley deserves the adjective *lush*.

Champlain is not just any lake. It's shaped like a skinny Y, the long upright strokes branching apart at Grand Isle, North Hero, Isle La Motte, and the other northern islands. Beyond, the lake's western arm narrows and drains north into the Richelieu River, then to the Saint Lawrence and the ocean; the eastern arm, the "inland sea," ends in the marshy expanse of Missisquoi Bay, which bulges into Canada. Never broader than 11 miles (just above Burlington), the lake is often much narrower, and south of the bridge to Crown Point, New York, it's sel-

PRECEDING PAGES: *Gifford Woods State Park protects sugar maples more than 300 years old, one of the few virgin forest stands extant in Vermont.*
LEFT: *A cottonwood frames a vista of Lake Champlain near Sand Bar State Park; outcrops here may be fossils of the world's oldest coral reef.*

dom wider than a good-sized river. Although narrow, Champlain is deep—390 feet deep off Split Rock Point. At the southern end, the lake runs into the Lake Champlain Barge Canal, which connects it with the Hudson River and ultimately New York City.

Lake Champlain is a natural corridor along which much history has passed. The scores of prehistoric Native American sites that dot the surrounding lowlands testify to the central role the lake and its wildlife played in the lives of early human inhabitants. It served as a border between the Algonquin and Iroquois nations prior to Samuel de Champlain's exploration of the lake in 1609. During the eighteenth century's French and Indian Wars, it was the easiest path between French Quebec and the English colonies; later it became the vital line dividing New England from the rest of the original states, a line the British in Canada tried desperately to sever. For all its present tranquillity, the Champlain Valley has seen more turmoil and bloodshed than any other area in Vermont, New Hampshire, or Maine: naval battles at Valcour Island and Plattsburgh, New York, clashes at Ticonderoga, Bennington, and Castleton—even a famous raid by Confederate irregulars on little Saint Albans in 1864!

Geologists believe that the lake originated in early Paleozoic times, between 375 and 335 million years ago. During this period the land experienced various kinds of faulting and thrusting, cracking into huge blocks that then heaved themselves on top of one another along the eastern edge of the Adirondacks (which, at nearly 4.5 billion years old, are among the oldest mountains on earth). The Champlain basin formed as these long, massive blocks dropped down between the Adirondacks to the west and the Green Mountains to the east, creating a trough for a freshwater inland sea.

Today Lake Champlain covers 440 square miles, and its drainage basin some 8,000 square miles. From ancient faulting and glaciation, the western (New York) side of the lake is steeper and rockier than the Vermont lowlands, which rise gradually to the east toward the foothills of the Green Mountains. The lowlands formed the bottom of a postglacial lake and then sea some 10,000 years ago. In the nineteenth century, the fossilized bones of a whale were discovered near Charlotte, suggesting that the area had been submerged. Such plants with maritime connections as false heather and beach pea still grow in

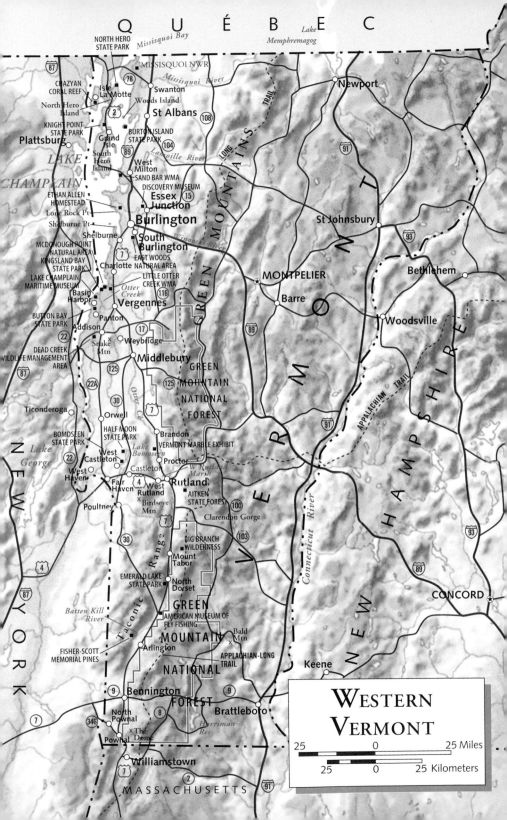

Q U É B E C

NORTH HERO
STATE PARK
Missisquoi Bay

Lake
Memphremagog

MISSISQUOI NWR
Missisquoi River

87

78
Swanton
Woods Island

Newport

CRAZYAN
CORAL REEF
Isle
La Motte

St Albans

108

North Hero
Island
2

91

KNIGHT POINT
STATE PARK
Grand
Isle
89

BURTON ISLAND
STATE PARK

104

Plattsburg

South
Hero
Island

West
Milton
SAND BAR WMA

St Johnsbury

LAKE

DISCOVERY MUSEUM

93

CHAMPLAIN

ETHAN ALLEN
HOMESTEAD

Essex
Junction

15

Lone Rock Pt
Shelburne Pt

Burlington

Bethlehem

Shelburne

South
Burlington

MCDONOUGH POINT
NATURAL AREA
KINGSLAND BAY
STATE PARK

7

Winooski River

EAST WOODS
NATURAL AREA

MONTPELIER

Woodsville

Charlotte

Barre

LITTLE OTTER
CREEK WMA

116

LAKE CHAMPLAIN
MARITIME MUSEUM

Otter
Creek

Basin
Harbor

Vergennes

89

BUTTON BAY
STATE PARK

Panton

22

Addison

17

Weybridge

DEAD CREEK
WILDLIFE MANAGEMENT
AREA

Snake
Mtn

87

Middlebury

125

GREEN

22A

MOUNTAIN

Ticonderoga

30

NATIONAL

7

Orwell

FOREST

125

Lake
George

HALF MOON
STATE PARK

BOMOSEEN
STATE PARK

Brandon

22

West
Castleton

Lake
Bomoseen

VERMONT MARBLE EXHIBIT

West
Haven

Castleton

Proctor

100

Fair
Haven

4

W Rutland
Marsh

Rutland

West
Rutland

AITKEN
STATE FOREST

Poultney

Birdseye
Mtn

Clarendon Gorge

103

30

7

BIG BRANCH
WILDERNESS

Mount
Tabor

EMERALD LAKE
STATE PARK

North
Dorset

89

GREEN

4

Batten Kill
River

AMERICAN MUSEUM OF
FLY FISHING

MOUNTAIN

CONCORD

87

FISHER-SCOTT
MEMORIAL PINES

Arlington

Bald
Mtn

APPALACHIAN-LONG
TRAIL

NATIONAL

Keene

7

9

FOREST

9

Bennington

346

North
Pownal

8

Brattleboro

Herriman
Res

7

The
Dome

Pownal

Williamstown

7

2

91

M A S S A C H U S E T T S

LONG
TRAIL

GREEN
MOUNTAINS

VERMONT

APPALACHIAN
TRAIL

NEW
HAMPSHIRE

Connecticut River

NEW
YORK

Taconic
Range

25   0   25 Miles

25   0   25 Kilometers

ABOVE: *Not great fliers, wild turkeys often turn tail and run to avoid danger, letting out a* put-put! *as a distress call. The well-known gobble is limited to the male, while the females, seen above, typically cluck.*

isolated colonies along the lake, evidence of the region's ancient oceanic heritage. Its flanking mountain ranges give the valley a slightly milder climate than surrounding areas, and abundant limestone in the soil supports flora and fauna different from those in eastern Vermont, as well as species, such as the black gum tree, that are rarely seen in northern New England.

Among the unlikely wildlife found in this valley are the wild turkeys that thrive in the oak-hickory forest of the state's southwestern corner and the unusual fish that can still be found in Lake Champlain—the "living fossils" belonging to lines that are extinct elsewhere. These include the bowfin, the ling, the sheepshead, the long-nose gar (which looks like a cross between a swordfish and a pickerel), and the lake sturgeon. This giant bottom feeder (specimens of 150 pounds have been caught) must move upstream in larger rivers to spawn. For many decades dams have blocked the way and the lake sturgeon, barred from its breeding grounds, is now listed as an endangered species in Vermont.

The waters of Lake Champlain are home to an amazing variety of fish, which interest anglers, scientists, and naturalists alike. Some species love the deep, cold waters of the main part of the lake; others prefer the shallower, warmer inshore waters. Of the cold-water species, the landlocked salmon is probably most prized as a game fish. Nearer shore, often associated with marshes, are such warm-water representatives as largemouth bass, pike, pickerel, and yellow perch

Vermont's gentle lakeside terrain, through which so many rivers meander into the lake, offers an impressive array of wetlands. Some 100,000 acres of biologically rich marshes and swamps, about half of the state's total wetland area, occupy the quiet interfaces between land and water, lake and river, attracting an abundance of waterfowl. Marshes are among the richest ecosystems in the world, and those at Lake Champlain feature a variety of herbaceous, grassy plants—wild rice, pickerelweed, arrowheads (whose nutritious, fleshy tubers are a favorite food of muskrats and ducks), bur reed, cattails, sedges, and rushes—that nourish and protect nesting waterfowl. Most abundant are ring-billed gulls, relative newcomers (first appearing in the 1940s) whose numbers have ballooned to more than 15,000. Although feeding mostly inland on just about anything (landfills, newly plowed fields) they compete for nesting space—and often battle—with rare common terns (listed as endangered), black-crowned night herons, and a few other species.

The Champlain marshes form a major branch of the Atlantic Flyway. As they make their way to and from the vast tundra breeding grounds in the Arctic, migrating birds seem to favor the Vermont side of the lake, where the terrain is flatter and the marshes more extensive than on the steep-walled New York shore. While most birds migrate through, many species stay to breed, nest, and raise their young. In the open water are diving varieties such as buffleheads, goldeneyes, and ring-necked ducks; more ocean-oriented species (old-squaws, scoters) visit occasionally. In the cover of wetlands, protected inshore waters, and adjacent fields are the surface feeders—mallards, black ducks, blue- and green-winged teal, wood ducks, Canada and snow geese, and many others.

Kayaking or canoeing these calm waters makes an ideal outing for

OVERLEAF: *Fireweed blooms along Equinox Skyline Drive near Manchester. The Taconics' well-rounded silhouettes reveal their age; the mountains have been eroded and molded by glaciers for some 400 million years.*

the casual explorer or serious birder. One of the more captivating sights is the muskrat lodges constructed of cattails. Muskrats actually build two lodges, one for feeding and a larger one for raising their young. Interestingly, once the muskrats abandon the lodges, their arch enemies, the minks, often take possession. Amphibians also throng the marsh—in spring, the "quack" of the wood frog and the chorus of peepers (tree frogs) can be deafening.

The southern part of western Vermont differs from the northern part in significant ways. The Champlain Valley proper, to stick to local terminology, runs north from Brandon some 100 miles to the Canadian border and averages about 20 miles wide. South of Brandon to the Massachusetts border (roughly 75 miles) is an extension known as the Valley of Vermont (although the name is rarely used in common parlance). Sometimes less than a mile wide, the plain in this region is framed by the Taconic Range to the west and the Greens to the east.

The Taconics are a lesser-known chain of mountains that follow the New York–Vermont border for almost 80 miles, from Brandon south to Pownal, and then continue along the New York–Massachusetts line. Fairly steep-sided and irregularly shaped, this low string of tree-covered mountains was formed some 440 million years ago. Today the tallest, beautiful Equinox near Manchester, is 3,816 feet above sea level. The bedrock of the Taconics is older than and different from that of the Greens. Formed from ancient seafloor sediments, Taconic rocks include limestone, marble (its metamorphic derivative), and slate. All have been quarried extensively. Indeed, deposits in the West Rutland–Proctor area contain some of the highest-quality marble in the United States, and its stone appears in many public buildings in Washington, D.C., and elsewhere. Historically, the valley has also been the scene of numerous mining operations. The large china-clay (or kaolin) deposits near Bennington, for instance, produced Bennington's famous stoneware pottery.

Because limestone and marble have such high calcium-carbonate content (from the shells of prehistoric sea creatures), rocks in this region dissolve comparatively quickly in water. Consequently, the moun-

---

RIGHT: *Although they die back in the fall, in spring and summer water lilies populate Vermont's slow-moving streams and the edges of still lakes, such as this quiet pond in Emerald Lake State Park.*

tains are honeycombed with caves and countless clear springs, which work their way through cracks and crevices and then bubble to the surface. The calcium thus freed sweetens the soil and supports an unusually diverse array of wetland plants. The relatively milder climate fosters still greater diversity: Hill forests sustain chestnut oak, flowering dogwood, mountain laurel, and mayapple, all unusual in Vermont and more common to the west and south.

Although western Vermont attracts throngs of summer visitors, it is easy to find peace and space, particularly in late fall or early spring. The relatively mild weather makes the summer and autumn seem longer than in higher, colder areas. The wildlife management areas and marshes open to the public never seem crowded, even at the height of summer, providing solitude and tranquillity only a short distance from the road.

In this chapter we begin at the narrow base of the Valley of Vermont on the Massachusetts border and proceed north, often on Route 7 or back roads that parallel it, to the Canadian border. Along the way the itinerary frequently jogs west to visit the lowlands, shoreline, and islands of Lake Champlain. Those venturing out onto the lake are advised not to take it for granted. Sudden gale-force winds are notorious, and operators of small boats must exercise caution. Still, the lake is at its most

ABOVE: *The diurnal woodchuck builds a heavy layer of fat that helps to sustain it through winter hibernation, when its heartbeat drops from 100 to just 4 beats per minute.*

LEFT: *Known for its trout, the boulder-strewn Big Branch Creek rushes through a wilderness area of the Green Mountain National Forest.*

majestic during a northwest gale—at least from a distance! As comber after comber sweeps down from Canada, the water becomes a long, slanting gallery of sunlight, whitecaps, and spray.

THE TACONICS AND THE SOUTH

Thanks to the state-straddling Taconic Mountains on the west, there

ABOVE: *Once prized for its medicinal qualities, the fall-blooming fringed gentian is now rare and should not be gathered.* **RIGHT:** *At Bald Mountain Natural Area in Aitken State Forest, purple loosestrife, reed canary grass, and wild parsnip (with its edible root) bloom in a sunlit clearing.*

is no jarring shift in scenery as one crosses from northwestern Massachusetts into southwestern Vermont: The hilly, meadow-dotted landscape simply continues. From Route 7, the main north-south road in the Valley of Vermont, views of the Taconics are wonderfully panoramic. Although no single hiking trail traverses the entire Taconic ridgeline in Vermont, many of the peaks are accessible by local back roads and foot trails.

A trail up the aptly named mountain **The Dome❖** is reached by taking White Oak Road in Williamstown, Massachusetts; the trailhead is about a third of a mile north of the state line in Pownal, Vermont. The shape represents an overturned anticline, or arch, of stratified quartzite rock, and the exposed summit provides a striking vista of this part of the state. A longer hiking route, the **Taconic Crest Trail,** edges north along the ridges of the Taconics, whose plunging gorges and steep valleys make them appear dramatically high, and south into the Berkshires of Massachusetts. The trailhead is accessible from the Hoosic River bridge on Route 346 in North Pownal.

Anyone seeking spectacular mountain views without hiking can drive

up **Equinox Skyline Drive** (off Route 7A between Arlington and Manchester), a five-mile toll road up the most impressive of the Taconic peaks, Equinox, the highest mountain in Vermont outside the Green Mountains. Below is the sweeping landscape of southern Vermont, and marching off in the distance are ranks of mountain ranges—the Berkshires to the south, the Adirondacks to the west, the Greens to the east. Skinner Hollow, on the mountain's eastern flank, lends a certain drama to the entire Manchester-area landscape and is an excellent example of a cirque, a steep-walled, bowl-shaped depression carved by a local valley-confined glacier after the main ice sheet retreated.

Through Arlington flows the world-renowned **Batten Kill River❖**, one of the shrines of American trout fishing and as beautiful and clear a stream as the state contains. (The **American Museum of Fly Fishing❖** in Manchester has displays on the sport's history.) West off Route 7A two miles north of Arlington is the 13-acre tract of the **Fisher-Scott Memorial Pines❖,** a national natural landmark, a designated Vermont natural area, and the home of some of the largest white pines in Vermont, measuring up to 40 inches in diameter and 120 feet tall.

Farther down the ravine are some enormous hemlocks. The tract is named in part for Dorothy Canfield Fisher, the novelist who once made this village her home and often wrote about the region. The group of nearly 200-year-old pines is a rare remnant of the old subclimax forest that covered this part of New England before settlers cleared the land. On a windy day, their tossing top branches color the sky with fluid strokes of green.

Emerald Lake State Park❖ on Route 7 in North Dorset occupies a quietly impressive spot: At this point the Valley of Vermont is only a few hundred yards wide, framed by the Taconics rising sharply on the west, the Green Mountains on the east. Otter Creek, the longest river entirely within the state, originates not far south of the park, creating a series of interesting wetlands on the southern end of Emerald Lake. In the park, five miles of interconnecting marked trails lead hikers through some gorgeous forest land. A small (four-acre) but impressive old-growth stand includes white ash, hemlock, bitternut hickory, and other species. The lake, typical of those formed by deposition of glacial till and damming, is fairly shallow, with a sandy bottom and heavily vegetated edges.

Many side roads branch off Route 7, the main highway up Vermont's west side, into the nearby mountains. One of the most scenic drives is east up U.S. Forest Road 10, which begins in the little village of Mount Tabor. The rushing stream on the left is the Big Branch, which soon leaves the road and cuts through a deep gorge full of huge boulders; in the pockets between the boulders, it is said, live some of the wildest, prettiest rainbow trout in Vermont. The **Big Branch Wilderness**—an area forever without roads, motorized equipment, or human development—is one of six wilderness areas (with a combined total of nearly 60,000 acres) in the **Green Mountain National Forest❖**. A hiking trail cuts down from the picnic area to the river.

On Route 30 north of Route 4, at the northern, more subdued end of the Taconics, are two state parks linked by state land and containing interesting natural and human history. **Bomoseen State Park❖,** on the lake of the same name (at 2,415 acres, the largest lake entirely within Vermont and often rather busy), is near a significant mid-1800s slate-quarrying and -processing site: A self-guided **Slate History Trail** passes the old quarry; the foundations of a slate-cutting factory and homes of slate workers are just outside the park entrance. The region to the south

ABOVE: *A coiled timber rattlesnake remains motionless waiting for unwary prey such as chipmunks or squirrels. These shy, long-lived snakes often winter in dens crowded with rattlesnakes, copperheads, and rat snakes.*

and west of the park (between Fair Haven and Poultney, and into New York) remains one of the country's important slate centers, the only one that produces green, purple, mottled, black, and red (the latter only in New York) stone. (The active quarries in the area can also be visited. In addition, the **Vermont Marble Exhibit**❖ in nearby Proctor, just north of Rutland, has displays about the history, formation, and uses of marble, as well as demonstrations by marble artisans.)

A short walk from the park entrance, past the slate factory and houses, is unspoiled, undeveloped **Glen Lake.** On the perimeter trail look for beaver activity near Moscow Pond, and slate bluffs along the fault line on the eastern side of the pond.

Between Bomoseen State Park and its northern neighbor **Half Moon State Park**❖ are 2,000 acres of forest preserve and trails well worth walking. This is prime wild turkey and deer habitat, where oaks (several species), hickories, beeches, and hop hornbeams produce the seeds or nuts so desirable to wildlife. On the high ground the forests occasionally open up into unusual "balds" of rocks topped with

35

lichens, offering fine views of the surrounding hilly country.

Although Rutland (population 18,230) is Vermont's second-largest city, there are some rural retreats just minutes from downtown. **Bird Mountain❖** or **Birdseye Mountain** in Ira (south side of Route 4A, 2.6 miles west of West Rutland) is one of many 2,000-foot ledgy knobs visible from town. Its **North Peak Trail** begins here and climbs steadily and easily to views overlooking the Castleton River Valley below. Hawk Ledge, reached by the **Castle Peak Trail,** is named for the peregrine falcons that have historically nested here. Successfully reintroduced in the East, peregrines are returning to several Vermont locations after a decades-long absence; they have nested at Bird Mountain for the past two years, and at certain times access to the area may be restricted for their protection.

Within the city limits of West Rutland and visible from Route 4A is a large cattail marsh in an abandoned marble quarry where the waters of the Castleton River have been impounded. In spring and summer, the **West Rutland Marsh❖** contains many rare and interesting birds: Virginia rail, soras, common moorhens, least bitterns, uncommon or rare warblers, and many others. Bird-watchers can stay dry while observing (or at least hearing) the birds from the gravel roads around and through the marsh.

ABOVE: *With its enticing pool of sticky liquid, the carnivorous pitcher plant traps insects and digests them for their nitrogen, which is scarce in the bog.*

LEFT: *Cattails and milkweed provide natural camouflage for waterfowl at the Dead Creek Wildlife Management Area.*

A short distance southeast of Rutland is **Aitken State Forest❖.** The **Bald Mountain Hiking Trail** features three rock promontories offering excellent views of the Green Mountains and the Taconic Range; the Red Rocks Vista is particularly splendid, providing outlooks south and west to the Otter Creek Valley. At **Clarendon Gorge,** south of the Rutland airport on Route 103, the Miller River has cut through soft rock that formed between harder varieties. The water has left a wide, high-walled (up to 75 feet) gorge, as well as an impressive string of pools and potholes, forming **Clarendon Gorge Wildlife Management Area❖.**

SOUTHERN LAKE CHAMPLAIN: BRANDON TO BURLINGTON

In the vicinity of Brandon, the valley opens up considerably; the Taconics disappear on the west, replaced by teasing views of the blue Adirondacks across Lake Champlain. Here the Champlain Valley proper is marked by bigger farms, apple orchards, and the openness of low plains and broad meadows. To the northeast in Addison is the **Dead Creek Wildlife Management Area❖,** the largest state-operated waterfowl area in Vermont. The nearly 3,000 acres of wetlands here are partly created by water-control dams along Dead Creek. Small-boat access is possible where Route 17 crosses the river, and canoeing the shallow waters is the best way for birders to find their quarry. Especially in spring and fall, the area often teems with ducks, geese (both Canada and snow), wading birds such as black-crowned night herons and American bitterns, and songbirds of various kinds. In years when Dead Creek is drawn down to control encroaching vegetation, migrating shorebirds in unusual numbers and species visit the exposed mudflats, attracting bird-watchers from great distances.

In the narrow uplands above the marsh, deer, otters, and mink are often spotted. The cattails in the center of the marsh, with their flowery spikes, grow too thickly to attract nesting birds but are a staple in the diet of muskrats, which also use the stems to build their lodges. Beyond the marshes of Dead Creek are scattered remnants of the forest that once dominated the upland landscape: most visibly, oaks (white, swamp white, red, and bur) and shagbark hickories.

Just to the east and overlooking Dead Creek is the abrupt rocky promontory of 1,300-foot **Snake Mountain❖.** The peak straddles the Addison-Weybridge town line, its isolation and relative height making it a recognizable landmark for miles around. A long, winding ridge

---

RIGHT: *The corklike bark of the paper birch insulates it from cold northern temperatures. Native Americans stretched the pliable bark over cedar frames to make their sturdy, lightweight canoes.*

38

with outstanding views of the lake, the mountain is actually part of the north-south Champlain Thrust Fault, which runs the length of the state. The fault has eroded in many places, leaving peaks such as Snake Mountain as islands in a flat sea of fields. In fact, Snake Mountain, Mount Philo to the north, and others were real islands, their summits poking above the surface of prehistoric Lake Vermont during early post-glacial times. Most of Snake Mountain is owned and managed by the Vermont Fish and Wildlife Department, and hikers may explore the old carriage road (now a trail) off the Mountain Road Extension, east of Addison on Route 22A. The trail passes through forests and small pockets of wetlands, offering outstanding views of the Champlain Valley and mountains beyond. Looking out, one can easily imagine the waves of long-gone Lake Vermont lapping at the shores below.

Although a disappointingly small amount of Lake Champlain shoreline is in the public domain, **Button Bay State Park**❖, west of Vergennes, occupies a crescent-shaped, south-facing bay right on the big lake and is of considerable geologic interest. The bedrock here is limestone of various formations and ages; some contains fossil corals, large sea snails, and other organisms dating back 450 million years, when Vermont was at the bottom of a shallow equatorial ocean. Visitors can see the fossils along the shore trails at **Button Point Natural Area**❖, a 25-acre preserve at the northern end of the park. The ancient corals are best viewed on the rocky outcrops of **Button Island,** an offshore section of the natural area. Trails also lead through an impressive old-growth forest of oaks, hickories, white and red pines, and white cedars that occupies the interior portion of the natural area. An attractive nature center within the natural area contains much information on its geology and natural history, including how the curious buttons—

ABOVE: *Now uncommon in Vermont, the black-crowned night heron, a wetland wanderer, stands "hunched in the white gown of his wings,"* wrote poet Mary Oliver.

LEFT: *An eastern cottonwood shades the rocky beach of Lake Champlain's North Hero State Park, where map turtles lay their eggs each summer.*

sedimentary concretions in the clays that give the place its name— were formed. Because Button Point is a state-designated natural area, collecting fossils is prohibited. The nearby Lake Champlain Maritime Museum, on the grounds of the Basin Harbor Club, a venerable summer resort, traces the human history of the lake.

Traveling northeast on back roads from Basin Harbor, visitors encounter the extensive Lower Otter Creek wetlands, more than 450 acres at the confluence of Otter Creek (the longest river entirely within the state), Dead Creek, and Lake Champlain. Still farther northeast in the town of Ferrisburg is **Little Otter Creek Wildlife Management Area**❖, a broad, attractive marsh that is one of Vermont's more accessible birding

41

ABOVE: *Magnificent flocks of migrating snow geese fill Vermont's skies during spring and fall. The snow geese breed in the Arctic, winter on the Atlantic coast, and use the state's grassy ponds in transit.*

areas. Some 1,000 acres of state-owned wetlands border the lake and are home to many species of wildlife, including the uncommon insect-eating black tern. In recent years, the endangered osprey has begun to nest on several platforms erected on telephone poles in and near the marsh.

Nearby, next to a portion of the lake bearing its name, is **Kingsland Bay State Park❖.** The site of a historic Revolutionary War–era inn and more recently a girls' summer camp, the park contains many unoccupied buildings and is not yet fully operational. However, one can stroll trails beside the lake and through wooded **McDonough Point Natural Area❖** under old oaks, hickories, pines, and maples. In spring, the forest floor is covered with a sea of delicate white trillium blossoms. The area is also sprinkled with calcium-loving plants that thrive on the limestone-derived sweet soils here.

Less than an hour's drive north, perched on a hillside overlooking the lake, is Burlington, Vermont's largest city, which contains several natural areas worth visiting. University of Vermont–owned **East Woods Natural Area❖**, off Route 7 in South Burlington, is a 100-acre undisturbed northern forest used extensively for research and teaching. It supports a variety of hardwoods and conifers, many of great size and age, and a rich understory of shrubs and herbaceous plants. Just north of town and visible from Interstate 89 is 40-acre **Centennial Woods❖**, another university natural area, where tall, old-growth white pines flourish in the sandy soils deposited millennia ago when this land was covered by the Champlain Sea.

Within the city limits and near the university campus is an unusual quarry that has been acquired by the university and designated a natural area—**Redstone Quarry Natural Area❖**. Here, geology students and others come to see and study the red quartzite and other ancient rocks that were once the sediments of a shallow ocean. One can still discern, preserved in rocks half a billion years old, places where currents rippled the sand, raindrops dimpled the surface of the mud, and marine worms dug their burrows.

Another outstanding geologic area, one that enjoys an international reputation among geologists, is **Lone Rock Point❖**, just north of Burlington Harbor. Here, on property owned by the Episcopal Diocese (permission required for entry), is one of the best views of a thrust-fault formation in the country. Particularly clear when viewed from the lake, the great over-thrust block of the Champlain Thrust Fault rises clearly above the beach. The tall vertical cliffs show where the old (550 million years) gray-white dolostone has been sharply thrust up and over the younger (450 million years), darker Iberville shale.

Visitors to the Burlington area can also enjoy a variety of indoor and outdoor centers that present bits of Vermont's natural and human history. Visitors may view a small fossil and mineral collection (including bones of the Ice Age whale and mammoth unearthed during the last century) at the **Perkins Geology Museum.** Just off Route 127 is the **Ethan Allen Homestead❖**, restored residence of one of Vermont's founding fathers and the legendary leader of the Green Mountain Boys prior to and during the Revolutionary War (a nature trail goes around the property along the scenic Winooski River). The **Discovery Museum❖** in neighboring Essex Junction features hands-on natural history displays for all ages. While in Essex Junction, take a walk around the perimeter trail at nearby **Indian Brook Preserve❖**, a natural area owned by the town.

NORTHERN LAKE CHAMPLAIN: BURLINGTON TO THE BORDER

North of Burlington, Lake Champlain is bisected by a low-lying series of islands traversed by Route 2. The last bit of United States mainland that Route 2 crosses before the causeway to the big islands is a silver-maple–swamp-white-oak wetland delta, built upon sediments deposited by the Lamoille River as it enters the lake. Most of the delta is the state-owned **Sand Bar Wildlife Management Area❖** (1,668 acres), and access is restricted in certain places and at certain times of year to protect the waterfowl that use it. At various locations, ducks, great blue and black-crowned night herons, diverse species of rail, and a great variety of songbirds afford excellent bird-watching.

The big islands—Grand Isle, North Hero, and Isle La Motte—are relatively flat and checkered with apple orchards and farms; with the Adirondacks rising like the teeth of a huge saw to the west and the Green Mountains looming more gently to the east, the effect is both pastoral and dramatic. Views from the eastern shores are also remarkable, including the added attraction of the brilliant lake waters rolling up in a sparkling parade. At the southern end of North Hero, **Campmeeting Point Natural Area❖**—a long, narrow pebbly shore—stretches around much of **Knight Point State Park❖.** In this fine example of an unusual Lake Champlain natural community, beach pea and other rare plants grow in the sparse soil between cobbles. The natural area is backed by a remnant forest of large oaks, hickories, and maples; a trail follows its perimeter, offering both pleasant views and access to the shore.

North Hero State Park❖ to the north contains an excellent wetland forested with silver maple, swamp white oak, and green ash—and often teeming with mosquitoes in the spring. Large map turtles (*Graptemys geographica*), inhabitants of the open water, come ashore here in the summer to lay their eggs in the sand and gravel of the beach (sections of the park are off limits to visitors during this time).

Still farther north, and slightly off the beaten track to Canada, is Isle La Motte, accessible via Route 129. Its geologically famous **Chazyan Coral Reef❖** appears as flat-domed, bald outcrops of gray limestone in the island's fields. These fossil corals are among the oldest in the world, dating back to Ordovician times some 550 million years ago, when this area was a continental shelf in a warm saltwater sea. The corals and many other types of fossils (crinoids, trilobites, sea snails) are easy to see when walking in the fields—with permission of the landowners—and inspecting the rocks up close. Elsewhere on the island are abandoned limestone and marble quarries, where the stone for Rockefeller Center and other important buildings was cut.

In addition to the 3 main islands, 77 smaller ones, most in Lake Champlain's wider northern half, range in size from 1,000 acres (Valcour) to a few square feet. **Burton Island State Park**❖ (240 acres) in Saint Albans Bay, accessible by boat or park ferry or from Kamp Kill Kare State Park on the adjacent mainland, contains a marina, campground, old fields of a former farm, and a perimeter nature trail that passes through a peaceful forest of large oaks, hickories, and green ash, skirts cobble beaches, and leads to scenic overlooks.

Nearby **Woods Island** (107 acres) and **Knight Island** (170 acres), more primitive state parks, each provide only a few campsites and no facilities of any kind. Similar in appearance to Burton Island, both support many rare plant species, moderate-sized wetlands, and more extensive forests, all traversed by fine hiking trails. Registration for camping on Woods is at Burton Island, on Knight at Knight Point State Park. Visitors must use their own boats to reach Woods Island; they may take a park boat to Knight Island.

Several of the smaller, undeveloped islands—even the tiniest rocky islets—are critical sites for birds that nest in colonies, some of which, such as the common tern (a state-endangered species), breed and nest nowhere else in Vermont. **Young Island**❖ (ten acres), west of northern Grand Isle, **Rock Island**❖ (two acres), at the mouth of Saint Albans Bay, **Hen Island**❖ (one acre), just east of Knight Point State Park, and **Popasquash**❖ (two acres), three miles north of Woods Island near the Vermont mainland, are four such important sites. Black-crowned night herons (endangered in Vermont), which are largely nocturnal and best known for their harsh, barking call, have been sighted on Young Island. During the tern breeding season, all islands are off limits to visitors, but the birds are easily viewed with binoculars from boats or the nearby shore.

45

The state's only national wildlife refuge is **Missisquoi National Wildlife Refuge❖.** On the mainland at the northern end of the lake, the refuge occupies nearly 6,000 marshy acres on the huge delta where the Missisquoi River slowly empties into Lake Champlain. One of the largest and most important wetland complexes in the region, it contains extensive silver-maple–swamp-white-oak swamps, wild rice and other grassy, sedgy marshes, and a 1,000-acre pitch-pine-shrub–sphagnum-moss bog. Interspersed with the wetlands is considerable upland, much of it managed to provide feeding and breeding habitat for birds and mammals within and passing through the area.

The Missisquoi refuge is a tremendously rich area for wildlife. Among the many species of ducks that nest or eat here during migration are wood ducks, blacks, goldeneyes, and hooded and common mergansers; both Canada and snow geese stop down on their migrations. In the late summer (mid-August to the end of September), upwards of 35,000 migrating ducks and geese may be in the refuge at any one time, filling the air with a happy confusion of beating wings and noisy honks. On **Shad Island,** the refuge also protects the state's largest rookery of great blue herons (more than 300 nests of twigs sit high in the trees). Rail, gallinules, and others stay within the protection of the marsh reeds; songbirds by the score are everywhere; walleyes and the rare muskellunge populate the river; beavers, muskrats, otters, and other mammals live within the refuge's boundaries. Many areas are off limits for all or part of the year, and waterfowl hunting occurs around its edges in the fall. Visitors should check at refuge headquarters for information, places to go, and restrictions.

Black Creek and **Maquam Creek** provide good opportunities for bird observation and photography, as does Mac's Bend Road along the river. Boaters can launch canoes from First Landing; blueberry lovers would be wise to visit the bog off Tabor Road in July or August, when the luscious purple berries are ripe and picking is permitted. Visitors should remember that the refuge is managed for wildlife and be careful not to disturb nesting birds.

RIGHT: *Cinnamon ferns, buttonbush, water lilies, and common arrowhead flourish at Missisquoi National Wildlife Refuge. The marshes provide breeding grounds for waterfowl, and food and rest for migrating ducks.*

CENTRAL VERMONT:
THE GREEN MOUNTAINS

Vermont is known as the Green Mountain State, a reference both to the verdure that inspired its name and to the north-south backbone that defines its literal as well as its spiritual geography. The mountains roll the length of the state—160 miles—and 100 miles beyond in a seemingly endless series of ups and downs, wildly green in summer and muted brown when they emerge from their blanket of snow in early spring. Starting at the Massachusetts border as the Hoosac Range, the Greens run north to Quebec, where they become known as the Notre Dame Mountains. The summits are visible from almost every part of the state, standing out in a bold line when viewed from Route 7 to the west, rising gradually out of lesser hills when seen from the Connecticut River Valley to the east. (In fact, the Green Mountains are but a segment of the Appalachian Mountain chain, which extends from the Smokies of North Carolina through the Gaspé Peninsula in Canada.) From 20 to 35 miles wide, they occupy a sizable portion of the land base and contain the six highest peaks in the state, all more than 4,000 feet tall. Before quick transportation and paved roads, their height, terrain, and climate were true barriers to east-west movement and communication.

Technically, the Greens, after forming a definite ridge for the first 60

LEFT: *State tree and symbol of Vermont, stately sugar maples (which produce 35 percent of the nation's maple sap) transform the mountainous landscape into brilliant mosaics of red, gold, and orange each fall.*

miles north from Massachusetts, split into three mountain ranges near Pico Peak in Sherburne. The Hogback Range begins in Brandon and parallels the Main Range a short distance north; the Main Range continues north to Lincoln and on toward the northeast; the Lowell Mountains, or Worcester Range, as they are known locally, start at Stockbridge. At regular intervals the north-south axis is bisected by east-west rivers and passes, including Bolton Gorge (traversed by I-89), where the Winooski River shears through the Main Range and where in less than four miles the Greens drop from more than 4,000 feet on Camels Hump to nearly sea level.

Containing remnants of the most ancient rock in New England, the Green Mountains are actually the remains of a prehistoric plateau, uplifted by enormous folding of the earth's crust on a north-to-south axis approximately 450 million years ago and weathered and sculpted by erosion ever since. Even in their present configuration they are old mountains, and some of the major rivers passing through them are even older. Flowing from east to west, the Winooski, Lamoille, and Missisquoi "sawed" their way through as the mountains were being pushed up.

Though variations are many, the most basic rocks of these mountains are metamorphic schists—originally, eroded materials of previous mountains and seaborne sediments heated and compressed into the fine-grained, convoluted, folded, and fractured rocks we see today. Their often striking green color comes from a constituent mineral, chlorite.

The summits of two of Vermont's highest mountains, Mansfield (the highest, at 4,393 feet) and Camels Hump (fourth highest, at 4,083 feet), support small and precarious vestiges of the once-prevalent alpine tundra (sometimes called arctic-alpine tundra). These barren-land zones above timberline—250 acres on Mount Mansfield and 10 on Camels Hump—resemble the true Arctic in appearance, ecology, and natural history, with some significant differences.

The frost-free growing season is short, often less than 90 days. The soils are thin, sparse, nutrient-poor, and tenuous on steep slopes. Plants are extremely hardy and generally dwarfed. Growing in dense clumps, they hug the ground to avoid ferocious winds, abrading snow and ice, and exposure. Unlike the true Arctic, however, precipitation is abundant in the form of rain, snow, and—most importantly—dew from the regular cloud cover. On the other hand, precipitation.during

the critical growing season is often quickly lost due to runoff on the steep slopes or drying by high winds. Common here, but very uncommon for the region, are such Arctic species as Bigelow's sedge, alpine bilberry, mountain sandwort, highland rush, and others whose main range is a thousand miles to the north.

Living among the plants are the very few animals that can survive in harsh conditions with such meager food supplies: Mammals such as red-backed voles subsist on seeds and plant materials, and shrews prey on other small mammals and abundant summer insects; migratory birds such as dark-eyed juncos may nest here and eat seeds and fruits on the ground. In the craggy ledges of cliffs near the tundra (and elsewhere high in the mountains), ravens now nest regularly, soaring on rising winds over and around the summits as they search for food.

From timberline around 4,000 feet, where vegetation is stunted and tangled and the terrain virtually impassable off trails, to 3,000 feet, where trees are taller and more widely spaced, is Vermont's high-elevation boreal, or subarctic, forest—the realm of balsam fir, red spruce, and a moisture- and shade-loving understory of mosses, lichens, and wildflowers such as goldthread, Canada

RIGHT: *A tiny bog atop the summit of Mount Mansfield supports a diversified community of firs and sedges, including the delicate white-flowered cottongrass.*

mayflower, and bunchberry.

Year-round residents, bird or mammal, are few in this exacting environment. In winter, birds include the familiar black-capped chickadees (and more rarely the brown-capped, now known as the boreal) and red-breasted nuthatches, which work tree bark and branches for seeds, grubs, and hibernating insects. The most common mammals are red squirrels, which are smaller and shier than the familiar gray squirrels of city parks and like to store mushrooms on tree trunks to dry, and snowshoe (or varying) hares, whose fur changes from brown to white in winter. More exotic species do pass through this zone: Moose frequently move up from the lower forests to browse here in winter, and predators such as goshawks, bobcats, and fishers (large, dark, weasel-like creatures) venture higher in search of prey.

Spring brings not only the pesky, stream-born blackflies, but a host of birds that stay to nest or pass through on the way to Canada. As many as 14 species of warblers are vernal visitors; a few, such as blackpoll and Nashville warblers, remain for the breeding season. The

ground-nesting Bicknell's gray-
cheeked thrush and, more common-
ly, Swainson's thrush are the highest-
elevation thrushes here, their
distinctive flutelike songs evocative
of their cousins in the lower, deciduous forests. Many ornithologists consider the song of the hermit thrush,
Vermont's state bird, the most beautiful, with its precise musical phras-
ing and reedy tremolos. Colored a
soft brown and smaller than a robin,
the hermit thrush has the endearing
habit of restlessly flicking its tail as it
searches the forest floor for insects.

Down slope from 3,000 feet, the
boreal forest gives way, sometimes
gradually, sometimes more abruptly,
to the northern hardwoods that so
dominate the Vermont landscape
(indeed, hardwood forest occupies
as much as 70 percent of the 4.5
million acres of forest in the state,
and that 4.5 million acres represent
75 percent of all Vermont land). In
the spring, before the trees of the
hardwood forest are fully leaved,
the forest floor is home to a delicate
array of wildflowers. The pale
spring sunshine reaching through
the branches reveals the lavender,
pink, and purple of hepatica and
spring beauties; the white, yellow,
and deep blue of violets; the creamy
sprays of foamflowers; the bur-
gundy of red trilliums.

The predominant species in an

ABOVE: *Although at home on land,
the river otter's rudderlike tail,
webbed feet, and fish diet reveal
that it's most comfortable in water.*

LEFT: *Unlike the wolf, the coyote is
thriving near developed areas,
where its nighttime barks and
howls are increasingly heard.*

BELOW: *The marten often perches
in coniferous trees, a strategic
position from which to pounce on
its favorite prey, the red squirrel.*

established hardwood forest are sugar maple, red maple, beech, yellow birch, eastern hemlock (a softwood), and a mixture of many others, depending on locale. For example, on rich, moist sites, white ash is a common tree; in places newly exposed by logging or windthrow, quaking and bigtooth aspen may grow quickly; on burned sites, paper birch is the pioneer; in abandoned fields, sun-loving white pine abounds. In the southern half of the state, oaks are often a significant part of the forest.

The sugar maple, of course, is the tree most often associated with Vermont. The state ranks first in the country each year in maple sap production (more than 500,000 gallons were gathered in 1992, 35 percent of the United States total). The weather-beaten sugarhouse with its stacked cords of firewood is a familiar sight on Green Mountain back roads. The sugar maple is also the star attraction of Vermont's annual foliage display. As the days shorten and weather turns cooler in the fall, trees form an abscission layer between their leaves and stems, cutting off the supply of nutrients and moisture to the leaves. As the green chlorophyll breaks down, other pigments present in the leaves, such as xanthophylls, are revealed, and the leaves turn yellow or brown. The brilliant reds of the sugar maple are the result of a pigment called anthocyanin, which is created when sugar builds up in the leaf because the abscission layer prevents the sugar from traveling to the stem.

The happy effect, as anyone who's visited these mountains in autumn knows, is slope after slope of brilliant color, as if the leaves, rather than dying, were blossoming in a vivid new incarnation. "Leaf peepers" from all over come in autumn to drive the back roads; indeed, in the most popular spots, it's not uncommon to see a particularly spectacular tree ringed with photographers! One caution: Foliage season, beginning in September, brings huge numbers of tourists to the Green Mountains, and anyone visiting during that period should make hotel or campground reservations ahead of time.

A more easily available food supply makes the wildlife of the northern hardwoods more diverse and plentiful than it is in the spartan

LEFT: *Covering 2,046 acres, Harriman Reservoir was created when the Deerfield River was dammed. Haystack Mountain rises in the distance.*
OVERLEAF: *Woodlands near Harriman support a rich transition forest where ferns and hobblebush flourish beneath yellow and gray birches.*

boreal forest above. Small mammals are many, including several species of shrews, mice, voles, and bats; red, gray, and flying squirrels—all or one—are usually present; and the New England cottontail rabbit may be crouching in brushy understory cover to hide from its predators.

Many of the larger mammals of the northern hardwoods, predators and herbivores alike, are here for the second time around, so to speak. Such forest-identified species as white-tailed deer, moose, black bear, fisher, beaver, bobcat, and others dwindled when early settlers assiduously cut the forests of the 1700s and 1800s to make way for their fields. As a result, many animals became virtually extinct in the state during that time and have returned or been restored only in the past 75 years of forest regrowth. Some, like the deer and fisher, had human help in recolonizing old ground. In 1878 a small herd of deer was imported from New York to reestablish the species throughout its former range—an experiment so successful that the Green Mountains today have one of the largest deer populations in the United States. The mountain lion is a sad-

ABOVE: *Despite its brilliant plumage, the scarlet tanager is more often heard than seen, as it carols high in the dense forest canopy.*

LEFT: *Canoes and kayaks are a familiar sight in Jamaica State Park's West River. National races are held annually in its boulder-strewn waters.*

der story. The last mountain lion, or catamount, was shot in 1881 near Barnard, and though tantalizing rumors of catamounts have cropped up since, there have been no confirmed sightings in more than a century.

Like the mammals, birds are also plentiful and varied. In the exuberant rush of spring come species by the score: wood warblers, thrushes (hermit, wood, and the veery), flycatchers, sapsuckers and flickers, broadwinged hawks, and many others. Some stay through summer to nest and raise young, others move on. By fall they have departed, leaving the quieter woods to the resident seed-and-bud eaters: the ruffed grouse (partridge), the wild turkey, and the ever-present white-breasted nuthatch and black-capped chickadee, the familiar bird that remains when so many other species head south. Their vigilant predators, such as the great horned owl, the barred owl, and the sharp-shinned hawk, winter with them in the woods.

The Green Mountains are sufficiently high to impede the prevailing western winds; thus the air is forced up and over the ridges and cooled, thereby reducing its ability to hold water. In winter, the resulting precipitation arrives as snow, and the north-facing slopes of these mountains experience the harshest weather in the state. Seventy-five years ago, winter brought quiet and isolation to the Vermont mountains. Then in 1933 the nation's first ski tow began operating in Woodstock, and the skiing industry established trails on many Green Mountain slopes. In the early 1990s, relatively snowless winters forced many smaller ski areas below 2,000 feet to shut down; but mammoth snow-making operations such as Killington thrive whatever the weather.

Hikers and animal watchers might prefer the slopes without the massive ski development, but even in summer, human activity and presence in the forest is vital to the state's economy. Forest-related industry accounts for about a tenth of all jobs in the state, and maple sugaring, hunting and fishing, and tourism—from skiing (downhill and Nordic) to fall color sightseeing to backcountry hiking—are all inextricably connected to and dependent upon the forested landscape.

At the height of the Great Depression in the 1930s, a paved highway along the crest of the Green Mountains, similar to Virginia's Blue Ridge Parkway, was proposed. The plan was narrowly defeated, leaving Route 100's quiet, meandering path through the hill towns and villages the major artery along the mountains. Our route for most of this chapter, Route 100 is arguably the most scenic highway in the state.

THE SOUTHERN GREEN MOUNTAINS

Across southern Vermont the Green Mountains sprawl irregularly. Because much of this mountain area has historically been inaccessible, more wild country is found in southern Vermont than in any other portion of the state except the region known as the Northeast Kingdom.

The **Green Mountain National Forest❖,** established in 1932 with the modest acquisition of 2,000 acres, spreads over 346,000 acres in the southern half of the state. This expanse—in two large blocks—represents half of all public land in Vermont and 5 percent of the state's total area. It offers countless opportunities for outdoor enthusiasts, from backcountry hiking trails to more modest nature trails, from wilderness exploration to highway vistas, from remote ponds, bogs, and numerous other natural areas to big tracts of forestland.

Some of the largest bodies of water in the state are in this region, surrounded by some of the most untamed country. One such site is **Harriman Reservoir❖**, just north of the little village of Whitingham on Route 100. The biggest impoundment in Vermont, it covers 2,046 acres and backs up to the national forest on its east side. Created by a hydroelectric dam across the Deerfield River, the reservoir occupies a broad six-mile-long wild valley that is an excellent place to see deer, wild turkey, and beaver. The **Atherton Meadow Wildlife Management Area❖**, at the reservoir's southern end, includes a large beaver meadow, a hemlock-hardwood forest typical of this area, and some quaking aspens near its marsh. Abundant here are salamanders, including the red-backed variety, whose colors change as elevation varies. The Harriman Trail, beginning at Wilmington on the reservoir's northern end, follows the bed of an old railroad, providing views of the mountains across the lake and passing stone walls, cellar holes, and other bittersweet reminders of the settlers who once tried to farm here.

Though somewhat smaller (1,568 acres), **Somerset Reservoir❖**, to the north at the headwaters of the Deerfield River, is even more remote and wild. A hiking trail leads from Somerset Reservoir to **Grout Pond Recreation Area❖**, which is also accessible by dirt road. Set like a punchbowl in a circle of young trees, the scenic 70-acre undeveloped pond was once a major logging site but has now grown back to forest. (The U.S. Forest Service maintains such recreation areas throughout the national forest, and several offer particularly attractive features, whether a pond, a waterfall, or a quiet patch of woods.) **Molly Stark State Park❖**, a short distance east off Route 9, includes a nature walk and a longer trail up Mount Olga (2,415 feet) to a fire tower with expansive views of the southern Greens.

Through this area passes the **Long Trail❖**, the oldest long-distance hiking trail in the United States. Beginning at the Massachusetts border and following the Green Mountains all the way to Quebec, 265 miles away, the Long Trail originated in 1910, when 23 Vermont residents formed the Green Mountain Club. With 175 miles of side trails and 62 rustic cabins and lean-tos, the trail gives hikers access to the heart of the Green Mountains and its major peaks. It was a major inspiration in the creation of the longer Appalachian Trail (AT) and forms a 100-mile portion of it from Massachusetts to the Killington area, where the AT branches to the east and the Long Trail continues north along the central ridgeline of the Greens. The trail is usually divided into three sections. The southern part crosses many mountains associated with ski areas, such as Stratton, Bromley, and Pico. The central section extends north of Route 4, where the well-defined ridgeline offers hikers views over Lake Champlain to the west and on a clear day, the big peaks marching northward to Mount Mansfield. The northernmost 55 miles of the trail traverse large tracts of undeveloped forest and isolated peaks.

The Long Trail manages to combine accessibility and remoteness. An afternoon's drive to the trailhead and a short hike via a feeder trail bring a hiker to the Long Trail. Establishing a campsite by an unspoiled pond, climbing to the ridgeline and seeing the first distant views, discovering evidence of an old abandoned hill farm, spotting a scarlet tanager or perhaps even a peregrine falcon—these rewards of a typical Long Trail journey lure hikers back season after season and make many vow to explore the trail end to end someday.

The ideal time for hiking is early summer to late fall—snow and ice make hiking difficult and destructive to fragile soils until late May, and by November the weather is getting colder, and hunting season begins. Expert cross-country skiers frequent the steeper slopes, but long sections of the lower feeder trails along unplowed forest roads are suitable for ski tourers of all levels. *Backpacker* magazine calls the Long Trail one of the world's ten best hiking trails, and today efforts are underway to protect every mile of it from Massachusetts to Canada. Just north of Somerset the trail passes some remote and pristine ponds, each ringed with boreal and bog vegetation of the higher elevations. Cabins and lean-tos provide places to stay overnight near Bourn and Stratton ponds.

Just off Route 100 in Jamaica is **Jamaica State Park❖,** site of national canoe and kayak races in the spring. A trail beginning at the swimming area follows the bed of the abandoned West River Railroad (built in 1879 to connect the Connecticut River and Lake Champlain) up to spectacular **Hamilton Falls Natural Area,** which features a series of wide, deep potholes at the upper end and long cascades descending open rock face. The waterfall is one of the highest in Vermont and—

RIGHT: *The Ottauquechee (Native American for "swift running stream") River tumbles through ancient bedrock at Quechee Gorge. Towering hemlocks thrive in the moist conditions of the 160-foot-deep ravine.*

judging by the number of fatal accidents here—one of the most dangerous to the unwary. A short distance east along Route 30 is **Townshend State Park❖,** where a trail through the hemlocks leads to the top of one of Vermont's several Bald Mountains, which is easily climbed in little more than an hour and affords views of Mount Monadnock in New Hampshire.

On either side of Route 100 between Tyson and Killington Peak is **Calvin Coolidge State Forest❖,** 17,949 acres in scattered blocks that contain some important natural areas. With a 3,720-foot summit, **Shrewsbury Peak Natural Area** offers an exemplary high elevation and a spruce-fir boreal forest ecosystem; in the 45-acre old-growth stand of **Tinker Brook Natural Area,** large red spruces and hemlocks line the creek.

In central Vermont, the Green Mountains rise toward pyramid-shaped Killington Peak (4,241 feet), which springs abruptly from the ridgeline and is either enhanced or marred—depending on your point of view—by the ski trails draped across its slopes. Here the Long Trail presents several side trails, permitting hikers to ascend one way and descend another (avoid the shadeless ski trails, which can be blisteringly hot in the summer sun).

Practically in the shadow of Killington Peak and near the northern junction of Routes 4 and 100 is small **Gifford Woods State Park❖,** whose 16 acres seem much larger because they adjoin the northern sector of the Green Mountain National Forest. The park was built in the 1930s within an old-growth northern hardwood stand, and some impressive trees remain. But directly across Route 100 is a larger vestige of the original stand, now set aside as a state natural area, where there are magnificent aged sugar maples, hemlocks, yellow birches, and other trees and a rich understory of wildflowers and ferns thriving in moist, fertile soils.

Route 4 crosses Sherburne Pass, one of the few major breaks in the Green Mountain barrier. Farther east is Woodstock, a handsome, well-preserved village set in the Ottauquechee River Valley, where the Green Mountains gradually fall away into the hills of the Vermont piedmont to the east. On the village outskirts, the **Vermont Institute of Natural Science** has its headquarters, classroom, and library in a renovated barn. There are trails around the 77-acre preserve, and a main attraction is the **Vermont Raptor Center❖,** a living museum where owls, hawks, and eagles that have been permanently injured in car accidents or other mishaps are housed in "flight habitats," spacious outdoor enclosures that are designed to reproduce the conditions the birds prefer. On a recent visit, occupants ranged in size from a small northern saw-whet owl to a beautiful bald eagle. Each year the center works to rehabilitate and release in the wild more than 400 less seriously injured or orphaned birds.

Woodstock was the home of George Perkins Marsh (1801–82) the writer often considered the father of the conservation movement. His book *The Earth as Modified by Human Action* advocated conservation practices a century before they were fashionable; his *Man and Nature* was one of the first works to recognize the complexity of nature's interrelationships—the concept later termed *ecology*. The **Billings Farm and Museum❖**, just north of Woodstock, is on the site of Marsh's former home. Appropriately enough, its exhibits explore the interrelationship of circa-1890 farmers in this region with the land they worked. Much of this area will be included in the National Park Service's new Billings-Marsh National Historic Site, the first place so designated in Vermont. The park will be open to visitors upon the death of the owners, Laurance and Mary Rockefeller, who have donated the property.

The hills between the Ottauquechee and the White River are some of the loveliest in Vermont. The open, sun-bathed meadows, stately maples, and weathered barns testify that the land here has been loved and carefully tended for generations. **Quechee Gorge,** to the south along Route 4, is a famous landmark (Vermont's "Grand Canyon" in tourist-speak) where the Ottauquechee River pours through a mile-long gorge 160 feet below the highway bridge. Although the way down looks impossible, an easy trail leads to the riverbank. The gorge is a fine example of glacial meltwater cutting through metamorphic rock some 60,000 years ago.

THE NORTHERN GREEN MOUNTAINS

Middlebury Gap is another of the dramatic east-west passes across the Green Mountains. The road that follows it, Route 125 between Hancock in the east and Middlebury in the west, rises to an elevation of 2,149 feet near the famous writers' colony at Bread Loaf. Like the other mountain passes, it was probably carved by streams before the last Wisconsin glaciation and retained its east-west alignment after the glaciers passed. The exposed rock alongside the road is mostly fine-

grained gray gneiss. Route 125 passes some interesting natural and cultural history sites. **Texas Falls❖** in Hancock includes not only falls but also two nature trails through an evergreen forest thick with ferns, as well as dramatic large potholes worn smooth by millennia of swirling water. To the west over the summit of Middlebury Gap is the **Robert Frost Wayside Area❖,** near the poet's former summer home in Ripton; the Robert Frost Interpretative Trail combines a traditional nature trail with appropriate mounted excerpts from Frost's poems.

West of the gap and just off Route 116 is **Battell Biological Preserve❖,** maintained as a research and natural area by Middlebury College. Its 400 acres are home to old-growth northern hardwoods, including some impressive big trees. East of the gap, farther north on Route 100, is scenic six-mile-long **Granville Gulf Reservation.** Here the mountains rise steeply on either side of the road, and in **Moss Glen Falls State Natural Area❖** a stream plummets down the sheer cliffs. At the north end of the reservation is another stand of old-growth hemlock and red spruce that has remained untouched on the craggy slopes.

With its remarkable silhouette, unusual summit alpine area, absence of ski development, and beautifully forested slopes, **Camels Hump,** east of Huntington, is the most distinctive peak in Vermont. The Long Trail is only one of several that lead to its 4,083-foot summit, which is surrounded by the 17,000-plus acres of **Camels Hump State Forest❖.** Its silhouette inspired Samuel de Champlain to lyrical accuracy when he named it *Le Lion Couchant* (the Sleeping Lion). About 1800 it began to be known as Camels Rump, but Victorian cartographers, reputedly aghast, changed the name to the current, more genteel version. The 5,304 acres above 2,500 feet, mostly boreal forest and alpine tundra, form the largest state natural area in Vermont. Of special interest is the 10-acre alpine area above the tree line—one of two tundra regions in Vermont—which contains plants usually found hundreds of miles to the north, such as mountain cranberry, alpine bilberry, and mountain sandwort. Because of the fragility of this community (its soil is very thin), a

LEFT: *The fragile tundra vegetation on the summit of Camels Hump is a relict of the Ice Age, when arctic plants were common in Vermont.*
OVERLEAF: *Mount Mansfield towers over Cambridge's snow-covered fields. A profile can be seen in the ridge; the chin is the highest point.*

ranger is on duty during the peak hiking season to see that the flora remains untrampled and to teach hikers more about this unique ecosystem. On the slopes of Camels Hump, where more than 100 inches of precipitation can fall in a normal year, University of Vermont scientists did much of the early pioneering research on acid rain.

The **Birds of Vermont Museum** in Huntington presents handsome displays of all the breeding birds of Vermont (as well as many others) in re-created natural habitats, prepared by well-known bird carver and naturalist Bob Spear. There are nature trails on the grounds.

Just north of Camels Hump the mountains drop precipitously to the Winooski River water gap, where the river valley ambles east to west through the mountains. Here, I-89 follows the river from Montpelier toward Burlington straight across the western thrust belt of Vermont— as geologist Bradford B. Van Diver puts it, "slicing through practically everything in true interstate style." At Exit 12, road cuts reveal dark brown schists striped with white quartz, their striated surfaces showing evidence of the Winooski glacier that made this valley so angular and striking. Also apparent are terraces marking the successive river floodplains formed when the Winooski flowed through high ground near Exit 11, and a more greenish schist between Exits 10 and 8. A recent state plan to blow up the road cuts for the sake of neatness was fiercely opposed by amateur geologists.

ABOVE: *Teaberry, or wintergreen, has spicy, bright red fruits that can be spotted in oak woods or near evergreens in the winter. Its extract is used in chewing gum, candy, medicine, and tea.*

RIGHT: *Stunted balsam fir trees and low-lying alpine bilberry are among the alpine tundra vegetation growing on the summit of Mount Mansfield. Hikers need to remember that one stray step can wipe out a fragile plant colony.*

North of I-89 is another large consolidation of state-owned land, **Mount Mansfield State Forest**,

33,000 acres extending roughly from the interstate highway to Route 15 south of Johnson, some 17 miles. The southernmost block surrounds large **Waterbury Reservoir,** built by the Civilian Conservation Corps (CCC) in the early 1930s to prevent a recurrence of the disastrous and deadly Winooski River Flood of 1927.

The reservoir and surrounding forest conceal a long history of human settlement and activity. **Little River State Park❖,** on the western side, has a fascinating self-guided history hike that reveals the evolution of the area: trails that were once town carriage roads; old cellar holes of abandoned hillside farms; graveyards in the forests; pastures long grown up to trees—reminders of the farmers who tried to pry a living from this thin soil before most of the land was flooded by the dam in 1930. There are also the remains of a large CCC camp built here in the mid-1930s. A bit farther north is **Nebraska Valley❖,** accessed via Moscow Road (off Route 100). The valley—which follows Miller Brook upstream to its source, **Lake Mansfield❖**—is a beautiful glacial cirque, or natural amphitheater carved by a glacier. A delta, a kame terrace, lateral and terminal moraines, a tarn, and a cirque basin, all evidence of glacial action, are visible from the valley road.

Just northwest of the village of Stowe, Mount Mansfield, with its long ridges and distinctive wedge-shaped summit, supports a ski area with all the attendant development, but it also offers much unspoiled mountain terrain, especially on the west-facing slopes, and miles of foot trails, some reaching to the summit. The mountain's long ridge presents a profile that is often described as a face looking up—forming, from south to north, the forehead, nose, upper lip, lower lip, chin (highest point), and Adam's apple. (Others have seen different images. Native Americans called it "Mose-O-Be-Wadso," translated "mountain with the head of a moose.") One of the most interesting—and fragile—features is a 250-acre alpine area above the timberline containing those rugged species that can thrive in a growing season sometimes as short as 90 days. The **Mount Mansfield Auto Road** loops its way 4.5 miles through the state forest to a point just below the summit; visitors can ride the Mount Mansfield Gondola partway up as well. While riding look for black, crowlike ravens soaring on the updrafts.

Skiing has a long history in Stowe. Several Swedish families settled here in 1912, bringing skis with them, but not until 1933 did the CCC design and construct the famous Nose Dive Trail on Mansfield; the first single chair lift followed in 1940. Altitude ensures snow—120 inches fall on the summit in a good year. Closer to town off Route 108, the **Stowe Recreation Path**❖ is one of the few greenways in the country built almost exclusively on private land but open to the public: More than five miles of trail along the West Branch River are available for walking, running, biking, and cross-country skiing.

Parallel to and east of the dominant Green Mountains, a subrange, the **Worcester Range**❖, extends from I-89 north to Elmore Mountain on Route 15. A good deal of it is state forest and natural area, including **C. C. Putnam State Forest** and **Elmore State Park.** Its main peaks, somewhat lower than the central Green Mountains, are in the mid-3,000-foot range; Hogback is the highest at 3,740 feet. Hiking trails lead to the summit of Mount Hunger from either side and continue partway along the ridge. However, there is presently no trail from Worcester Mountain to Mount Elmore; access to the latter is from the state park.

Northwest of Stowe, Route 108, the road through **Smuggler's Notch**❖, is perhaps the most twisting and precipitous short drive in Vermont; the steep, moist cliffs tower over the switchbacking highway, slowing cars to a crawl. The notch, part of the route between Canada and the States used by contraband smugglers during Jefferson's Embargo Act in the early 1800s, is an exciting natural area. Peregrine falcons' nests perch on the cliffs (which may be out-of-bounds to hikers during breeding season); in winter, ice climbers tackle the sheer walls. Alpine plants— including such rare species as purple mountain saxifrage and the carnivorous butterwort, which catches insects on its greasy leaves—find conditions on the cliffs equally to their austere liking. Vertical scars caused by recent landslides carrying a freight of uprooted trees and scoured debris are visible from the road; in summer, children enjoy scrambling among the rocky "caves" and crevices near the parking turnoff.

In contrast to the mountain country just to its south, the Lamoille River Valley seems exceedingly lush and pastoral. Here, in the northern part of the Green Mountains, summits are irregular and less well defined than in areas to the south. Jay Peak, reaching 3,870 feet near the Canadian border, is the last high mountain. To the east on Route 14 north of Hardwick is **Craftsbury Common,** a village whose hilltop setting above ponds and lakes, quiet lanes, and neat village common makes it one of the most beautiful in Vermont. There is much outdoor activity here in all seasons, primarily centered on Sterling College, a small school committed to natural resources education, and the **Craftsbury Sports and Learning Center❖**, which maintains 62 miles of trails. Part of the old Bayley-Hazen Military Road to Canada, cut through the forests in 1770, can still be followed today as a pleasant hiking trail. Nearby in this lovely region is the **Wild Branch Wildlife Management Area❖**, which along with the Nature Conservancy's **Bar Hill Nature Preserve❖** in Greensboro helps maintain important habitat for bear and other area wildlife, while providing opportunities for study and recreation. The Bar Hill preserve contains a birch-beech forest very typical of this region.

The most scenic way to loop back south to explore the Connecticut River Valley is a slight detour down Route 14 through the Calais area, one of the lesser-known, unspoiled pockets of the state characterized by rolling hills and small ponds. Off a woods road trail past the Calais

Elementary School is the Nature Conservancy's **Chickering Bog❖**. This splendid preserve is more precisely a fen, a peatland receiving nutrients from the groundwater passing through the calcium-based rocks of the region. Unlike a bog, its dominant plants are sedges (not sphagnum mosses), northern white cedar (not black spruce), and tamarack. It supports a much richer flora than a bog, containing many rare and unusual plants. A nature trail, which at first passes through the woods and damp areas that sustain plants such as joe-pye weed and jack-in-the-pulpit, ends at the fen, a spongy mat of peat. A boardwalk allows visitors to see the natural area without getting wet or trampling its fragile organic soils. Interpretative brochures are available in conspicuous boxes along the trail.

ABOVE: *The great horned owl's diet includes lizards, skunks, and herons. Highly adaptable, this owl is at home in swamps, deep woods, and city parks.*
RIGHT: *Vermont's Long Trail passes over the spectacular gap of Smuggler's Notch, once a route for bootleggers and Canada-bound escaped slaves.*

EASTERN VERMONT:
THE CONNECTICUT RIVER VALLEY
AND THE NORTHEAST KINGDOM

The Connecticut River, New England's longest and largest, begins in a pond 120 yards across near the Canadian border. From this tiny Fourth Connecticut Lake in the boreal forest north of New Hampshire, first as a stream between other small lakes, widening as it goes, it travels south 410 miles. For 235 miles of its course it forms the border between Vermont and New Hampshire (New Hampshire legally owns the waters), then proceeds through Massachusetts and Connecticut, where it finally empties into Long Island Sound. For most of its length the river is the locus of a region that remains remarkably self-contained, the long corridor of its valley changing little. Not as high as the Green Mountains to the west, not as spectacular as the Whites just a short distance to the east, the hills of the Connecticut River Valley are gentle and accessible, stepping down to the river in gradual wooded increments.

The area that feeds the Connecticut covers more than 11,000 square miles. Most of the drainage is from the Vermont Piedmont, east of the Green Mountains and south of the Northeastern Highlands (also known as the Northeast Kingdom). The Piedmont is the largest of Vermont's physiographic regions, and such rivers as the West,

---

LEFT: *Boulder Beach in Groton State Forest is strewn with glacial erratics, ancient rocks torn from ridges and deposited in valleys below. Geologists now use these boulders to map the trails of past glaciers.*

Williams, Black, Ottauquechee, White, and Passumpsic are major eastward-flowing arteries that pump into the Connecticut. The river for much of its length follows an old fault line from the mountain-building era some 500 million years ago.

In French, the word *piedmont* literally means "foot mountain," and, with scattered exceptions like Mount Ascutney, the phrase exactly describes the area's terrain: rolling hills (generally less than 1,500 feet) grading down from the high Green Mountains to the terraced Connecticut River Valley. During postglacial times, a moraine in the vicinity of Middletown, Connecticut, dammed the river valley, creating a long, narrow lake (Lake Hitchcock) that inundated the valley and stretched north more than 200 miles to the Thetford area of Vermont. When the dam eventually broke and the water rushed out, the river dropped to roughly its present level, leaving many extraordinary terraces along its banks. Today the river has a narrow but clearly defined floodplain, where deposits of silt and fresh organic matter have created some of the richest farmland in Vermont. The riverbanks are usually clay, making treacherous footing for walkers but also providing an impressionable surface that is liberally covered with the tracks of the many animals who make the riverside their home.

While the vegetation of the Piedmont—and thus also its wildlife—generally mimics that of the Green Mountains (northern hardwoods, mixing with oaks and hickories in the more southerly zones), the more benign Connecticut River Valley sports some species less common elsewhere, such as black birch, hackberry, black gum (in some swamps), and others. At some locations are plants growing nowhere else in the state; even a species of nationally rare mussel lives on one small segment of the river's bottom. Bald eagles, extremely rare visitors to the state, have occasionally appeared at reservoirs on the river as well, especially in winter.

The marshes where tributary rivers empty into the Connecticut, the backwaters of bays, and the bankside thickets of wild honeysuckle are all prime bird- and animal-watching locales. Sitting quietly on the banks, or better still, coasting slowly along the shore in a canoe or kayak, one is almost certain to spot a variety of creatures. Raccoons come nightly to search for amphibians and small fish; beavers build lopsided lodges against the steep banks; river otters, the largest members of the weasel family in Vermont, make "toboggan slides" in winter

QUÉBEC

Lake Memphremagog

St Albans

89

2

104

Essex Junction

Burlington

7

Vergennes

17

125

Middlebury

GREEN MOUNTAIN NATIONAL FOREST

7

4

Rutland

Williamstown

7

2

Bennington

9

8

GREEN MOUNTAIN

NATIONAL

APPALACHIAN-LONG TRAIL

FOREST

103

100

Woodstock

Hartland

4

100

Ascutney

Weathersfield

Springfield

SPRINGWEATHER NATURAL AREA

100

Dummerston

30

Brattleboro

Guilford

Vernon

FORT DUMMER STATE PARK

Maynard Miller Black Gum Swamps

Newport

SOUTH BAY WMA

100

91

LONG TRAIL

Barton River

Lamoille River

Barton

14

Hardwick

15

Passumpsic River

Lyndonville

Black River

PEACHAM BOG NATURAL AREA

14

GROTON STATE PARK

GROTON STATE FOREST

MONTPELIER

Barre

89

302

SEYON RANCH FLY FISHING AREA

110

HULBERT OUTDOOR EDUCATION CENTER

Ompompanoosuc River

132

Thetford Center

UNION VILLAGE DAM REC AREA

107

MONTSHIRE MUSEUM OF SCIENCE

Quechee Gorge

91

Norwich

White River Junction

ASCUTNEY STATE PARK

Mt Ascutney

WILGUS STATE PARK

Connecticut River

West River

Keene

9

BILL SLADYK WMA

Holland Pond

Norton Pond

114

3

Island Pond

BRIGHTON STATE PARK

105

WENLOCK WMA

Lake Willoughby

WILLOUGHBY STATE FOREST

Victory Bog

114

VICTORY BASIN WMA

St Johnsbury

FAIRBANKS MUSEUM

2

Barnet

Wells River

302

Woodsville

Newbury

25

Bradford

Fairlee

North Thetford

APPALACHIAN TRAIL

Bethlehem

WHITE MOUNTAINS

NEW HAMPSHIRE

93

89

CONCORD

Bloomfield

105

26

MAIDSTONE LAKE STATE PARK

Maidstone Lake

Guildhall

North Concord

93

3

2

Connecticut River

NEW YORK

MASSACHUSETTS

2

91

EASTERN VERMONT

25   0   25 Miles

25   0   25 Kilometers

to slip down the banks; weasels and muskrats are also in evidence—as are tamer animals. Many a canoeist, rounding a bend, has been startled by a wading Holstein cow having a drink.

Frequently sighted birds include great blue herons, spotted sandpipers, bitterns (who like to stay 20 yards ahead of a canoe, wait until the boat reaches them, then fly off that same short distance to start the game of tag over again), and, in the sandy cliffs that are common here, acrobatic bank swallows. The Connecticut River Valley is on a major flyway for migrating birds, and during the autumn and spring many species travel the corridor from north to south and back again.

ABOVE: *Nineteenth-century artist John James Audubon (or perhaps his son John) painted the American bittern on the East Coast in 1832–33. Thoreau called this large, furtive marsh bird "the genius of the bog."*
RIGHT: *Groton State Forest's 200-acre Peacham Bog supports many sedges and shrubs, including leatherleaf; its numerous tamarack, balsam, and spruce trees make it one of the largest wooded bogs in Vermont.*

Human beings have long been close companions of the Connecticut, and not always to its benefit. Native Americans settled along it to take advantage of the remarkable fishery—especially the teeming spring runs of Atlantic salmon and American shad swimming upstream to spawn in tributaries. By 1814, early dams and industrial pollution had already wiped the salmon run out—one of the first environmental catastrophes the young country experienced. In 1966, federal, state, and local agencies joined forces with conservation groups and power companies to begin an ambitious restoration program: establishing salmon hatcheries, planting smolts (young salmon) in tributary streams, and constructing fish ladders around the dams. More than $700 million has been spent in this effort—with slow but encouraging results. For the first time in almost two centuries, salmon are using the Connecticut River as a corridor north. In the early 1990s nearly 500 adult salmon returned to the river from their ocean haunts off Greenland in the North Atlantic.

Another anadromous fish (one that lives in saltwater but spawns in fresh), the shad, has benefited from the fish ladders and improved water quality as well and now returns by the thousands. Both species have worked their way as far north as central Vermont and New Hampshire.

Although the Connecticut River Valley retains its gentle, meandering character all the way to the Canadian border, upstream toward Essex County, the land just west of the river changes dramatically. This area is known as the Northeast Kingdom—the 600 square miles of wild, forested hills that form Vermont's northeastern corner just below Quebec. George Aiken, Vermont's former governor and longtime U.S. senator, is credited with coining the term *Northeast Kingdom* for the area, which differs in geography, appearance, and culture from the rest of the state. Although there is no fixed boundary for the kingdom, it is generally recognized as Essex, Orleans, and Caledonia counties. In topography it has much more in common with the northern tip of neighboring New Hampshire and the forests of Maine than with the rest of Vermont. The weather is the most severe in the state: On December 30, 1933, the thermometer fell to minus 50 degrees Fahrenheit in Bloomfield, still the record low for all of New England.

Perhaps not so ironically, this region is different geologically and biologically from the rest of Vermont. Many of the relatively low and rounded mountains are essentially the western extension of New Hampshire's White Mountains, granites much younger (200 million years old at most) than the metamorphic rock of the Green Mountains. Indeed, the mountains give this region its other name, "the Granite Hills." Hard and resistant to weathering, the rocks yield little in the way of nutrients, so soils here are not very fertile. The addition of a demanding northern climate makes this a true boreal environment. Almost everywhere else in the state, such conditions exist high in the mountains; here a boreal environment occurs at low elevations, and at its heart in Essex County, in huge unbroken tracts of land.

Logging is the mainstay of the economy here, and most of the land is owned by timber companies. Conservation efforts focus on the Northern Forest, which extends from upstate New York through the Northeast Kingdom into New Hampshire and Maine—the largest area of wild land remaining in the Northeast. Various strategies for this forest are being debated in this critical time for future planning.

The route for this chapter follows the course of the river. We begin in the south on the narrow piedmont between the Green Mountains and the Connecticut River and proceed north mainly on Route 5 and I-91, which cross and intertwine all the way to the Canadian border. On side excursions we visit various sites in the Northeast Kingdom after the river angles east at Barnet.

The main highway along the Connecticut is I-91, and north of Brattleboro the road is often high enough above the river to provide good views of the terraced floodplains along its banks. Occasionally, along the road cuts, sections of "varved" (distinctly laminated) clay deposited by the river at its prehistoric height are exposed. By studying these deposits, geologists have determined that the last Wisconsin glacier receded from south to north, taking 4,300 years to retreat the 200 miles from Middletown, Connecticut, to Saint Johnsbury, Vermont, a rate of about 245 feet a year.

LEFT: *Forming the border between Vermont and New Hampshire, the Connecticut River, seen here from Putney, Vermont, winds its way south, cutting a smooth strip in the New England bedrock.*

THE CONNECTICUT RIVER VALLEY

A canoe or kayak is by far the best way to explore the river and its wildlife. A number of public access sites make the Vermont side of the river much more convenient to boaters than the New Hampshire side, where public access points are few and far between.

Each access point offers a boat launching ramp and space to park cars; some provide a toilet. Listed from south to north, they include **Old Ferry Road Access Area,** off Route 5 in Brattleboro; **Putney Landing Access Area,** off Route 5 near the Dummerston-Putney town line; **Hoyt Landing Access Area,** in Springfield just off Exit 7 of I-91; **Hammond Cove Access Area,** off Route 5 in Hartland; **Ompompanoosuc River Access Area,** where the river of the same name enters the Connecticut under Route 5 north of Norwich; **North Thetford Access Area,** in the quiet hamlet of North Thetford just east of the railroad tracks off I-91; and **Haverhill Bridge Access Area,** one of the prettiest sites, in Newbury off Route 5, just under the bridge to New Hampshire.

Other launching points are connected with the occasional state park on the river, and many towns have their own undeveloped "landings" where access can be gained. It's best to inquire about these sites at the town clerk's office or ask local landowners for permission to cross their fields to the river. In the stretches of river impounded by dams, the banks are very steep, and just a few feet from shore the water reaches depths over most people's heads; below the dams, the water level can rise unexpectedly when water is released, so boaters, swimmers, and anglers should keep a wary eye on water levels at all times. An old fishing trick is to stick a branch in the mud to serve as a gauge.

The Connecticut River Valley comprises more than the river. In extreme southeastern Vermont, off I-91, the town of Vernon protects the unusual **Maynard Miller Black Gum Swamps❖,** part of its town forest. Named after a local farmer who has taken great interest in the swamps and their preservation, they are apparently holdovers from the era when Vermont's climate was warmer than it is today. The largest number of southern plants—such as black gum (tupelo), mountain laurel, and

---

RIGHT: *In late afternoon a golden glow brightens the summit of Mount Ascutney. To the east sunlight fans over the gently rolling hills of the Connecticut River Valley and the White Mountains beyond.*

86

ABOVE: *Nicolino Calyo painted* View Along the Connecticut River *about 1850. Born in Italy, Calyo traveled down the river in a 17-foot raft to capture scenes such as this one of Mount Ascutney and Windsor, Vermont.*

Virginia chain fern—in the state grow here as a community. With their nearly horizontal branches and deeply furrowed bark, black gums grow to an impressive old age—400 years in some cases—and they live here surrounded by a luxurious assortment of mosses and ferns. The area has such an otherworldly, prehistoric feel that a dinosaur would look right at home. A few large, old, but sterile American chestnuts, extinct almost everywhere else, still cling to existence here. Visitors should check at the town clerk's office in Vernon for directions and information.

South of I-91 Exit 1 in Guilford is **Fort Dummer State Park❖,** site of the first permanent white settlement in Vermont (1724) and one of the few state parks on or near the river. Several miles to the north on the town borders of Springfield and Weathersfield is the **Springweather Nature Area❖,** a 70-acre preserve, walking area, and viewing point for nearby Mount Ascutney. It is managed as an environmental education area by the Ascutney Mountain Audubon Society on land owned by the Army Corps of Engineers. Several self-guided, color-coded nature trails follow the ecotone, or boundary between different habitats such as forests and fields. Many birds flourish here, including song sparrows, with their streaked brown-and-white underparts; field sparrows; and yellow-throated warblers, which are particularly fascinating to watch during spring breeding, when males fly up out of the meadow grass in a noisy display to attract females.

Pyramid-shaped Mount Ascutney (3,144 feet) is the most conspicuous mountain in the middle third of Vermont's Connecticut River Valley. It's a classic monadnock—a cone of hard, resistant, originally subsurface rock (in this case granite), left exposed and isolated as the softer, less-resistant rock encasing it eroded away. In fact, Mount Ascutney has more in common with the White Mountains of New Hampshire than with the very rocks around it. **Ascutney State Park**❖ (off Exit 8 of I-91) offers two different ways to reach the summit: via a 3.8-mile paved toll road and via hiking trails. A particularly popular route is the Wethersfield Trail, on the southern slope. On the way up look for scour marks left by the last glacier on the summit rocks, indicating just how high the ice sheet rose here. Its commanding and isolated height above a major corridor of the Atlantic Flyway makes Mount Ascutney a favorite spot for birders, particularly in the spring: Ravens and other boreal species have been seen here. Black-throated blue warblers—the tamest of warblers, easily identified by the males' unmistakable blue-gray color—are abundant too. Emulating the birds, hang gliders like to launch themselves off West Peak toward the river, taking advantage of updrafts from the valley floor. Three miles south, perched directly on the river and on sharply cut terraces overlooking it, is small but attractive **Wilgus State Park**❖, offering good access to the river for canoeing and canoe or car camping.

In a steep-banked oxbow, or U-shaped bend, of the Connecticut outside Norwich is the **Montshire Museum of Science**❖, one of the best nature centers in northern New England. Among the many interpretative displays on the region's flora and fauna (including interactive exhibits appealing to children) is a freshwater aquarium containing brook and brown trout, bass, perch, and other fish from local waters. Self-guided nature trails thread through the woods and wetlands; wildlife tours led by the museum's naturalists to many areas of the

---

Overleaf: *A good vantage point for observing wildlife is from the water. With planning, canoeists can paddle the Vermont section of the Connecticut River camping at such places as Wilgus State Park, shown here.*

Northeast are open to members and nonmembers alike.

One Vermont tradition is the swimming hole—the deep pool in a cold, rushing river that, in a state with no ocean, acts as the local beach. There are several of these along the Ompompanoosuc River by the **Union Village Dam Recreation Area❖,** off Route 132 in Thetford Center. A self-guided nature trail here traverses the old farm fields growing back into forest. About 10 miles north in Fairlee, at the north end of Lake Morey, the 1,000-acre **Hulbert Outdoor Education Center❖** conducts a variety of nature-related educational programs for children and adults.

ABOVE: *Known as the fire throat, the male Blackburnian warbler frequents the tops of conifer trees and uses his distinctive wiry song and bright colors to attract a mate.*

RIGHT: *Beside the tranquil Mollys Falls Pond near Groton State Forest, a sugar maple dressed in brilliant fall garb glows among evergreens and meadow flowers such as white pearly everlasting.*

North of Bradford the river plain widens, the constraining ridges fall away, and more expansive views open out toward New Hampshire's White Mountains to the east, as if a giant had shaved down the intervening ridges with a sharp plane. This area is a transitional zone between the piedmont country of the south and the more rugged landscape of the Northeast Kingdom. Just north of Route 302 along the headwaters of the Wells River is **Groton State Forest❖,** one of the largest (some 33,000 acres) publicly owned areas in Vermont. As seen on many bare peaks, the bedrock here is granite, originating as huge, molten domes (plutons) emplaced in the preexisting bedrock some 200 million years ago. Subsequent erosion of the surrounding rocks has exposed these rounded peaks. The granites of Groton are actually kin to those of the White Mountains of New Hampshire: They are part of the same formation and approximately the same age.

Set amid a series of low hills and ridges, Groton affords enough variety to reward many full days of exploration. Roads, hiking trails, and even an old railroad bed provide access to six large ponds and many

ABOVE: *Hardy hay-scented and boulder ferns are relatives of tree-sized fern species that flourished in swamps at least 200 million years ago.*

smaller ones, one of the largest bogs in Vermont, and one of its last stands of old-growth hardwoods. First-time visitors can stop at either the **Big Deer Campground❖,** at the head of Lake Groton, or the Groton Nature Center, a short distance beyond, to pick up unusually detailed trail maps, history guides, and keys to the birds, plants, and animals found here. Several trails leave the Nature Center; one goes 2.5 miles to **Peacham Bog Natural Area❖,** a 200-acre raised bog where layers of saturated peat have built a dome-shaped mass. The highly acidic bog, one of the largest in the state, supports plants such as black spruce, tamarack, leatherleaf, sedge, and rhodora.

More than 100 species of birds have been recorded in Groton. Of particular interest are the abundant warblers and flycatchers, insect-eating birds that thrive in the mixed forests. Hawks can be sighted from the low, open hilltops during their fall migration. Boreal species, including the boreal chickadee and Wilson's warbler (a yellow-breasted bird with a distinctive black crown patch that does most of its insect hunting less than a dozen feet above the ground), inhabit the spruce-fir forest around Peacham Bog.

ABOVE: *Amid boulders and fallen leaves, a paper birch gracefully sheds thin spirals of its distinctive bark in Groton State Forest.*

A gem in the forest's center, **Lord's Hill❖** is a protected 25 acre old-growth northern hardwood forest and designated state natural area. Individual trees here have reached state-record size and represent a diversity of species: white ash, yellow birch, sugar maple, basswood, hop hornbeam, and others. Inquire at the nature center or campground offices for hiking directions.

Peaceful and beautiful **Seyon Ranch Fly Fishing Area❖** is in the southern part of the forest. Here, Noyes Pond is closely controlled: Anglers are restricted to fly-fishing (with barbless hooks only) from a limited number of park rowboats (advance reservations are recommended). A comfortable lodge is available for overnight accommodations, meals, meetings, or other gatherings. Seyon Ranch and the outlying area are also used in winter as an environmental education center for schoolchildren from across the state.

OVERLEAF: *The forest continuously recycles and regenerates. Nutrients from dead leaves reenter the food chain; fallen trees are attacked by fungi, bacteria, and insects. Eventually, saplings begin to fill the void.*

THE NORTHEAST KINGDOM

North of Groton State Forest lies the Northeast Kingdom—600 square miles of rugged hills, ponds, rivers, and coniferous woods that seem painted with a different brush from the rest of the state. Poorer, tougher, grittier, this rugged corner of Vermont lacks the neat villages and farms so typical of the rest of the state. Even casual travelers quickly perceive that this is a working landscape, an impression reinforced by the house trailers, logging trucks, and cheap cafés that line the highways. The late Wallace Stegner, a well-known western novelist who summered here for years, noted that the Northeast Kingdom is "still a frontier. It's special in Vermont: the least developed part, the wildest and roughest."

A paucity of fertile soil concentrated around the Connecticut River floodplain and in a few sheltered valleys, the predominance of the logging industry, the demanding northern climate, and an isolated position north of the main transportation routes have made the Northeast Kingdom the poorest, least populated part of Vermont. Those who manage to survive here—animals, plants, and humans—are the ones who have adapted best to the unforgiving severity of the land. Viewed on a late October afternoon, however, when the crepuscular sunlight breaks down through the clouds and fans over the ridges, this is as majestic a landscape as Vermont possesses. Perhaps because many of its major rivers flow north, the area seems to lie tipped toward Canada, barely connected to the rest of the United States. In numerous villages, French is spoken as a matter of course because so many immigrants have come from Quebec to work in the woods and factories. The watersheds split fairly evenly down the center of the Northeast Kingdom; streams in the south and east flow primarily into the Connecticut and Long Island Sound, and those in the west and north flow into big Lake Memphremagog and in turn into the Saint Lawrence.

At the junctions of Routes 2 and 5 and Interstates 91 and 93 lies Saint Johnsbury, the Northeast Kingdom's largest town (population 7,600) and home of the **Fairbanks Museum and Planetarium❖**. Established a century ago by the philanthropy of Thaddeus Fairbanks, inventor of the platform scale and founder of the Fairbanks Company here, it is the state's largest natural history museum. Exhibits are devoted to local, regional, and even exotic animals, geology, and minerals, as well as Vermont history (especially as related to land use). The museum—which also offers many educational programs, from planetarium shows to lectures to school group visits to field trips—is an excellent place to begin an exploration of the Northeast Kingdom.

North of Saint Johnsbury and nearby Lyndonville stretches the rural and wild country of the Northeast Kingdom. Northeast of Saint Johnsbury, along the headwaters of the Moose River off Route 2, is the **Victory Bog❖,** a vast expanse of marshes, swamps, bogs, and connecting streams, interspersed with uplands of mixed hardwoods and softwoods. The area is rich wildlife habitat for moose, bear, coyote, deer, fisher, otter, birds by the score, and many others. One of local novelist Henry Frank Mosher's best stories, "Kingdom County Come," is about a terminally ill man who has loved the bog his whole life and crawls into an empty beaver lodge in the bog's center to die in dignity, alone. It is difficult to get around in the complex of wetlands (especially during blackfly and mosquito season); one of the few points where the bog is accessible is the **Victory Basin Wildlife Management Area❖** (5,000 acres), off Route 2 in North Concord (maps of the area are available). During the autumn, after leaves have dropped off the deciduous trees, the tamaracks have a foliage season of their own. They are the only conifers in the Northeast that shed their needles every year; the needles turn bright yellow before they fall, transforming hillsides and swampy areas into beautiful, austere displays of color.

The Connecticut River, whose width remains relatively constant through most of the state, narrows to the size of a trout stream above Guildhall. (Indeed, the fishing from here all the way to the source is some of the best in New England. Wild brown trout weighing more than 14 pounds are taken each year, many through the winter ice.) Tracing the river's course, Route 102 heads north to the Canadian border, skirting the perimeter of vast timberlands owned primarily by large industrial pulp and paper companies. **Maidstone Lake State Park❖** is a public holding within these private lands. Although the park is just two miles from the Connecticut River as the crow flies, earthbound visitors, who negotiate a six-mile dirt road, arrive feeling that they have penetrated the deepest spruce-fir country.

The park is on large and scenic Maidstone Lake, whose deep, cold waters hold landlocked salmon and lake trout. There are several trails in the park, and endless opportunities for walking and hiking outside it

ABOVE: *Known as the fool hen, the spruce grouse is so trusting that it often allows humans to come within a few feet before retreating into the cover of the woods.*

RIGHT: *Passive defenses such as cryptic coloration, or camouflage, are common among animals. This week-old white-tailed deer can blend into a variety of backgrounds, such as a field of daisies.*

OVERLEAF: *Trails winding through Willoughby State Forest offer views of distant mountains and a small woodland pond. A beaver dam probably caused the water to rise, killing the trees closest to the shore.*

on timber company roads and trails. The shoreline of Maidstone Lake conceals the nests of common loons, endangered in Vermont. The female of each pair lays two olive-brown eggs in a large mat of weeds and branches in easy reach of the water. Moose Trail, one of three trails that circle the lake, offers excellent opportunities to spot the chocolate-colored, clumsy-yet-graceful mammals for which the trail is named and which are becoming increasingly common here.

Branching off in Bloomfield, Route 105, which follows the Nulhegan River west from the Connecticut, crosses the divide over to the Memphremagog watershed and bisects the largest unbroken expanse of boreal forest in the state, some 250,000 acres of timber company–owned lands. Here, in the red spruce–balsam fir uplands and black spruce wetlands, live some of the state's most unusual boreal birds, some of which are found nowhere else, including spruce grouse, gray jays, and blackbacked woodpeckers.

Roads in this region cut straight through moose country—indeed, after dinner local residents park their jeeps on sidings and wait patiently for moose to appear to lick the winter road salt that has leached down the banks. These big creatures can be a serious driving hazard for the unwary; there are fatal moose-car collisions every year, and although the state has gone to great lengths to make moose areas obvious, drivers

should exercise caution at all times. The stretch of I-91 between Lyndonville and Barton has a particularly bad reputation for moose-car collisions. Also, on logging roads open to the public, logging trucks have the right of way, so drivers must be vigilant and careful. In addition, visitors easily can become confused and lost in the backcountry, where myriad roads and trails cover so much territory. The best strategy is to determine one's route before setting out.

South of the town of Island Pond on Route 105 is the **Wenlock Wildlife Management Area❖,** nearly 2,000 acres along the Nulhegan, featuring boreal bird species more common in Canada than Vermont. The rarest here is the spruce grouse, a dusky, quiet bird that favors the edges of bogs and is known for—and vulnerable because of—its extraordinary tameness (which gives it the nickname "fool hen"). Wenlock contains the state's biggest deer wintering area, a vital refuge for animals from miles around. Moose Bog, a large area with a floating sphagnum-sedge mat surrounding open water, sits hidden in a spruce-fir basin south of the road.

Nearby is **Brighton State Park❖,** which includes a small museum and self-guided nature trails through the mixed forests and around

101

Spectacle Pond. Across the pond from the campground and accessible by trail is **Spectacle Pond Natural Area❖,** home to majestic red and white pines and an understory of sheep laurel, leatherleaf, and other boreal wildflowers.

Up Route 114 just south of the Canadian line is the **Bill Sladyk Wildlife Management Area❖.** Occupying nearly 10,000 acres west of Route 114 between Norton Pond and Holland Pond, this is one of the largest and wildest wildlife management areas in Vermont, actually touching the Canadian border in places. Visitors will find pristine expanses of boreal and mixed forestland, wetlands of many types, and several small and untouched remote ponds, all of which can be reached on foot (some more easily than others) or in cars via woods roads and trails. Here and elsewhere, local sporting groups have been backpacking wild trout fingerlings in to stock remote beaver ponds, ensuring some excellent fishing in years to come.

Lake Memphremagog—nicknamed Magog locally—is the second-largest lake in which, as the old Works Progress Administration guide puts it, "Vermont has an interest." Roughly a quarter of the lake's 60 square miles are in the state; the rest lie in the province of Quebec. Memphremagog (Algonquian for "beautiful waters") has long been a corridor between Canada and the United States—a particularly important one for smugglers who did a great deal of nocturnal boating during Prohibition. In 1759, Major Robert Rogers (whose exploits were the subject of Kenneth Roberts's best-selling book *Northwest Passage*) led his famed Rogers' Rangers through the area to and from his raid on the Indian village of Saint Francis in Canada during the French and Indian Wars. In the nineteenth century the lake was a major waterway for the movement of logs, and it remains today an important fishery for landlocked salmon, rainbow trout, and others.

There are boat launching sites in the Newport area. The public park just north of where the Clyde River empties into the lake is one of the few landlocked-salmon fishing areas in the Northeast. Every autumn the rule is "catch and release"—all salmon caught must be returned immediately to the water. The lake is fed by two important rivers at its southern end, the Black and the Barton. **South Bay Wildlife Management Area❖** (1,559 acres) is at the mouth of the latter as it empties into the South Bay of Memphremagog. Around it is an extensive and wildlife-rich marsh, an excellent place for waterfowl, marsh birds such as bitterns and rail, and even osprey. One can canoe in from the lake or other access points or walk along the railroad tracks at the eastern edge of the marshes.

For those heading south toward Saint Johnsbury on Route 5, the most spectacular part of the trip lies ahead: dramatic **Lake Willoughby,** which many consider the most beautifully situated lake in Vermont. Willoughby is long, deep, and narrow, flanked by precipitous cliffs that rise a thousand feet, creating a fjordlike effect that is in startling contrast to the softer lines of most Vermont landscapes. The notch is so raw that the glacier that carved it could have retreated just yesterday. In fact, Willoughby was formed in a classic way: An ancient river followed a crustal fault line through the granitic bedrock; much later, passing glacial ice carved the river valley deeper and wider, smoothing the mountains on either side. The glacier's retreat left the drainages dammed with sand and gravel.

Besides their awe-inspiring appearance, the 1,000-foot-high cliffs dropping precipitously to the lake support rare arctic plants (e. g. yellow mountain saxifrage, green alder), which cling to an ages-old existence in the cliff crevices and on the fallen boulders at the talus base. Peregrine falcons, absent from the cliffs for more than 25 years, have returned for the past 10 to nest successfully. The cliffs, part of **Willoughby State Forest❖** and a state natural area, can be viewed from several hiking trails on either side of the lake, up Mount Pisgah (2,751 feet) on the east side and Mount Hor (2,648 feet) on the west.

Willoughby is a favorite of anglers, who troll for lake trout and landlocked salmon. Its outlet, the Willoughby River, is the site of one of the best-known spawning runs of rainbow trout in the United States. The Barton River upstream passes through the village of Orleans, where it is joined by the Willoughby River, coming from the east. Within the town limits is Willoughby Falls, a series of low falls, pools, and cascades. Here, in mid- to late April, Lake Memphremagog's steelhead rainbow trout jump the falls as they migrate up to the headwaters of the Willoughby River to spawn. Each year anglers and spectators line the banks, the former to try their hand at catching them, the latter to admire the big fish close-up as they leap through the cascading waters and rest in quiet pools. Such seasonal migrations—of fish, of birds, of mammals—lend their own ambience to the untamed quality of the Northeast Kingdom.

NEW HAMPSHIRE

WESTERN NEW HAMPSHIRE:
MONADANOCK AND THE UPPER VALLEY

The western hills of New Hampshire, overshadowed by the higher White Mountains to the north and the popular lake district to the east, comprise one of the least visited corners of New England. This area contains a high density of protected natural areas, large tracts of wild, wooded upland seldom visited outside hunting season, and the cellar holes and old stone walls that remain as bittersweet reminders of the farming communities that existed here 150 years ago. Anyone driving to this region from Vermont will see an immediate difference between the two states, at least outside the towns. Here the hills are steeper, the farms less common, the streams more precipitous, the landscape more neglected.

Bounded by I-93 and the Merrimack River on the east, the Connecticut River on the west, the White Mountains on the north, and the Massachusetts border on the south, the western hills are a series of long ridges averaging 2,000 feet in elevation and pocketlike valleys averaging 350 feet in elevation. A group of unrelated mountains rise just far enough above the surrounding hills to act as landmarks for navigation and magnets for nature lovers and hikers. These mountains include Mount Cardigan near Canaan, Mount Kearsarge near New

PRECEDING PAGES: *Cathedral Ledge, near Conway, New Hampshire, provides a sweeping vista of wooded valley and distant mountains.*
LEFT: *Forest, bog, water, and sky coalesce into a splendid summer still life in this painterly view of Pillsbury State Park near Washington.*

London, Mount Sunapee near the lake of the same name, and, most famous of all, Monadnock Mountain, called Mount Monadnock by locals, in the southwestern corner of the state.

Monadnock has become a generic term, defined in the dictionary as "a single remnant of a former highland, which rises as an isolated rock mass above a plain." Monadnock rises above the town of Troy in a fine pyramid that belies its modest elevation of only 3,165 feet. With a core of harder rock (the Littleton formation schist that occurs so frequently in New Hampshire) than the surrounding hills, the mountain was better able to resist the eroding pressure of the last great ice sheet some 10,000 years ago. But isolated as it is in the landscape, Monadnock suffers no isolation when it comes to visitors: It is reputed to be the second most frequently climbed mountain in the world after Fuji in Japan, with as many as 10,000 hikers reaching the top on a single day. As the country's closest "big" mountain to Concord, Massachusetts, Monadnock was often visited by transcendentalists such as Emerson and Thoreau. Author Mark Twain, viewing the peak from the nearby town of Dublin, extolled:

"In these October days Monadnock and the valley and its framing hills make an inspiring picture to look at, for they are sumptuously splashed and mottled and betorched from sky-line to sky-line with the richest dyes the autumn can furnish; and when they lie flaming in the full drench of the mid-afternoon sun, the sight affects the spectator physically, it stirs the blood like military music."

The western hills, perhaps better than any other region in northern New England, illustrate the slow progression of once-cleared land back to forest. The original mixed hardwood and softwood forest of the 1700s was cut down by the first European pioneers to clear the land for pasture and crops; by 1830, nearly 80 percent of the area had been cleared of trees, mainly to make room for sheep and dairy farming. By 1850, when many farmers were abandoning their land for, literally, greener pastures in the West (it has been estimated that 95 percent of New Hampshire's soil remains not arable), sun-loving white pines were large enough to harvest as timber. This left room for the understory hardwoods to grow—a forest that still characterizes the region today, when more of western New Hampshire is wooded than at any other time since the first European settlers arrived.

Within a patchwork of woodlots, overgrown farms, depopulated old

QUÉBEC

Pittsburg

Bloomfield

Groveton

Berlin

WHITE
MOUNTAIN
NATIONAL
FOREST

St Johnsbury

MONTPELIER

Barre

Bethlehem

Franconia

WHITE MOUNTAIN

Mt Washington
6288

Woodsville

North
Haverhill

BEDELL BRIDGE
HISTORIC SITE

Haverhill

WHITE

MOUNTAINS NATIONAL

Reed's
Marsh

Orford

WHITE
MOUNTAIN
NATIONAL
FOREST

FOREST

NEW

Lyme

HAMPSHIRE

PINE
PARK

Newfound
Lake

Hanover

White River
Junction

CARDIGAN
STATE PARK

Canaan

Mt Cardigan

Lake Winnipesaukee

ENFIELD
WMA

Crafton
Pond

RUGGLES MINE

Grafton

ST GAUDENS
NAT HIST SITE

GILE STATE
FOREST

Wilmot

Laconia

APPALACHIAN-LONG
TRAIL

JOHN HAY
NWR

New London

WINSLOW
STATE PARK

Sunapee
Lake

Mt Sunapee

Newbury

ROLLINS
STATE PARK

Rochester

PILLSBURY
STATE PARK

Warner

CHRISTA MCAULIFFE
PLANETARIUM

Washington

FOX
STATE FOREST

CONCORD

Allenstown

CHARLES L PIERCE
WILDLIFE SANCTUARY

Hillsboro

Portsmouth

Stoddard

MCCABE
FOREST

DEERING
WILDLIFE
SANCTUARY

BEAR BROOK
STATE PARK

Deering

Great Bay

WANTASTIQUET MTN
STATE FOREST

Antrim

MEETINGHOUSE POND
WILDLIFE SANCTUARY

WAPACK
NWR

Manchester

MERRIMACK RIVER
CONSERVATION CENTER

Keene

Marlborough

Peterborough

MILLER
STATE PARK

Atlantic Ocean

Brattleboro

Chesterfield

PISGAH
STATE PARK

Mt Monadnock
3165

Troy

Gap Mtn

MONADNOCK STATE PARK

PONEMAH BOG
BOTANICAL PRESERVE

Nashua

Hinsdale

RHODODENDRON
STATE PARK

Fitzwilliam

Jaffrey

Hollis

BEAVER BROOK NATURAL AREA

MASSACHUSETTS

ABOVE: *With leathery leaves resistant to water loss, the native lowbush blueberry thrives in bogs. The fruit has hundreds of seeds, too tiny to detect in the mouth.*

RIGHT: *Strong fliers, vivid monarch butterflies migrate thousands of miles to Mexico each fall. On their way back north, they reproduce and die; their offspring then complete the springtime journey.*

mill towns, and small villages, this portion of New Hampshire offers a variety of flora and fauna. Plants of the field, those able to tolerate sun and wind, grow extensively in recently cleared areas. These include familiar milkweed, the nonnative shepherd's purse, the ubiquitous dandelion, goldenrod, and thistle, and, most favored of all, the berries—blackberries, raspberries, and blueberries. Many favorites of the backyard birder frequent this region, including the grosbeaks, the song sparrow, which favors the shrubs and small trees on the forest edge, and the mockingbird, which has slowly extended its range northward over the past several decades. The cardinal is also expanding its range northward, lured by the proliferation of bird feeders and the increased planting of ornamental trees bearing seeds and fruit.

Insects abound as well. One of the most remarkable is the bright orange and black monarch butterfly, which summers in New Hampshire. Supplemented by those individuals that emerge from metamorphosis late in the season, the monarchs migrate to Mexico and Central America during the early fall, flying by day, congregating on trees and ledges at night. People who have monitored this migration have seen a dramatic decrease in the number of butterflies over the past few years, possibly due to the destruction of their habitat in the south. Among common insects is the honeybee, which was transported to this country in 1638 by the settlers of Massachusetts Bay. Regarded as less benign is the eastern tent caterpillar, whose tents, in times of heavy infestation, cover a remarkably high percentage of

112

trees and can cause heavy defoliation.

Plenty of large mammals roam these hills, including deer, black bears (which have been known to make foraging raids on domesticated beehives down in the valleys), a growing moose population, and coyotes, lured back by the increased forest cover. More common are the smaller mammals, such as the vegetarian meadow vole, the short-tailed shrew, and the hairy-tailed mole with its extraordinarily rapid metabolism that makes it eat ravenously. Frequently spotted are the familiar raccoon, porcupine, skunk, cottontail rabbit, chipmunk, and red squirrel. The last two like to gnaw the plastic tubing used to collect sap from maple trees and thus have become a problem. Opportunities for viewing all these species in their natural settings are offered by an ample network of old woods roads.

Visitors must be cautious, avoiding any wild animals acting suspiciously tame, particularly raccoons. An outbreak of rabies spread into northern New England during the early 1990s, and raccoons are extremely susceptible to this disease. Campers in particular should not leave food or garbage in the open, where it may attract wild animals.

The flattest and most heavily farmed land in this region is the strip along the Connecticut River in the west. Still, the floodplain and valley here are not as wide as on the Vermont side of the river, and not until north of Woodsville do the ridges hemming in the river really subside. Relatively few tributary rivers flow in the southern two-thirds of the valley, and those that do are shorter and more tumultuous than on the Vermont side.

Western New Hampshire, like much of northern New England, has benefited from the efforts of conservation organizations to protect land. One particularly effective organization has been the nonprofit Society for the Protection of New Hampshire Forests, organized in 1901 when much of the state's forestland had been denuded by farmers and in lumbering operations of the most exploitative sort. This society and similar organizations—such as the Audubon Society, the Nature Conservancy, and ad hoc, local organizations, often formed locally to protect a specific feature—have succeeded in preserving much of this region from the heavy suburban pressure of the state's southeast.

Beginning in southwestern New Hampshire, this chapter's route travels east to the Merrimack River and I-93 before proceeding west on or parallel to I-89 through the Sunapee Lake region. From the central region, the route continues north to Mount Cardigan and west to Hanover on the Vermont border.

MONADNOCK AND THE SOUTH

Southwestern New Hampshire is a sprawl of hills that requires frequent checks of the road map to navigate. The best driving route starts in the southwestern corner and works its way east, then northwest.

Across the Connecticut River from Brattleboro, Vermont, is one of New Hampshire's lesser-known natural areas: **Wantastiquet Mountain State Forest❖** on Route 119 in Hinsdale, featuring the small mountain that rises above this part of the Connecticut. The red pines here provide relief even on the hottest days; an easy climb to the granite ledges near the summit is rewarded by excellent views. Thoreau, having climbed Wantastiquet during a trip here in 1856, observed: "This everlasting mountain is forever lowering over the village, shortening the day, and wearing a misty cap each morning."

A short distance to the east is a real surprise: an undeveloped forest of more than 13,000 acres that is as close to wilderness as can be found in the southern tier of New Hampshire. **Pisgah State Park❖,** located off Route 63 two miles east of Chesterfield, is deliberately being left in a

114

primitive condition—a parking lot and pit toilets constitute its only improvements. The forest offers excellent hiking on old woods roads, cross-country skiing, and even a small stand of old-growth white pine the loggers somehow missed. Ponds are scattered throughout; swamps and marshes are favored birding spots. To the northwest of the mixed hardwood forest, a series of ridges culminates in Mount Pisgah (1,300 feet). Pisgah doesn't have the extensive trail system of the Whites in the North, and as a result it is a particular favorite of experienced bushwhackers.

Keene is the busy market town in this part of the state, but just east of it off Route 101, in the village of Marlborough, is the quiet **Meetinghouse Pond Wildlife Sanctuary❖,** maintained by the Audubon Society of New Hampshire. This 202-acre preserve includes unspoiled and eminently canoeable Meetinghouse Pond, a sphagnum bog, and beautiful wildflowers, including the rare spotted wintergreen. The Rocky Ridge Trail is a fairly rugged hike up from Meetinghouse Pond to a beaver pond, back past the boat landing, and on through an impressive stand of 160-year-old red oak, which survived not only the loggers but also the general devastation caused here by the infamous 1938 hurricane (to this day, New England's worst natural disaster). Here and elsewhere in the western hills, many of the oldest, largest trunks decaying on the ground in the woods fell during this storm.

The entire southwestern corner of New Hampshire is dominated by solitary Monadnock Mountain (often referred to as Grand Monadnock). **Monadnock State Park❖** off Dublin Road takes up 900 acres on the southeastern side of the mountain; the picnic area and trailheads are reached over the Poole Memorial Road originally cut in 1802. The Society for the Protection of New Hampshire Forests also owns 4,000 acres on the mountain, so much of it is permanently protected. Normally, a mountain with a height of only 3,165 feet would not have a timberline. But in 1810, to drive sheep-eating wolves from their dens, settlers set fires so hot and intense they destroyed all the soil on the top 500 feet of the mountain. What remains is bare ledge, permitting views in all directions. Close to Boston, Monadnock has always been a magnet: Henry David Thoreau,

---

OVERLEAF: *At sunset, Mount Monadnock broods over Perkins Pond.*
Rising above the rolling hill country of southern New Hampshire, the
isolated landmark has long been irresistible to hikers and naturalists.

camping here in 1860, found it too crowded for his taste!

Since its first recorded ascent in 1706, millions have climbed Monadnock, many of them children on their first "big mountain" hike. At one time there were more than 80 trails on the mountain, but—with the burning of one of the hiking centers, the Halfway House, in 1954—only about a dozen are permanently maintained today. Some of these trails begin at the park's visitor center, an interpretative museum with hiking and historical exhibits. One of the oldest and most attractive trails is the White Dot Trail, which provides the most direct route to the summit. The two-hour hike to the top begins by the visitor center off Route 124 two miles west of Jaffrey. The peak is also the southern terminus of the Monadnock-Sunapee Greenway, a 51-mile through hiking trail linking these two New Hampshire mountains, and the northern terminus of the 160-mile Metacomet Trail, which heads south to Meriden, Connecticut.

In Monadnock's shadow is **Rhododendron State Park❖,** one of the gems of the New Hampshire park system, located off Route 119 approximately one mile west of Fitzwilliam. The 16-acre colony of wild rhododendron, *Rhododendron maximum,* protected here is by far the largest such cluster in New England, and as such, designated a national natural landmark. Threatened with logging in 1902, the land was bought by Mary Lee Ware, a botanist who loved rhododendron. She gave it to the Appalachian Mountain Club with the stipulation that it be permanently protected; the AMC later donated the land to the state. Rhododendrons are much more common in the mountains of North Carolina and other southern areas, but they do well in the acid soil and deep humus found here, at the northern limit of their range. The one-mile Wildflower Trail is especially spectacular in mid-July, when the rhododendrons are in blossom. But there are other wildflowers here as well, blooming three seasons a year, from jack-in-the-pulpit to lady's slipper to the late-blooming pipe and woodland asters.

Another natural area in the famous mountain's shadow worth visiting, the **Gap Mountain Reservation❖** sees far fewer visitors than Monadnock. This preserve has more than a thousand acres of hardwood forest, bogs, blueberry bushes, and mountain ridges. Gap itself is a low mountain (1,862 feet), but the north and middle peaks are open and have fine views. The best access from the west is Quarry Road, a half mile south of Troy on Route 12.

Miller State Park❖, three miles east of Peterborough off Route 101, the main road through south-central New Hampshire, is the oldest park in New Hampshire, created in 1891. The park sits atop **Pack Monadnock Mountain** (2,288 feet), the smaller sister to Grand Monadnock 12 miles to the west, and includes a paved toll road leading from Route 101 to the open South Peak summit, where the views from the fire tower are extensive. On clear days, the skyscrapers of Boston are visible on the horizon, 55 miles away. Nearly 1,700 acres on the slopes of North Pack Monadnock (reachable by a trail from the summit of the South Peak) are protected in the first national wildlife refuge ever established in New Hampshire: **Wapack National Wildlife Refuge❖.** This refuge lies beneath a busy hawk migration route and is visited by migrating songbirds, including tree sparrows, wrens, and thrushes.

Just before Route 101 reaches Manchester, three natural areas offer havens in a part of the state that is under increasing development pressure. The **Heald Tract❖** on Route 31 includes unspoiled Heald Pond, an apple orchard, and a large tract of woods, maintained by the Society for the Protection of New Hampshire Forests. A short drive north in Amherst is the Audubon Society of New Hampshire's **Ponemah Bog Botanical Preserve❖,** featuring a kettle-hole pond and a quaking bog (so called from the gelatinous mix of dry land and water that "quakes" when you step on it), with a boardwalk that lets you explore without damaging any plants. (An aside: Bog water is highly acid because of the slowly decaying peat it contains, but the problem of acid rain in southern New Hampshire has become so severe it has prompted concern that even the bog ecosystem may be adversely affected.) It is worth braving the bugs in mid-May to see the beautiful rhodora at their flowering peak. The third preserve in this increasingly populated part of the state is **Beaver Brook Natural Area❖,** on Ridge Road in Hollis south of the Route 130–Route 122 intersection. Here the nonprofit Beaver Brook Natural Association maintains 1,700 acres of field, forest, and wetlands. Thirty miles of trails and woods roads are open here during daylight hours year-round for hiking, cross-country skiing, and snowshoeing. Numerous educational programs, many designed for children, explore aspects of the natural world, ranging from maple sugaring to spotted owl habitats. The checklist of plants includes more than 400 species; among the more unusual

119

ABOVE: *The rhodora, with bright lavender flowers emerging in early spring, is one of many heaths that grow well in the acid soils of bogs and along trails on rocky slopes.*

RIGHT: *The lady's slipper is the region's tallest native orchid. Despite foliage that can cause a poison ivy–like rash, the plant has been picked excessively in recent years.*

are dogwoods, orchids, fringed gentian, and leatherwood. In addition, at least 100 species of birds have been spotted here.

The Manchester-Concord corridor along the Merrimack River and I-93 is New Hampshire at its most crowded, but even here are places of natural interest. Off Fletcher Street near Manchester's famous old textile mills is the **Amoskeag Fishways❖**, a fish ladder constructed around the dam as part of the effort to restore Atlantic salmon to the Merrimack. The underwater viewing window is open daily in May and June, when several species of anadromous fish return from the ocean to spawn. Twenty minutes to the north in Concord, the state capital, two of the state's leading conservation organizations have their headquarters set in small natural areas within the city limits. On Portsmouth Street along the river the Society for the Protection of New Hampshire Forests has its **Merrimack River Outdoor Education and Conservation Area❖**. The area includes the society's passive solar headquarters, 95 undeveloped acres on the Merrimack's floodplain, and two miles of nature trails. The Audubon Society of New Hampshire's headquarters at Silk Farm (on the road of that name) offers nature exhibits, trails, and educational programs, centered around the white pines and oaks of Great Turkey Pond. Also in Concord, on Institute Drive, is the **Christa McAuliffe Planetarium❖**, created to honor the schoolteacher who died in the *Challenger* space shuttle disaster. East on Route 28 in nearby

Allenstown is **Bear Brook State Park❖,** the state's largest developed park. Its 10,000 heavily forested acres can be crowded near Catamount Pond but are quiet and peaceful elsewhere, with miles of old logging roads for hiking and skiing, and self-guided nature trails.

I-89 is the major route bounding this region back toward the northwest, but a worthwhile detour on Route 202 leads to several natural sites centered in the Hillsboro area. The **McCabe Forest❖** on Elm Street in Antrim is one of the most interesting reserves belonging to the Society for the Protection of New Hampshire Forests (SPNHF), with two miles of trail on the Contoocook River. On Clement Hill Road the **Deering Wildlife Sanctuary❖,** in the village of the same name, is crisscrossed by a network of foot trails leading through orchards, a beaver swamp, hemlock groves, and a fine stand of white pine. In June, look for bluebird nests from the trails along the edges of the fields, which are private property. The **Fox State Forest❖** in Hillsboro has a nature education center, a quaking bog, and some rare black tupelo trees.

A bit farther to the east, along Route 123 in Stoddard, is the SPNHF's **Charles L. Peirce Wildlife and Forest Reservation❖,** named after a local mapmaker and historian. Here more than ten miles of hiking trails and woods roads wind through a fine hardwood forest dotted with beaver ponds. One trail, the intriguingly named Trout-n-Bacon Trail, climbs to views on Bacon Ledge and then on to remote Trout Pond.

This is one of those hidden corners of New Hampshire that tourists often bypass. One of the best-kept secrets in the entire state is **Pillsbury State Park**❖ on Route 31 near the little village of Washington. Except for a handful of campsites and a picnic area, this 5,000-acre collection of woods, ponds, wetlands, and hills is totally undeveloped. Quiet now, like much of this area it was once heavily settled, and the outlets of many of these ponds were once dammed to supply power to various mills, the stonework of which can often still be found. The last of the mill owners, Albert Pillsbury, was one of the founders of the Society for the Protection of New Hampshire Forests, and in 1920 he deeded this land—growing back to forest—to the public. In 1933, 12 Rocky Mountain elk were released in the park. The last animal

Above: Often nesting in abandoned woodpecker holes, the brightly colored eastern bluebird "carries the sky on its back," wrote Henry Thoreau.

Left: Once clogged with sawdust from timber mills, the restored ponds of Pillsbury State Park now reflect its forested hills.

Overleaf: A cairn of piled stones near the top of Mount Kearsarge marks the trail to the summit. The summit's rock is laced with glacial striae, deep scratches revealing the area's frozen past.

was seen in 1955, although there are occasional rumors of one being spotted. For a glimpse into the past, walk about a hundred yards north of the entrance and follow a woods road a short distance into the forest. There, half-hidden in the underbrush, is a fine old cellar hole, complete with withered apple tree, a haunting reminder of the people who once made this forest their home.

ABOVE: *The red squirrel has a varied diet that includes pinecones, mushrooms, and even eggs and young birds. During the fall, it stores up to a bushel of pinecones per cache in the forest floor.*

RIGHT: *A harvest moon rises over a mixed transition forest, more obvious in the autumn when white birches and fiery maples are silhouetted against the darker evergreens.*

THE UPPER VALLEY

Near Sunapee Lake, I-89 crosses the divide separating the Merrimack River watershed to the east and the Connecticut River watershed to the west. The area directly to the northeast and southwest of I-89 on the Connecticut River side is a mix of hill and lake country not as spectacular as the White Mountains to the north yet offering a rich diversity of terrains, habitats, and waters. Near I-89 this is called the Sunapee region; closer to the Connecticut River, residents speak of living in the Upper Valley, although the river extends northward a hundred miles before reaching Canada.

The landmark that towers over the interstate here is **Mount Kearsarge** (2,937 feet), another of the isolated mountains common in the lower half of New Hampshire. In **Winslow State Park❖,** off Route 11 three miles south of Wilmot, an auto road climbs Kearsarge's northwest slope, making this a nice drive for those who are unable to hike. The road leads to a prominent shoulder below where the old Winslow House Hotel flourished in the 1860s; those wishing to gain the actual summit can hike a steep mile-long trail that leaves from the parking area. Another road also climbs the mountain, this one leaving from **Rollins State Park❖** in Warner off Exit 9 on I-89 and following the route of an old carriage road to the summit.

Big Sunapee Lake, southwest of New London, is 9 miles long, with Mount Sunapee (2,734 feet) and its ski area rising above the southern end. "Discovered" as early as 1630 by a scout for a Boston exploring party, the lake was the hunting ground for the Penacook Indians. With the French and Indian Wars over, the Penacook were soon displaced by white settlers, who began clearing the land around Newbury. When

a railroad reached this town in 1849, Sunapee's popularity as a summer resort was assured.

This is a busy, heavily developed lake, but at least one mile of shoreline has been left unspoiled: the **John Hay National Wildlife Refuge❖** off Route 103 in Newbury. On the site of the estate of historian and politician John Hay, the refuge protects 163 acres of forested upland above the lake, with scattered softwood stands that include trees more than 200 years old. The house itself—where Hay entertained such guests as Theodore Roosevelt—is open to the public, and the extensive formal gardens are in the process of being restored to their original glory. The property abuts 600 acres owned by the Society for the Protection of New Hampshire Forests, and plans call for the combined areas to be used as an environmental education center.

Off Exit 12 from I-89 in New London is the **Philbrick-Cricenti Bog❖**, which—with its nearness to the interstate and its boardwalk—is one of the most accessible sphagnum bogs in northern New England, and a

ABOVE: *The now-abundant wood duck nests in tree cavities, sometimes as high as 60 feet above swamps and ponds. At roosting sites, the multicolored drake lets out a rising* ter-we-ee.

LEFT: *Ralph Waldo Emerson might well have been admiring a New England woodland in autumn attire when he observed, "The simple perception of natural forms is a delight."*

good spot to see lake-to-forest succession at work. For geologists, this portion of the interstate has some spectacular road cuts, with much of the rock being porphyritic, dotted with large rectangular crystals of white feldspar that seem to float in a gray layer of mica. Red garnets up to an inch in diameter are found here as well.

Lovers of back roads should get off I-89 at Exit 17 and head east on Route 4 toward the Canaan-Grafton area. **Mount Cardigan** (3,121 feet), standing alone, soars above this part of the state, with its distinctive bare, scalloped summit rising to the point of the fire tower on top. Most of the nearly 30 miles of trails on this mountain originate from the Appalachian Mountain Club's **Cardigan Lodge❖** on the eastern side of the mountain, which provides meals and accommodations for the public. On the opposite side of the mountain is perhaps the easiest route to the summit: the West Ridge Trail, leaving from **Cardigan State Park❖,** four and a half miles east of Route 118 in Canaan. The views—and the blueberries—are both abundant enough so that the summit is filled with hikers most summer weekends.

Grafton on Route 4 is a quiet hamlet quite removed from time, and the surrounding countryside is wild and little known. **McDaniel's Marsh** off George Hill Road in the southwest part of town is a 300-acre open marsh. A bit closer to town, north of Route 4A on Grafton Pond Road, is **Grafton Pond❖,** one of the most beautiful, unspoiled lakes in New Hampshire. The 935 acres surrounding the pond's seven-mile shoreline were given to the Society for the Protection of New Hampshire Forests in 1984 by an anonymous donor, thus ensuring protection for the pond, its islands, and its rocky shores. This is one of the best wildlife viewing spots in the state; moose, otters, deer, and bears are all common here, to say nothing of the pond's feisty population of smallmouth bass. The big story from the ornithologist's point of view are the loons; there are usually several nesting pairs here, watched over in part by the Audubon Society of New Hampshire's Loon Preservation Committee, a statewide group of volunteers who mark off loon nesting sanctuaries, oversee nests to ensure they are not hassled by motorboats, and conduct an annual loon census to monitor the health of the population throughout New Hampshire. The small parking area on Grafton Pond's western shore provides the ideal place to launch a canoe or kayak.

Grafton is also the site of the mountaintop **Ruggles Mine❖,** a large open mine that bills itself as the oldest mica, feldspar, and beryl mine in the country. Mica, also known as isinglass, is valued for its transparency and was once mined here for windows; today it is used in insulation and electrical equipment and by the space industry because it is nonflammable. Just over the town line near Enfield Center off Route 4A, the **Enfield Wildlife Management Area❖** comprises nearly 3,000 acres of northern hardwoods and several ponds, including 17-acre Cole Pond, which is restricted to fly-fishing for trout.

This area of New Hampshire was one of the hardest hit by depopulation in the nineteenth century; between 1807 and 1823, 136 families left Grafton for states to the west. It is impossible to travel far in these woods today without coming upon old stone walls, vine-choked cellar holes, or withered apple trees bearing varieties of fruit with names not even the oldest inhabitant can recall. **Gile State Forest❖** south of Grafton on Route 4A is another good example of old farmland going back to forest, with cellar holes and stone walls testifying that this was once all cleared and settled land.

I-89 continues to the Connecticut River, where Route 12A is the most scenic route to the south, staying for the most part close to the river on the floodplain. In Cornish, a short way from the river, is the **Saint Gaudens Historic Site**❖, former home of the late sculptor whose work includes the Shaw Memorial in Boston. Within the grounds is the **Blow-Me-Down Natural Area** along the cool, shadowy brook of the same name (Blow-Me-Down is a corruption of a local name, "Blomidon"). Of special interest here are the rare sycamore trees, a species that can grow as high as 100 feet, making it one of the tallest eastern hardwood trees.

In Hanover, Route 10 becomes the river route and is, among other things, one of the levelest biking routes in this hilly state. Hanover is both a busy college town and the center for much outdoor activity. The **Appalachian National Scenic Trail**❖ crosses from Vermont into New Hampshire via the Ledyard Bridge across the Connecticut, and hikers with heavy backpacks are a common sight downtown. The Appalachian Trail, or AT as it is nicknamed, is the well-known 2,140-mile-plus hiking trail that leads from Springer Mountain in Georgia to Katahdin in Maine. In 1968, with the passage of the National Trail Systems Act, it became the first federally designated national scenic trail in the United States. The New Hampshire portion of the trail runs for 157 miles in a southwest-to-northeast direction. While the most heavily hiked segment is in the White Mountains, much interesting terrain is encountered immediately northeast of Hanover, ranging from the **Velvet Rocks** in that town, a favorite short hike, to **Smarts Mountain** (3,238 feet) near Lyme, and **Mount Cube** (2,902 feet) near Orford, two peaks of considerable interest; the fire tower on the former and the open ledges of the latter provide some of the best mountain views south of the Whites. The Dartmouth Outing Club, which is headquartered in Robinson Hall on the Dartmouth campus, maintains much of the AT in this region. The Appalachian Trail Conference, along with federal, state, and local governments, has been active in recent years in establishing the AT on public property over its entire length, resulting in extensive rerouting; consult the ATC guidebooks for changes.

In Hanover itself, off Lyme Road along the Connecticut and near the golf course, is **Pine Park**❖, a beautiful forest of old-growth pine and

ABOVE: *Tree limbs with neatly gnawed edges and plentiful tooth marks are usually a sign of porcupines. Here a young animal, its quills relaxed, dines on a cluster of tasty maple leaves.*

RIGHT: *Ledyard Bridge carries the Georgia-to-Maine Appalachian Trail over the Connecticut River between Norwich, Vermont, and Hanover, New Hampshire.*

hemlock. Here trees tower more than 100 feet over walking paths that become cross-country ski trails in winter.

New Hampshire does not offer as many access points to the Connecticut River as neighboring Vermont does, and often the best spots to launch a boat or canoe can be discovered simply by asking at a local tackle shop or the town clerk's office. **Reed's Marsh❖** on Route 10 in Orford is a 64-acre backwater off the river that offers prime habitat for birds, including, in the spring, hooded mergansers. A canoe or small boat can be launched here, and panfish can be caught in abundance—not only by anglers, but also by the great blue herons that hunt the shallows. **Bedell Bridge Historic Site❖** sits on a prime example of Connecticut River floodplain in Haverhill off Route 10. Once the site of a covered bridge (destroyed in a violent windstorm in 1979, two months after it was laboriously restored), it is now a simple, quiet meadow where one can launch a canoe to explore this part of the river. Downstream the banks steepen, and the overhanging branches of the lush silver maples give the effect of being in a secret tunnel of green, lost to the outside world. In late July and early August the raspberries ripen, and paddlers can let their canoe drift while they reach up to the drooping vines and pick all the berries they want as they drift downriver.

The Upper Valley Land Trust has established a chain of primitive campsites along this part of the river for canoeists' and kayakers' tents. Look for signs designated CRPC (Connecticut River Primitive Campsite) on the river just below Horse Meadows; one is ten miles downstream in South Newbury, on the Vermont side of the river at Vaughan Meadows.

CHAPTER FIVE

NORTHERN NEW HAMPSHIRE:
THE WHITE MOUNTAINS

The White *Hills* they were called in Nathaniel Hawthorne's day, when the first tourists from Boston came to marvel at natural features like the Old Man of the Mountains with its brooding profile or the Flume with its mysterious caverns. And they would be called hills in many other places in the world, with their low altitude and modest extent. But for the dramatic way they have influenced the human imagination, for the manner in which they have come to symbolize an entire region, for their impressive ravines and glacial "notches," for their serious climbing routes, and most of all for their notoriously dangerous weather, these peaks well deserve the loftier term, and it's the White *Mountains* they are universally known as today.

The White Mountains have a character all their own. Starting in the west with big Moosilauke, extending northeastward in definite ridges all the way into Maine, they include nearly 50 peaks more than 4,000 feet high. Many have well-defined treelines above which grow rare mountain flowers and the twisted, gnarled krummholz (stunted forest) that can only be found in true alpine environments. The biggest mountain of all is Mount Washington—at 6,288 feet high, it is the highest mountain east of the Mississippi and north of the Carolinas, and one of the most famous and infamous summits in the world. Among its other

LEFT: *Silver Cascade rumbles through Crawford Notch State Park. For all its power, a waterfall is actually short-lived geologically, because erosion inevitably reduces its lip and creates a quieter, more level watercourse.*

distinctions, it has some of the strongest winds on earth: On a gusty April day in 1934, the weather observatory on the summit recorded a wind of more than 231 miles per hour, a world record that still stands.

The Whites (named, as far as anyone can discover, by early sailors who saw the mountains' snowy summits from the sea in early spring) combine grandeur with accessibility. They contain the oldest continuously maintained hiking trail in the country—the Crawford Path across the Presidential Range, first blazed in 1819—and more than a thousand miles of hiking trails of varying difficulty, from the easy walk up Mount Willard to the lung-busting, dangerous ascent of Huntington Ravine. A significant portion of the mountains lies within the White Mountain National Forest (WMNF), which, with almost 800,000 acres, comprises 12 percent of New Hampshire. Managed for multiple use like all national forests, it still has the recreational opportunities of a national park, especially on busy summer weekends. Route 302 and the Kancamagus Highway are typically thronged with tourists at those times. Yet it is relatively easy, via the hiking trails, to escape the rather crowded, unattractive towns at the mountains' fringes and immerse yourself in some of the finest mountain scenery in the East.

As with other forest areas in New England, much of this region had been completely logged by the turn of the century, and only through the timely intervention of early conservation organizations was much of it saved. Except in a few scattered valleys, "intervales" as they're called here, farming was hardly practiced. Tourism has been the main cash crop in the Whites since legendary seven-foot-tall Ethan Allen Crawford opened his first rustic inn in the notch that now bears his name. The nineteenth century was the golden age of the region's resorts, with huge hotels where families would stay for the entire summer; one from the turn of the century in Bretton Woods still stands. Among popular diversions were riding carriages and horses up paths carved to the various summits and staying overnight in "summit houses" on top. These are long since vanished, but their spirit lives on in a series of eight mountain huts operated by the Appalachian Mountain Club and open to hikers across the range.

What forces were responsible for the abrupt, massive shapes of these mountains? The Whites are part of one of the oldest mountain ranges on earth, the Appalachians, created from the pressure of the colliding

NORTHERN NEW HAMPSHIRE

25   0   25 Miles

25   0   25 Kilometers

QUÉBEC

Third Lake

CONNECTICUT LAKE STATE FOREST

Second Lake

First Connecticut Lake

Pittsburg

Lake Francis

COLEMAN STATE PARK

Richardson Lake

Umbagog Lake

DIXVILLE NOTCH STATE PARK

APPALACHIAN NATIONAL SCENIC TRAIL

Errol

Bloomfield

Groveton

Stark

Milan

Berlin

Lancaster

WHITE MOUNTAIN NATIONAL FOREST

Bethel

St Johnsbury

Randolph

Gerham

WHITE

PONDICHERRY WILDLIFE REFUGE

Twin Mountain

Mt Washington 6288

GREAT GULF WILDERNESS

PINKHAM NOTCH VISITORS CENTER

MOUNTAIN

KRETZFELDER MEMORIAL PARK

Bretton Woods

Presidential Range

Bethlehem

Franconia

MT WASHINGTON S P VISITOR CENTER

NATIONAL

SCOTLAND BROOK SANCTUARY

FROST PLACE

PRESIDENTIAL-DRY RIVER WILDERNESS

FOREST

Woodsville

CRAWFORD NOTCH STATE PARK

FRANCONIA NOTCH STATE PARK

Mt Kearsage

VERMONT

Mt Moosilauke

KANCAMAGUS

Bartlett

North Conway

Lincoln

Swift River

HWY

Lost River Gorge

Mt Chocorua

Sandwich Range

WHITE MOUNTAIN NATIONAL FOREST

SANDWICH RANGE WILDERNESS

Chocorua

APPALACHIAN TRAIL

West Ossipee

Ossipee Mountains

Hanover

Lake Winnipesaukee

MAINE

N E W

Laconia

H A M P S H I R E

Rochester

Connecticut River

CONCORD

American and African continents. Since then, the mountains have been shaped and battered by erosion; hot, syrupy granite magma rising toward the earth's surface has metamorphosed into the gneiss, marble, schists, and slate so typical of these mountains. Two million years ago, when the first of the great ice ages began, glaciers covered the landscape. At first these were alpine glaciers, originating high on the mountains' flanks, carving out, as snow enlarged them, glacial cirques such as Tuckerman Ravine. In the meantime, as the weather remained cold, a single massive ice sheet moved down from Canada, blanketing the valleys and rising until it covered even Mount Washington.

Continuing southward, the glacier dug out mountainsides and valley bottoms, creating the characteristic U-shaped notches such as Crawford and Pinkham. This ice sheet ebbed and flowed four separate times over the course of 2 million years; the last flow occurred 50,000 years ago during the Wisconsin Age. The retreat of this sheet as the weather warmed gave these mountains a final shaping, creating scree piles, talus slopes, deep scoured ravines, tarns and bogs, and, at least on top of Mount Washington, one of the truly greatest assemblages of boulders ever deposited in one spot. In the years since, wind, frost, and running water have been the prime sculptors here; mountains such as Flume, Tripyramid, and Washington itself bear the long rocky scars created by landslides when storms ripped whole sections of mountain slope away.

Without any high mountains to their northwest, the Whites receive the full brunt of the prevailing wind, as well as being exposed to powerful northeasters swirling in from the nearby ocean. The Mount Washington Observatory, established in 1870, has recorded winter conditions typical of Antarctica; winds of more than 100 miles per hour have been clocked every month of the year, and the mountain remains hidden in cloud cover at least 55 percent of the time. In the famous two-day storm of February 1969, 98 inches of snow fell on the summit, including 49.3 inches of snow during one 24-hour period, a record for all weather observation stations in the United States. Its sudden, violent storms have given Mount Washington, in the Appalachian Mountain Club's phrase, "a well-earned reputation as the most dangerous small mountain in the world," and many careless hikers and climbers have lost their lives here. The smaller peaks have their own share of bad weather. Anyone climbing above timberline should use common sense and discretion, and be

ABOVE: *Nineteenth-century tourists record their visit to the Flume, a narrow 800-foot granite gorge in Lincoln, New Hampshire. Near the boardwalk stood Flume House, a resort that charged a dollar a day.*

equipped for sudden storms during any season of the year.

The forest in the Whites is of two types: northern hardwood (birch, beech, and maple) at elevations of less than 3,000 feet, and boreal forest (mainly balsam fir and black spruce) at elevations of more than 3,000 feet. Indeed, anyone looking at the mountains from a distance can easily see the line separating them, the light green shading away to a darker color. Many trees in the boreal zone, under the constant assault of wind and cold, grow in gnarled, stunted mats called krummholz, with impressive tenacity.

OVERLEAF: *From Lakes-of-the-Clouds, the Ammonoosuc River leaps down a ravine between Mount Washington and Mount Monroe, only to become a meandering waterway in the meadows and hardwood forests below.*

139

ABOVE: *In the evening, great flocks of abundant white-throated sparrows gather in wooded thickets, where they create rich, gentle choruses as twilight falls.*

RIGHT: *Thick stands of slender birches, which often colonize an area after a fire, thrive in the White Mountain National Forest near Shelburne.*

A definite timberline comes above the krummholz, at elevations of 4,000–5,000 feet. Above this grow alpine plants such as lichen, sedges, mosses, and wildflowers, which had their genesis here during the last ice age. When the ice retreated, they stayed on, finding the high winds, moisture, and cloud cover perfect for their needs. The result is what botanists term an island of vegetation, consisting of arctic-alpine species at the southern limit of their range in the United States. Many early explorers of these mountains were botanists drawn by these plants' rarity; names such as Tuckerman Ravine, Oakes Gulf, and Boot Spur honor these pioneering scientists.

The best location for studying these alpine wildflowers is the Lakes-of-the-Clouds Hut, operated by the Appalachian Mountain Club. The wildflower display begins in May, reaches its peak in late June, and is usually finished by July. The Alpine Garden on Washington's eastern flank, a short hike from the auto road, is a particularly good spot to see the pink-magenta Lapland rosebay, the five-petaled white diapensia, the small pink flowers of alpine azalea, and—rarest of all—the dwarf cinquefoil, which grows nowhere else in the world. Admirers should remember not to walk on them—they survive wind better than they do Vibram-soled boots—and not to pick them, in accordance with WMNF regulations.

The altitude affects the White Mountains' fauna, too, particularly the birdlife. In the high scrub zone near timberline are species that are rare at lower elevations; these include the shy, ground-feeding gray-cheeked thrush, the yellow-rumped warbler, the blackpoll warbler with its sibilant call on one high pitch, and even the rare spruce grouse. The only species nesting above timberline are the junco and the white-throated sparrow. The WMNF has a checklist of 194 bird

species found in these mountains; of these, most are migrants, and only 21 species remain through the winter.

The White Mountains have a healthy population of black bears, although they are seldom seen. Moose are increasingly common, having moved back into this area from Maine in the late 1970s. Moose are famous for wandering into the most unlikely places during the fall rutting season; one was seen and photographed several years ago circling the buildings on Mount Washington's summit! Drivers should exercise caution at all times to avoid a collision with these animals, particularly in late spring and early summer, when the blackflies drive the moose out of the forest and the road salt washed into gullies attracts them to the roads. Anyone hiking even a short distance into the backcountry will almost inevitably see beavers. Once all but exterminated for their pelts, they are back in high numbers, and almost every stream seems to have a beaver dam or two in the process of construction or repair.

In the Whites, as in other mountain ranges, the highest summits attract the biggest crowds. Those seeking a little more elbowroom should visit off-season, particularly in May, when the still-leafless trees permit views and the blackflies have not yet appeared. But even at the height of summer, some areas of the White Mountains receive relatively few visitors. The Evans Notch area on the border of New Hampshire and Maine is one of these lesser-known regions, with some attractive, accessible mountains and some of the best blueberry picking in New England. The mountains north of Route 2 in the Pliny, Pilot, and Crescent ranges are seldom hiked. North of Route 110 begins New Hampshire's share of what is now referred to as the Northern Forest, a lightly populated land owned primarily by lumber and pulpwood companies. This region is similar in terrain, flora, and fauna to adjacent areas in Vermont and Maine, as well as the boreal forest that covers Quebec to the north. The main backbone of the Whites continues all the way to the Canadian border, but the mountains become more scattered here, wilder, with fewer maintained trails. Dixville Notch and Lake Umbagog are the chief points of interest on the eastern side of this rapidly tapering pyramid (at Pittsburg, New Hampshire is fewer than 20 miles wide). On the western side are the Connecticut Lakes, source of the Connecticut River, hunting and fishing country that offers some of the best opportunities for wildlife viewing in the state.

This chapter explores the White Mountains, starting from Route 10 at the Vermont border and proceeding northeast on Route 302, then east to White Mountain National Forest through Zealand Notch. The route continues clockwise through the forest to the scenic Kancamagus Highway, which travels north through Franconia Notch. Going east again, the route takes in the Presidential Range and concludes with the north country, including Lake Umbagog and the Connecticut Lakes near the Canadian border.

THE NOTCHES

Those approaching the White Mountains from the western border of New Hampshire on Route 10 won't see much of them until past North Haverhill, when suddenly the low intervening hills drop away to the east and there stands **Mount Moosilauke** (4,802 feet), with a commanding size and majesty. Drivers have a choice: to take Routes 25 and 118 directly east into the heart of the mountains or to continue north on Route 302 and approach them in a more roundabout manner.

The latter route leads past several natural areas worth visiting before reaching the mountains proper. The **Scotland Brook Sanctuary❖** in Landaff off Route 302 is a charming Audubon preserve of wetlands and spruce-fir forest in an area of old farmland going slowly back to the wild. At least 84 species of wildflowers are found here, 10 of which are orchids. The Lady's Slipper Trail is a gentle trail through the preserve's center. A short distance away, off Route 117 in Franconia, is the **Frost Place❖,** where Robert Frost lived and wrote for five years, now used as a retreat for poets. Visitors are welcome at selected times to wander the half-mile Poetry Nature Trail, with quotations from Frost's poetry mounted near the springs, brooks, and trees that inspired so much of his work.

On Route 302 is the old resort town of Bethlehem, which seems like an oasis of tranquillity compared to the more modern White Mountain resorts. Contributing to this atmosphere is the **Bretzfelder Memorial Park❖** in the heart of town; here three interpretative nature trails go through a fine 77-acre preserve of balsam woods and beech ferns; in August, this is an excellent place to find wild raspberries. The Society for the Protection of New Hampshire Forests has its North Country headquarters at the **Rocks Estate** in Bethlehem and maintains the Red Barns

ABOVE: *The beaver builds lodges as large as 6 feet wide and 40 feet high. A fast worker with strong teeth, it can fell a five-year-old willow in three minutes.*
RIGHT: *The distinctive V of Crawford Notch, a steep-sided mountain ravine that was sculpted by glaciers, rises beyond Wiley Pond in the nearby state park.*

Nature Trail through a managed forest area, a sugar bush (a woods in which sugar maples predominate), and a Christmas tree plantation, with good views of the Presidential Range just to the east.

East on Route 302, near the junction with Route 3 in Twin Mountain, is one of the northeastern approaches to the **White Mountain National Forest❖.** Managed for multiple use, the WMNF nevertheless is especially important for the outdoor recreation opportunities it affords visitors from the urban areas of the Northeast and the protection it gives to the most spectacular mountain landscape east of the Mississippi. In an effort to fulfill the latter responsibility, the federal government has designated five wilderness areas, encompassing 114,932 acres of the WMNF's 786,962 total. They are the **Pemigewasset Wilderness** (16,000 acres) east of the Franconia Range, the **Presidential–Dry River Wilderness** (27,380 acres) on the southern flank of Mount Washington, the smaller but equally spectacular **Great Gulf Wilderness** (5,552 acres) occupying a glacial cirque on the eastern flank of Mount Adams, the **Caribou–Speckled Mountain Wilderness** (41,000 acres) in the mountains along the Maine border, and the **Sandwich Range Wilderness** (25,000 acres) in the southern part of the WMNF south of the Kancamagus Highway. Special regulations are in effect here, among other things prohibiting the construction of roads, dams, or permanent structures, as well as logging and mining. Regulations also apply to hikers and campers; for instance, hiking groups of more than ten people are not permitted, and above treeline to protect the fragile soil and flora of the alpine zone, camping is prohibited except on two or more feet of snow (for complete rules, contact the WMNF). According to the Forest Service, the areas protected here

146

ABOVE: *At Sabbady Falls, lush mosses and hemlock roots intertwine above a pothole formed by rocks spinning in eddies of glacial meltwater.*

constitute roughly 53 percent of the wilderness left in the Northeast.

Smaller "scenic areas," some easily accessible from main roads and others requiring a hike, are also under special protection. The **Snyder Brook Scenic Area,** for example, with old-growth trees and a waterfall, is just west of Randolph off Route 2. The **Greeley Ponds Scenic Area,** near Mad River Notch, offers two remote ponds about an hour's hike from the Kancamagus Highway. The WMNF also operates 22 roadside campgrounds scattered throughout the forest.

The WMNF is currently trying to involve the public in volunteer efforts to maintain and protect the backcountry. Volunteers serve as campground or backcountry "hosts," patrol designated areas, and participate in adopt-a-trail projects. During the summer, the White Mountain Interpretative Association and the Forest Service present free evening nature programs at Jigger Johnson Campground along the Kancamagus Highway, Dolly Copp Campground along Route 16 near Gorham, and Russell Pond/Campton Campground on Tripoli Road off I-93.

The road toward **Zealand Notch** leaves Route 302 a short distance east of Twin Mountain at Zealand Campground. A "notch" in local par-

ABOVE: *Clear mountain water cascades over granite bedrock at Sabbady Falls off the White Mountain's Kancamagus Highway.*

lance is a glacially gouged mountain pass with steep sides. Zealand Notch fits this description well, although it is one of the smaller notches in the Whites. This area was once called New Zealand Valley, probably for its remoteness. Logging here was widespread and destructive during the early part of this century, and the land was seared by a series of huge forest fires. But the forest has recovered beautifully, as seen along the pleasant Zealand Trail, which leaves the end of Zealand Road on an old railroad grade and leads up to the steepest, most dramatic part of the notch. For those wanting a steeper climb, the Hale Brook Trail leaves from the same trailhead and quickly ascends to the bare summit of **Mount Hale** (4,054 feet), which has excellent views. Hale is one of the 48 "four-thousand footers" in New Hampshire—mountains that top out at 4,000 feet or higher. "Bagging" these peaks is a feat many area hikers strive to accomplish.

A short distance east of this area on Route 302 is one of the most spectacular mountain passes in the East: **Crawford Notch**❖ (in the state park of the same name). For three miles the sheer talus cliffs of Mount Webster, on one side, and mounts Willard and Willey, on the other,

149

press in upon the road. The north entrance to the park, called Gate of the Notch, is where an ice "tongue" off the main glacier carved out the valley, twisting around the hard knobs of granite on either side. Many White Mountain legends center around this famous notch, "that narrow rift," the poet John Greenleaf Whittier put it, between "mountain walls piled to heaven." Ethan Allen Crawford, the gentle giant who guided countless first ascents of Mount Washington, is the hero of several of these legends. Others focus on tragedies such as the Willey Slide, the basis of one of Nathaniel Hawthorne's best stories, "The Ambitious Guest." (During a torrential rainstorm in August of 1826, the whole slope of Mount Willey gave way in a landslide, killing nine members of the Willey family who lived at its base.) A number of hiking trails depart from the highway in Crawford Notch. One, the Crawford Path, which crosses the Presidential Range to Mount Washington, is considered to be the oldest continuously maintained footpath in America; it was cut by Ethan Allen Crawford with his father Abel Crawford in 1819.

Continuing east, Route 302 makes a clockwise circle around the southern half of the Whites. The Frankenstein Cliffs rising to the right, past the spectacular railroad trestle, are a popular ice-climbing spot during the winter. The valley floor widens considerably near Bartlett and becomes an extremely broad "intervale," or plain, in the North Conway area, with mountain views across the Saco River. Visitors who appreciate mountains more than shopping will want to hurry through North Conway, although rock climbers might want to take a crack at **Cathedral Ledge,** a 1,000-foot granite cliff above town; a road accessed from River Road takes the easier route up to the summit.

South of town and looping back to the west is the **Kancamagus Highway,** an officially designated scenic byway that travels 34 miles and climbs to a height of nearly 3,000 feet through some of the finest mountain scenery in New Hampshire. Although local roads reached Passaconaway (now the site of a campground) as early as 1837, it wasn't until 1959 that the various roads were linked into a highway. The U.S. Forest Service has picnic sites along the road, as well as overlooks,

LEFT: *Surrounded by brilliant autumn hardwoods, the Swift River has some of the best brook and rainbow trout fishing in the region. These prized game fish spawn in nearby streams and headwaters.*

ABOVE: *Bolts and rods now keep the Old Man of the Mountains, a well-known New Hampshire landmark, from slipping into the valley below. Frost heaves created his jutting brows and pointed chin.*

RIGHT: *Franconia Notch, a mountain pass traversed by I-93, is home to steep-cliffed Profile Lake. A clump of steeplebush blooms along the shore; bald eagles and moose live nearby.*

campgrounds, and scenic areas. The **Rocky Gorge Scenic Area** is a fine spot to admire the rushing water of the Swift River, but exercise caution on the rocks. The Forest Service also maintains several dozen hiking trails into the mountains that flank both sides of the road. Among other distinctions, the Kancamagus Highway has the reputation of being one of the toughest—and most beautiful—bike rides in the East. The auto-encased should keep in mind that traffic can be bumper-to-bumper on fall foliage weekends—this is not a road for drivers in a hurry.

Near the busy town of Lincoln, the Kancamagus Highway joins Route 3, which with I-93 leads north through **Franconia Notch❖** and the state park of the same name. Here to the east rise the steep, serrated ridges of the Franconia Range, including Mount Lafayette (5,260 feet), named after the patriot general in 1816. Across the valley—which is just wide enough here for the road—is dome-shaped Cannon Mountain (4,100 feet), remarkable both for the steep cliffs that fall down to Profile Lake and for the rock profile known as the Old Man of the Mountains. The latter, which looks from a distance like an old man of great dignity and wisdom, has become the state symbol of New Hampshire. The profile was the inspiration for Hawthorne's well-known story "The Great Stone Face," in which he writes:

"The Great Stone Face was a work of Nature in her mood of majestic playfulness, formed on the perpendicular side of a mountain by some immense rocks, which had been thrown together in such a position as, when viewed from the proper distance, precisely to resemble the fea-

tures of the human countenance. It seemed as if an enormous giant, or Titan, had sculpted his own likeness on the precipice. . . . The Great Stone Face seemed positively to be alive."

After a battle with conservationists that lasted decades, I-93 (also called the Franconia Notch Parkway) was finally completed through the notch in the late 1980s. Trailheads, sightseeing points, and such suffered much disruption but have now been sensibly resited. One of the park's best known features is the Flume, a narrow gorge with broad ledges worn smooth by rushing water and avalanche; a boardwalk goes through the steepest, most dramatic part. Nearby is the Pool, a pothole formation in the Pemigewasset River that is more than 100 feet in diameter and 40 feet deep. A paved bike trail now reaches the entire length of the notch, from the Flume to the Skookumchuck Trail. During summer and fall weekends, the Appalachian Mountain Club, the U.S. Forest Service, and the New Hampshire Department of Parks maintain a visitors' booth at the Lafayette Place Campground to provide information about hiking trail conditions, weather, and special regulations in effect. The Franconia Ridge Trail, which is almost entirely above timberline for two miles and has some of the narrowest, most exposed sections—and

ABOVE: *Snow may linger into the summer atop New Hampshire's Presidential Range. The 11 mountains in the chain are a jagged*

some of the grandest views—of any trail in the Whites, is a favorite hike.

A short drive away in Kinsman Notch on Route 112 is **Lost River Reservation❖,** a labyrinth of moss-covered boulders where the rushing river "disappears" and reappears as it tunnels its way downhill.

THE PRESIDENTIAL RANGE

The highest mountain in a range always fascinates and magnetizes climbers, hikers, and tourists alike. This is true with a vengeance when it comes to Mount Washington—the most famous and infamous mountain in the Northeast, for its height, the ferocity of its weather, the victims it has claimed over the years, and its lofty beauty.

Washington and the other mountains that flank it in the Presidential Range cover a vast area. Washington can be approached from all points of the compass via a large circle of roads around the range. Those coming from the west, completing the loop from Franconia Notch on Route 3 back to Route 302, have several options, including the Mount Washington Cog Railway. Completed in 1869, with a maximum grade of

154

jumble of boulders, scree piles, and treeless peaks. Their stark beauty, however, attracts thousands of visitors as soon as the weather allows.

13.5 inches to the yard near the trestle called Jacob's Ladder, it is matched in steepness only by similar railroads in the Alps. Steam trains depart from the base station at Marshfield, chugging their way up the western ridge of the mountain; look for signs on Route 302 for the access road. The railroad has become so closely associated with Mount Washington that it seems a perfectly natural part of the landscape.

Near the base station is the trailhead for the Ammonoosuc Ravine Trail, which climbs up and around the river of the same name with its many waterfalls. The top of the trail meets the Crawford Path; the combination of these two trails provides the shortest route up Mount Washington from the west—although not for the ill prepared. As the AMC guidebook to the range cautions: "Whether, as is often stated, Mt. Washington has the worst weather in the world is subject to debate. But the dozens of people

*OVERLEAF: **The Appalachian Trail crosses mounts Eisenhower and Franklin in the White Mountains. Despite the wind and cold, more than 100 plant species, including lichens, survive on the rocks and in the crevices.***

ABOVE: *Found on rocky heights, the dark red fruit of the mountain cranberry actually sweetens through the winter.*
LEFT: *Mount Washington is the southern limit for moss campion, a hardy alpine flower that grows in dense tussocks.*

who have died on its slopes in the last century furnish adequate proof that the weather is vicious enough to kill those who are foolish enough to challenge the mountain at its worst." Proper clothing, the appropriate guidebook, maps, and prudence are all necessary here, even in summer.

The mountain's eastern flanks are approached through yet another White Mountain notch: **Pinkham Notch,** where Route 16 is pinched between Washington to the west and the Carter Range to the east. Dozens of trails, many originating at Pinkham Notch Visitor Center, on Route 16, beckon the hiker here. Of special interest are the famous steep-walled ravines on this side of Washington and on Mount Adams to the north; these include Huntington Ravine, a favorite ice-climbing spot in winter, and Tuckerman Ravine, the glacial cirque high on Washington marked by a steep head wall. With the snow sometimes lingering long into June, Tuckerman Ravine is one of the meccas of American downhill skiing, even though there are no lifts here and skiers must hike up to the head wall's base to start each run.

Even older than the cog railway is the **Mount Washington Auto Road,** which dates back to 1861 when horse-drawn wagons took early visitors to the top of the mountain. This eight-mile toll road starts at Route 16 south of Gorham; those preferring to let someone else drive the twisting road can take a guided van. The ride up acts as a kind of geological field trip; the bedrock along the road is mica schist and quartzite, among the most durable rocks in New England. From the auto road, too, are excellent views of the huge glacial cirques where the mountains arc toward the northeast. One of these, the wilderness area of Great Gulf, is the largest cirque in the White Mountains and the destination and corridor for many trails.

The summit of Washington, well above treeline, holds the upper terminus of the cog railway, a parking area for the toll road, the **Mount Washington State Park Visitor Center❖,** and the weather observatory. All the views, especially toward the northeast, are spectacular, although even on cloudless days, the wind can be enough to make you walk stooped over. A little below the summit is the **Alpine Garden❖,** the most accessible area to view the alpine flora that blossoms here each summer.

Pinkham Notch Visitor Center❖, ten miles south of Gorham on Route 16, is the White Mountain headquarters of the Appalachian Mountain Club, an organization of outdoor lovers founded in 1876 that describes itself as "the place where recreation and conservation meet." The AMC has been in the forefront of building and maintaining White Mountain trails and additionally supports educational workshops, day programs, and guided hikes.

Perhaps the most popular of the AMC's various projects is their hut system—a series of mountain huts dispersed a day's hike apart over 56 miles of trail through the heart of the Whites. First established more than 100 years ago with a stone cabin on Mount Madison, the system today consists of eight huts reachable only by foot, where meals, educational programs, and accommodations are available to hikers whether they are club members or not. **Lonesome Lake Hut,** on the shore of the pond of the same name near Cannon Mountain, is the easiest hut to hike to and the most popular for young families. **Greenleaf Hut,** high on the western flank of the Franconia Ridge, offers views of nearby Mount Lafayette; **Galehead Hut,** near the mountain of the same name, is the

159

most isolated. **Zealand Falls Hut** is located on the northeastern edge of the Pemigewasset Wilderness, **Mizpah Springs Hut** on the southern flank of Mount Clinton above Crawford Notch. **Lakes-of-the-Clouds Hut,** the largest, highest, and most visited, is situated above treeline on a shoulder of Mount Washington. **Madison Spring Hut** is the oldest, built in 1888. **Carter Notch Hut,** easternmost of the chain, is perched below Carter Dome (4,832 feet). In the magnificence of their settings and the casual bonhomie of their atmosphere (hikers are friendly and eager to share stories with one another), these are the nearest thing this country has to the alpine huts of Europe.

The Presidentials can get crowded at certain times of the year. Those looking for more solitude should visit **Evans Notch** on the border of New Hampshire and Maine along Route 113. Although the mountains are not as high here as the big peaks, there are some attractive summits. A traverse of the **Baldface Range** takes a hard seven hours but rewards hikers with four miles of open ledges and unobstructed views; the trailhead is on Route 113 at a new parking area just north of the driveway to the AMC's Cold River Camp.

THE NORTH COUNTRY
There is a tendency to think of the Presidentials as the roof of New Hampshire, but 30 miles of fine mountain scenery and forest stretch northward from Route 2 to Canada. North of Route 110 is the North Country—a large expanse of sparsely settled boreal forest that, along with similar areas in Vermont, Maine, and New York, forms the southern band of the huge forest that covers much of Ontario and Quebec.

Conservationists are trying to protect much of the North Country, and one of their major successes has been the **Nash Stream Forest** off Route 110 between Groveton and Stark, where a large tract of forest is managed cooperatively by the WMNF and the state of New Hampshire. While plans for this area are still in the formative stage, several hiking trails will likely be maintained through the heart of this area, including ones on the matching Percy Peaks that dominate the view northward from Mount Washington.

A few miles to the east on Route 26 near Errol and the beautiful, brawling Androscoggin River, big **Lake Umbagog** straddles the border of New Hampshire and Maine. The opportunities for wildlife spotting

ABOVE: *A winter sunrise lights Mount Washington, the highest peak in the northeast, soaring a mile above the town of Jackson. The observatory at the top has recorded winds exceeding 200 miles per hour.*

around this unspoiled lake are outstanding—moose roam the shallows, loons are common, and in the opinion of many ornithologists, it is the best birding area in New Hampshire. Among other surprises, the lake has the only nesting bald eagles in the state. A significant portion of this land was designated a national wildlife refuge in 1992, and canoe access is available from Errol via the Androscoggin River. Wilderness campsites are available at **Umbagog Lake Campground❖.** Don't miss **Thirteen Mile Woods,** a scenic drive along the Androscoggin River between Errol and Milan reached via Route 16. The river is famous for its trout but hard to wade and deserving of respect.

　　Dixville Notch State Park❖, the most northerly of the state's notches, lies between Sanguinary Mountain and Mount Gloriette on Route 26. Steep, jagged cliffs of vertical strata rise abruptly on either side of the highway, squeezing it for nearly two miles. A short distance to the north off Route 26, **Coleman State Park❖** is one of the rare parcels of state land in a region where most of the forest is owned by timber companies.

ABOVE: *An expert climber, the lynx often posts itself in trees, where its antennalike ear tufts help it to locate prey. Large, furry paws enable the cat to make a silent, lethal approach.*

RIGHT: *Connecticut Lakes State Forest, a prime birding area near the Canadian border, encompasses the wooded shoreline of First Lake, the source of the Connecticut River.*

Little Diamond Pond here is a fine spot for trout.

Even farther to the north, where the state narrows to little more than a dozen miles across, are the headwaters of the Connecticut River. The Connecticut forms the border with Vermont for more than 200 miles south of here, but it starts out entirely within New Hampshire, passing through a series of lakes of steadily increasing size. The river's northernmost source, Fourth Connecticut Lake, is no more than a beaver pond, reached via foot trail from the U.S. Customs station on the Quebec line. Then the river flows south-southwest into Third, Second, and First Connecticut lakes and then into Lake Francis (where a state park provides good camping), all accessible from Route 3.

The **Norton Pool Natural Area❖,** a 143-acre parcel of virgin red spruce and balsam fir at Norton Pool on East Inlet Stream, is accessible from a road just above Second Connecticut Lake. The **Connecticut Lake State Forest❖** along 3 is one of the most unusual parcels of public land in the state, and—for the driver—the best place to spot moose. At night, lines of cars stop on the road as people snap pictures and gawk at obliging moose browsing contentedly.

Those looping back south toward the heart of the White Mountains should stop in the Whitefield area off Route 3 to visit **Pondicherry Wildlife Refuge❖,** an Audubon preserve accessible via trail from the Whitefield Airport. Moose, loons, and beavers are all spotted here frequently, and the wetlands provide excellent birding.

EASTERN NEW HAMPSHIRE: LAKES AND SHORE

F ew place names in America have as beautiful a cadence as those of the New Hampshire lakes. Sunapee, Winnisquam, Chocorua, Suncook, Winnipesaukee, and a dozen more—their rhythmic names retain the flavor of their Native American past and convey a rugged clarity characteristic of the lakes themselves, at their best.

New Hampshire has 1,301 lakes within its borders, and although the difference between what is called a lake and what is termed a pond is not always clear-cut, generally any body of water more than ten acres in size is called a great pond. Some ponds, in contrary New Hampshire fashion, are considerably larger than some lakes. The largest and best known of the lakes are grouped in a 50-mile-wide area from Newfound Lake near East Hebron in the center of the state to Province Lake on the border with Maine. Dominating the area is 22-mile-long Lake Winnipesaukee, the largest body of water in New Hampshire, nearly 300 feet deep and dotted with more than 250 islands. The lake district was already popular as a tourist destination when in 1982 it received a tremendous amount of publicity as the setting for the hit movie *On Golden Pond*, filmed at Squam Lake.

The relative paucity of state-owned land on the lakes has resulted

LEFT: *The wooded 60-mile shoreline of Squam Lake unfolds below Rattlesnake Mountain. Framing the view is a shapely red pine; its slender needles help conserve water by cutting down on evaporation.*

in continual conflicts here between those who want more public access to the lakes and those who want to restrict that access. Battles over mooring rights and jet ski use are only the latest skirmishes in the controversy. The fact that the state has always been legally responsible for the lakes themselves but not for their shores has hamstrung any effort to give the lakes more protection. Still, even with the increased development, the lakes are blessed with a remarkable purity and a relative lack of aquatic vegetation, permitting views of the rocky bottom in more than 40 feet of water. And while the lakes can get overcrowded in the summer, just a little ways up into the hills can be found the best of both worlds—fine views of the lakes and the quiet and solitude of the woods.

ABOVE: *In 1869 American painter Childe Hassam did this delicate wood engraving of picnickers and the White Island Light on the Isles of Shoals. Today the islands still support a variety of native and migrating birds.*

OVERLEAF: *When conservationist Aldo Leopold wrote of the marshland bog, "a sense of time lies thick and heavy on such a place," he might well have been describing this sunlit scene of grasses, sedges, and red maples near Sandwich.*

Judging by the trinkets sold in area gift shops, the loon has become the symbol of the lake district—and rightly so. Carefully protected and monitored by hardworking volunteers, more than 100 nesting pairs of loons visit New Hampshire. This heavy, goose-sized bird with its distinctive black-and-white collar prefers large ponds and lakes that give it the long "runway" it needs to become airborne. Famous for its laugh (described in the *Audubon Society Field Guide to North American Birds* as "wild and maniacal"), the loon is a shy, wild bird, easily frightened, and should be viewed only through binoculars from a distance.

Southeast of the lake district is one of New Hampshire's surprises: a seacoast, only 18 miles long but offering long strips of beach, extensive marshes, and, in the Great Bay, a huge estuarine area that effectively multiplies the length of the saltwater shoreline. Along the ocean itself

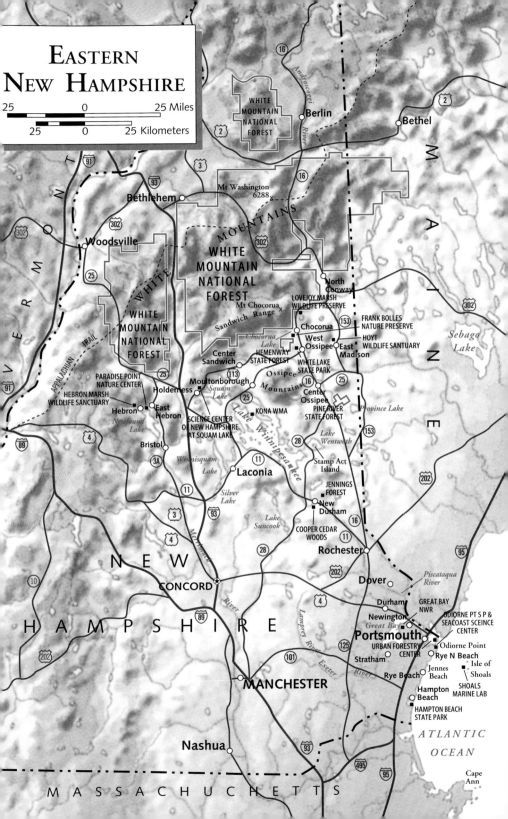

EASTERN NEW HAMPSHIRE

25   0   25 Miles

25   0   25 Kilometers

WHITE MOUNTAIN NATIONAL FOREST

Berlin

Bethel

Mt Washington 6288 ×

MOUNTAINS

Bethlehem

Woodsville

WHITE MOUNTAIN NATIONAL FOREST

WHITE MOUNTAIN NATIONAL FOREST

North Conway

LOVEJOY MARSH WILDLIFE PRESERVE

Mt Chocorua ×

Sandwich Range

Chocorua

FRANK BOLLES NATURE PRESERVE

Chocorua Lake

West Ossipee

East Madison

HOYT WILDLIFE SANTUARY

Sebago Lake

Center Sandwich

HEMENWAY STATE FOREST

WHITE LAKE STATE PARK

PARADISE POINT NATURE CENTER

Moultonborough

Holderness

Squam Lake

Ossipee Mountains

Center Ossipee

HEBRON MARSH WILDLIFE SANCTUARY

Hebron

East Hebron

Newfound Lake

SCIENCE CENTER OF NEW HAMPSHIRE AT SQUAM LAKE

KONA WMA

PINE RIVER STATE FOREST

Province Lake

Bristol

Winnisquam Lake

Lake Winnipesaukee

Lake Wentworth

Laconia

Silver Lake

Stamp Act Island

JENNINGS FOREST

Lake Suncook

New Durham

COOPER CEDAR WOODS

Rochester

CONCORD

Piscataqua River

Dover

Merrimack River

Durham

GREAT BAY NWR

Newington

Great Bay

ODIORNE PT S P & SEACOAST SCIENCE CENTER

NEW HAMPSHIRE

Portsmouth

URBAN FORESTRY CENTER

Odiorne Point

Rye N Beach

Stratham

Isle of Shoals

Lamprey River

Rye Beach

Jennes Beach

MANCHESTER

Hampton Beach

SHOALS MARINE LAB

Exeter River

HAMPTON BEACH STATE PARK

Nashua

ATLANTIC OCEAN

Cape Ann

MASSACHUCHETTS

VERMONT

MAINE

ABOVE: *The perfectly pointed tip of Mount Chocorua, New Hampshire's second most climbed peak, rises above the reflective blue surface of*

are five beaches: Jennes, Rye, Rye North, Seabrook, and Hampton. Seabrook is infamous in United States environmental history for its nearby nuclear power plant and the furious protests the plant's construction generated. Hampton Beach is known for the hordes of sunbathers that take up every last inch of sand on hot summer weekends.

Nine miles out to sea is a calmer oasis, the Isles of Shoals. Only three of the isles actually belong to New Hampshire, but all of them, reached via a ferry from Portsmouth, are considered by custom and history to be part of the state's domain. These islands, like the nearby areas of the New Hampshire mainland, are rich in birdlife, with migrating wildfowl passing through in spring and fall. The writer and bird conservationist Celia Thaxter, who lived in the isles in the last century and whose *Among the Isles of Shoals* is a gem of regional American literature, lamented the numbers of birds destroyed by colliding with the lighthouse there:

"Many a May morning have I wandered about the rock at the foot of the tower, mourning over a little apron brimful of sparrows, swallows, thrushes, robins, fire-winged blackbirds, many-colored warblers and flycatchers, beautifully clothed yellow birds, nuthatches, catbirds, even the purple finch and scarlet tanager and golden oriole, and many more beside." Her description testifies to the wide variety of birdlife that passes through this flyway even today, when the islands are popular destinations with birders. Many special excursions are offered by regional nature museums, the Audubon Society, and similar organizations.

This chapter heads south of the White Mountains through the lake

170

Chocorua Lake, one of hundreds of ponds and lakes that dot the rolling landscape between the White Mountains and the coast.

region to Lake Winnipesaukee. Farther south, the route proceeds past the Rochester-Dover area to explore the New Hampshire coastal plain, from the Great Bay to Portsmouth south to Rye. The chapter ends with a trip offshore to the Isles of Shoals and their abundant birdlife.

THE LAKES REGION

Approached from the White Mountains, the hills of the lake country look low in comparison; but to one driving north from the flat coastal plain of southeastern New Hampshire, the lake country's hills appear impressive. Newfound Lake, on the western edge of the lake country north of the crossroads town of Bristol on Route 3A, has low hills on each side. The lake itself is heavily developed, but one lovely stretch on the northern shore remains unspoiled: the **Paradise Point Nature Center❖,** operated by the Audubon Society of New Hampshire, located west of Route 3A in East Hebron. Here 3,500 feet of rocky lakeshore, fringed by an old-growth forest of hemlock, red spruce, and white pine, provides the setting for a small, attractive nature center with hands-on exhibits for children. Less than two miles down Groten Road toward the village of Hebron is the **Hebron Marsh Wildlife Sanctuary❖.** This combination of wetlands and open fields includes the mouth of the Cockermouth River and is a fine birding area, with an observation tower providing the best views. This is a good spot to see great blue herons, especially in the early morning as these gawky-looking yet graceful birds hunt for small fish.

A short drive east along Route 3 takes one to the town of Holderness

171

ABOVE: *One of the region's best-loved inhabitants, the common loon, marked by a white collar and checkered back, has an eerie wail. This deep-diving bird has been caught in nets 200 feet below the surface.*

RIGHT: *A rustic bridge crosses Chocorua Lake, where oxygen-rich waters make an ideal habitat for game fish such as salmon and trout.*

on Squam Lake, and the **Science Center of New Hampshire at Squam Lake❖.** This is another nature museum primarily for children, with displays in a protected 200-acre site. Squam Lake itself is largely given over to large estates, particularly on the northern and eastern shores, but there is a state-owned boat launch at Holderness, and anyone can explore the lake by boat or canoe. With its 26 islands and its unobstructed views of the mountains, it deserves its reputation as possibly the most beautiful of New Hampshire's lakes.

Continuing in a clockwise direction, heading east on Route 113 through lovely Center Sandwich (the nearby road through Sandwich Notch is one of the best-known scenic drives in the state), brings one to the Mount Chocorua region, with its mountains and smaller lakes. **Hemenway State Forest❖,** near the town of Chocorua, is a relatively undiscovered forest just south of the White Mountains. It includes the **Lovejoy Marsh Wildlife Preserve❖** and the **Big Pines Natural Area,** with 150-year-old conifers. **Mount Chocorua** (3,475 feet) is probably the second most climbed mountain in the state, after Monadnock. Its perfect pyramid shape makes it look like a mountain a child would draw, and its summit—a good climb, but not impossible—has been attracting hikers for years. One of the most popular routes is the Piper Trail, which leaves from Route 16 and ascends via switchbacks to the open ledges of the summit.

Right at the base of the mountain, the inevitable foreground in every postcard, is Chocorua Lake. On the northern shore of the lake off Route 16 are the **Frank Bolles Nature Preserve❖,** operated by the Nature Conservancy, and the **Clark Preserve❖,** owned by a local conservation

group. Together, they form a natural area that includes swamp, kettle holes, eskers, glacial erratics (rocks deposited by the melting Wisconsin Age glacier as it retreated northward), and a diversity of wildlife habitat.

White Lake State Park❖, on the small lake of that name off Route 16 near West Ossipee, is more than just another pretty beachside campground, thanks to the White Lake pitch pines on the western shore. These old-growth pitch pines, the needle-shedding *Pinus rigida,* are protected in a 72-acre national natural landmark. This species is relatively rare elsewhere in New Hampshire but common in this corner of the lake region, giving the air a pleasant resinous aroma on hot summer afternoons. The **Tamworth Black Spruce Pond Preserve❖** adjoins the state park.

Not far to the east is the **West Branch Pine Barrens❖** near Silver Lake. Pitch pines and scrub oaks flourish in the well-drained, sandy soil here. Nature writer Frank Bolles wrote of this area at the turn of the century: "Half the country between Ossipee Mountain and Chocorua is a sandy level covered with pitch pines and scrub oaks. It is a fine place for blueberries, firs, and pine warblers." The West Branch Pine Barrens is reputed to be the largest and best-preserved example of this kind of terrain in the northern United States and is protected by the Nature Conservancy.

To the east off Route 113 in Madison is another national natural landmark: the **Madison Boulder,** the largest known glacial boulder in North America. A dense mix of biolite, quartz, and feldspar, it measures 83 feet long and is estimated to weigh more than 7,000 tons. Northern New England is heavily littered with these glacial erratics, although few are this mammoth.

Nearby in East Madison off Route 153 is the **Hoyt Wildlife Sanctuary❖,** on the southeastern shore of the aptly named Purity Lake. The sanctuary, which covers 168 acres, includes a trail to No Bottom Pond—a kettle-hole bog filled with sphagnum moss, the home of carnivorous plants such as the round-leafed sundew and the pitcher plant, which get their nutrients by consuming insects. Here, too, is the Virginia chain fern, a plant rare this far north. The Esker Trail follows the top of a winding ridge, a glacial formation known in New England as a "whaleback," created when sediments were deposited along the course of a stream tunneling beneath melting glaciers. These eskers are usually 10- to 100-foot-high ridges that from a distance resemble railroad embankments. Eskers once provided high, dry routes through swamplands and were used as pathways by Native Americans and early settlers—and then later as the driest, most obvious paths for early roads.

Another, more prominent esker is located in the **Pine River State Forest❖** in Center Ossipee off Route 16. This esker, a serpentine, 5-mile-long, 120-foot-high ridge of gravel and sand left by the last glacier, parallels Pine River, which is a quiet and pastoral canoe route along Route 16.

Southwest of this area of smaller lakes is **Lake Winnipesaukee,** the largest body of water in New Hampshire. More than 130 different spellings of the lake's name are on record. Nearly as many translations of the original Native American phrase for it have been offered; the

---

RIGHT: *"Each year snow renews our sense of wonder," wrote naturalist Donald Stokes. Here laden branches arch gracefully over the steel gray waters of the Cockermouth River near Hebron, New Hampshire.*

most plausible is the simplest: "Good water with large pour-out place," referring to the outlet in the southwestern corner of the lake, long a valuable source of water power. The outlet was a favorite spot of the Indians, and the name of the present Weirs Beach in Laconia commemorates the V-shaped nets made of hemp they would place in the outlet to trap trout and salmon, which are still plentiful.

Perhaps the best way to explore Winnipesaukee is by small boat or canoe, launched from one of the numerous private or state-run ramps on the lake. This is usually a busy lake, but on an off-season weekday when the crowds are gone, Winnipesaukee reverts back to a huge, placid, island-dotted expanse. The **Kona Wildlife Management Area❖** in Moultonborough fronts the lake for 3,000 unspoiled feet on Braun Bay. The area is crisscrossed with old woods roads, which makes it easy to explore.

Lake Wentworth is a smaller lake just to the east of Winnipesaukee on Route 28. **Stamp Act Island❖,** at 100 acres the largest of the lake's 17 islands, once belonged to Governor John Wentworth, the last colonial governor of New Hampshire, who was active in pushing for the repeal of the infamous Stamp Act tax. Now operated as a preserve by the Nature Conservancy, the island is covered by a forest of beech and red oak and offers more than 11,000 feet of undeveloped shore frontage, including five natural beach areas. A special feature here is one of the last remaining great blue heron rookeries in northern New England. The island is closed to visitors from March through mid-July to avoid disturbing the nesting herons. It is reached by boat from Mast Landing on Crescent Lake just north of Wolfeboro Falls; the landing point is at Stamp Act Beach on the island's northern shore.

THE NEW HAMPSHIRE SHORE

South of the big lakes, the terrain starts to flatten out as it approaches the coast. **Cooper Cedar Woods❖** in New Durham features an extremely rare Atlantic white-cedar swamp. The white cedar is a medium-sized, reddish brown tree that favors swampy bogs in the coastal plain. The preserve, off Route 11, also includes a fine stand of black spruce, a bog, and another esker, with a well-marked interpretive trail leading through the heart of the woods. The Society for the Protection of New Hampshire Forests also maintains the **Jennings Forest❖** in New Durham, a 376-acre preserve on Middleton Road that includes a beaver meadow and 30 acres of wetland along Hayes Brook.

In the Rochester-Dover area to the southeast, the land flattens out even more. This is the Eastern Slope, New Hampshire's coastal plain. Just southeast of the university town of Durham on Route 4 is the **Great Bay,** New England's largest inland body of saltwater. When seen from a distance, the bay looks like a lake; but up close, the marks of tidal fluctuation are obvious. The Great

ABOVE: *The great blue heron stands four feet tall and has slow-moving wings that span seven feet. To hunt, it stands perfectly still in the water and then in a flash thrusts its daggerlike bill at unsuspecting prey.*

LEFT: *Located along the Atlantic Flyway, the Great Bay is a large inland saltwater body that attracts thousands of birds (herons, geese, and ducks), which use the area as a rest stop during the spring and fall.*

OVERLEAF: *In the tidal flats of Odiorne State Park, resilient saltmeadow and saltmarsh cordgrasses are vital food sources for animals and help build soil along the shore.*

Bay is fed by the Oyster, Exeter, and Lamprey rivers. The shoreline of the bay proper is more than 48 miles long, even longer when Little Bay to the north is added in. The **Great Bay National Estuarine Reserve❖** protects much of the bay. Access by boat and land is from **Adams Point,** a wildlife management area in Durham, or the **Discovery Center at Sandy Point** off Route 101 in Stratham. For boaters, numerous launching sites are scattered around the bay's perimeter. As befits its location along the Atlantic Flyway, this is prime birding territory, particularly during seasonal migrations. Reflecting this importance, New Hampshire's largest wildlife refuge was established on 1,000 acres of a former air force base: the **Great Bay National Wildlife Refuge❖** is located in Newington south of Route 4.

New Hampshire's short coastline has one oasis of both scenic and historic interest: **Odiorne Point State Park❖** on the ocean near Rye, reached on Route 1A. Ragged Odiorne Point with its jutting promontories was one of the first points of land to be settled in the United States. A Scotsman named David Thompson landed in 1623 to establish the first settlement in New Hampshire, selecting this point because of the harbor and the large salt marsh, which made it readily defensible. The last and only sizable piece of New Hampshire seacoast that has escaped development is protected within the 137 acres of this park, which is home to herons, northern harriers, snowy egrets, and black-backed and herring gulls in the marsh, and such intertidal species as sea stars, crabs, and sea urchins. Also in the park is the **Seacoast Science Center❖,** operated by the Audubon Society of New Hampshire in cooperation with private conservation groups and the state. This interpretative museum and nature center has exhibits on natural and coastal history as well as several foot trails. Rusting fortifications built here during World War II are visible from some of the trails; there are tidal pools and fine beachcombing near the water.

Just north of the park is the coast's one large city: Portsmouth, with its renowned harbor at the mouth of the Piscataqua River. The **Urban Forestry Center❖** on Elwyn Road, run by the state, features an arboretum, a hiking trail, a forestry learning center, and a wildflower garden—a natural oasis in the heart of town. Portsmouth is also the terminus for the boat running to the Isles of Shoals, the small chain of islets lying nine miles offshore. Of the islands, the most interesting is Appledore, al-

ABOVE: *Once a popular summer resort area, the windswept Isles of Shoals were an important subject for American impressionist painter Childe Hassam. He completed* White Island Light *in 1899.*

though public access to it is limited. Here the **Shoals Marine Laboratory❖,** operated jointly by Cornell University and the University of New Hampshire, serves not only as a unique offshore research station for oceanographers but also as an educational center offering members of the general public a variety of courses, on topics ranging from marine mammals and seabirds to general marine ecology and natural history.

Early English explorer John Smith visited these islands in 1614, and European fishermen almost certainly used the isles to dry their fish even earlier. In 1847, with the construction of the Appledore House Hotel, the island of Appledore became a resort. Until it burned down in 1914, the hotel served as a summer retreat for many late-nineteenth-century artists, writers, and musicians. Childe Hassam, the American impressionist painter, did much of his finest work on the island, painting ocean views as well as **Celia Thaxter's Garden.** The garden, described by Thaxter in her classic *An Island Garden,* is maintained today as faithfully as possible to its late-nineteenth-century splendor. Also of interest today is Appledore's huge gull colony, with approximately 3,000 pairs of herring gulls and the larger great black-backed gulls.

181

MAINE

CHAPTER SEVEN

INLAND MAINE:
THE FOREST PLATEAU

The old saying about Maine is that it's too large to explore adequately in one lifetime, but small enough to try. Compared to compact Vermont and New Hampshire, the landscape is on a much grander scale altogether. From Bethel near the western border with New Hampshire northeastward to Fort Kent on the Canadian line is a road distance of more than 300 miles, and for most of this distance the terrain is remarkably similar. The broad forest plateau interspersed with mountains gives the impression of one very slow, very huge, very shaggy undulation.

This is timberland, more than 17 million acres of it, forming the last great wild area on the eastern seaboard and the closest approximation to what the land looked like before white settlers arrived three centuries ago. In actuality it is not strictly wild; although the area is as forested as it was in the seventeenth century, the woods are second and third growth and are managed by private corporations and thousands of small owners to produce timber. A rapidly expanding network of logging roads crisscrosses the area everywhere. Still, except where logging has been recent, these woods convey the majestic and even intimidating solitude of Thoreau's day, and the words he used to describe the interior in 1846

PRECEDING PAGES: *The rising sun illumines the cliffs and waters of Maine's Quoddy Head State Park, the easternmost point of the United States.*

LEFT: *Glacial boulders such as these in Baxter State Park are often covered with velvety mosses, which form dense mats that absorb water.*

could be used with little change to describe it today:

"What is most striking in the Maine wilderness is the continuousness of the forest, with fewer open intervals or glades than imagined. . . . It is a country full of evergreen trees, of mossy silver birches, and watery maples, the ground doppled with insipid small red berries, and strewn with damp and moss-grown rocks—a country diversified with innumerable lakes and rapid streams, peopled with trout, with salmon, shad and pickerel; the forest resounding at rare intervals with the note of the chickadee, the blue-jay and the woodpecker, the scream of the fish-hawk and the eagle, the laugh of the loon, and the whirr of ducks along the solitary streams; at night, with the hooting of owls and howling of wolves; in summer, swarming with myriads of black flies and mosquitoes, more formidable than wolves."

Except for the potato fields of Aroostook County in the northeastern part of the state (and these, too, deserve the adjective *vast*), this has never been farming country; as a result, there is little of the familiar field, meadow, and barn scenery associated with so many other areas of New England. The weather, too, is rugged. Van Buren, near the New Brunswick border, averages 208 days a year with below-freezing temperatures and holds the record for the coldest reading in Maine's history: 48 degrees below zero Fahrenheit in January of 1925. Study a state map and you will appreciate how far north northern Maine extends; indeed, the shortest rail line from the Canadian Maritimes to Quebec cuts across the interior of the state.

With their wild character and their proximity to the urban centers of the East Coast, the Maine woods have long captured people's imaginations. At least two genuine American folk heroes originated here: the loggers, woods-wise and laconic, and the even wiser and more laconic Maine guides, telling stories around the campfire as they skillfully fry up a mess of trout for their "sports." These woods have also contributed to the country's notion of a sporting camp, which can range from a rustic fishing lodge on a lake that accepts paying guests, to a family's primitive hunting cabin on a jeep trail miles from the nearest road.

The Maine woods, in topographical terms, consist of a broad plateau running northeast from New Hampshire across the Rangeley Lakes and Moosehead regions, gradually sloping eastward toward the basin of the Penobscot River and northward to the Saint John River.

INLAND MAINE

25   0   25 Miles
25   0   25 Kilometers

NEW BRUNSWICK

CANADA

QUÉBEC

NEW HAMPSHIRE

ST JOHN RIVER

St John River

Allagash River

ALLAGASH WILDERNESS WATERWAY

Fort Kent
St Francis
Allagash
Van Buren
Caribou
Eagle Lake
Presque Isle
Ashland
AROOSTOOK SP
Squapan Lake
Machias River
Aroostook River

Eagle Lake
Chamberlain Lake

BAXTER STATE PARK
SOUTH BRANCH CAMPGROUND
North Brother ×
Doubletop Mtn ×
Great Basin ×
Katahdin 5268 ×
Sandy Stream Pond
Chimney Pond
ROARING BROOK CAMPGROUND
Patten
LUMBERMAN'S MUSEUM

Moosehead Lake
Nahmakanta Lake

Mt Kineo ×
Rockwood
Millinocket
MATTAWAMKEAG WILDERNESS PARK
Mattawamkeag

Jackman
Moose River
LILY BAY SP
APPALACHIAN TRAIL
Gulf Hagas
Greenville
Little Wilson Falls Gorge
Brownville
Milo

Attean Pond

Big Squaw Mtn ×
MOOSEHEAD MARINE MUS
Lake Moxie
Borestone Mtn ×
Monson

Dead River
Moxie Pond

BIGELOW PRESERVE
Eustis
The Forks
APPALACHIAN TRAIL
Stratton
Avery Peak ×
Carrabassett

Moxie Falls

HUNTER COVE SANCTUARY
Crocket Mtn ×
Mt Abraham × 4049
N New Portland

RANGELEY LAKE SP
Oquossoc
THE Aziscohos Mtn CMPG ×
Saddleback Mtn ×
Tumbledown Mtn ×
MT BLUE SP
Mt Blue × 3187
Weld
N New Portland
Skowhegan
Farmington
Bangor

Rangeley Lake

GRAFTON NOTCH SP
Andover
Newry
W Paris
Snow Falls Gorge
Weld
CHESTERVILLE WMA
Chesterville Esker
Waterville

Upper Richardson Lake

PERHAMS OF W PARIS QUARRIES

Webb Lake
Kennebec River

AUGUSTA

ABOVE: *For decades, rustic lakeshore camps (such as this one on Long Pond near Bemis) have dotted many of Maine's remote inland lakes, providing no-frills seasonal retreats for hunters and anglers.*

This area can be broken up into smaller chunks: the western region of high mountains and large lakes; the central interior of lower mountains and smaller lakes; and the 314 square miles of Baxter State Park. Then there is the Aroostook region, mostly forested but including along the fertile lowlands of the Aroostook and Saint John river valleys—an area that resembles Wisconsin more than it does New England—one of the most famous seed potato–growing areas in the world.

Viewed from on high, the landscape of interior Maine appears as if a giant's hand had scooped, gouged, folded, and patted it into a series of long ridgelike eskers, potholes, and moraines. The region's recent geological history dates from the last Pleistocene glacier. Although the preglacial landscape probably closely resembled that of today, with a similar drainage pattern carved into the bedrock, what is most evident today are the effects of the last glacier. For instance, many mountains in Maine have a uniformly sloping north side, but a rugged, jumbled south side—a shape created by the advancing ice sheet as it rose up the north slope, smoothed it, then plucked away the rock on the south side, leaving behind a precipitous "downstream" cliff. Glacial cirques are obvious in the form of steep-walled amphitheaters on mountains such as Katahdin, and Crocker Mountain in the Carrabassett area. One peculiarity to note: Scratches on bedrock in far northern Maine suggest the glacier flowed northwest here rather than south. A remnant ice cap probably still covered the Maine mountains quite a while after the Saint Lawrence River valley to the north had thawed, and gravity drew this ice toward the open river.

The forest covering this moist, cool region is primarily spruce—black, white, and red; also present are balsam fir (favored for Christmas trees), hardwoods, hemlocks, the swamp-loving tamarack, and northern white cedar. The white pine, which appears on the state seal and gives Maine its nickname, once grew in stands more than 250 feet high, and while few giants remain, white pine is still common. As on the White Mountains to the west, there are alpine species of flora on Katahdin and other high peaks, but most of the plant life in this area falls within the Arcadian classification. The area's abundant bogs support sphagnum moss, Labrador tea, bog rosemary, little cranberry, leatherleaf, and skunk cabbage. While the prime blueberry-growing barrens are to the south east in Washington County, berries are common everywhere, particularly on sunny hillsides—good browsing terrain for black bears.

Two animals once common in the Maine woods are now extinct there: the wolf and its favorite prey, the caribou. Efforts to reintroduce the latter into interior Maine have failed, in part due to the increased numbers of a predator that, migrating here from the West, has replaced the wolf in the food chain: the coyote. Moose, so perfectly adapted to combing the shallow lakes for food, do well here, too; bulls feed in the shallows, dipping their heads below the surface to emerge with jawfuls of dripping vegetation. White-tailed deer, bobcats, fishers, martens, red and gray squirrels, the various voles, porcupines—they are all found here, too, as are beavers, their lodges and dams liberally dotting the landscape. The birdlife is similar to that found in adjacent areas and includes spruce

OVERLEAF: *A moose feeds in Sandy Stream Pond in Baxter State Park. Excellent swimmers, these huge relatives of the deer will often retreat to cool waters to avoid blackflies and mosquitoes or to graze on aquatic plants.*

LEFT: *North America's most common wildcat, the bobcat is the only Maine predator that regularly kills deer, often attacking their bedding areas at night.*
RIGHT: *The powerful black bear, seen here feeding on dandelions, is an insatiable omnivore, finding delicacies at anthills, rodent burrows, and fruit trees.*

grouse and ruffed grouse, evening grosbeaks, loons and grebes on the ponds, the gregarious Canada jays or "camp robbers," and a bird of the true North, the raven, soaring on the updrafts over the peaks.

Two fish should be mentioned as well. One is the brook trout, the native salmonoid so closely identified with these woods, which is still abundant, although nowhere near the size it once was. The other is the landlocked salmon. As its name implies, this is a close relative of the anadromous Atlantic salmon, one whose route to the sea was cut off thousands of years ago by gradual changes in the geology of the region, causing the fish to evolve separately in Maine's interior lakes.

For many people, the best way to explore the interior of Maine is still, as it has been for centuries, via canoe. The Allagash, the Penobscot, the Saint John—many of the most famous canoe routes in America are here, with the established campsites, launching sites, and portages that make them possible. Guided trips are popular, and many people set out on their own, for day trips or longer.

Anyone venturing into these woods should understand that they differ in important respects from other wild areas of northern New England. Less of the land is public; most of it is commercial forestland operated by private landowners to whom the roads, complete with

gates and bars, belong. By custom and by law this land is open to recreational use by the public, but the lumber corporations have rules and regulations regarding campsites, fire use, road travel, and such, and those venturing deep into the interior should familiarize themselves with these before starting out. Care must be taken in driving the logging roads, as one is likely to meet logging trucks, many traveling at high speed.

Care must also be exercised by anyone venturing off these roads. This is a complex area, with a maze of streams and bogs. It is much easier to get lost here than it is in less rugged areas of New England, and the distances to any kind of assistance are correspondingly greater.

This chapter explores Maine's vast inland regions, moving from west to east. Beginning on Route 2 from New Hampshire, about halfway between the coast and the Canadian border, the route moves through the western highlands and Rangeley Lakes area, then proceeds north to Moosehead Lake, Baxter State Park, and the Allagash Wilderness Waterway, ending in the remote Aroostook region.

THE WESTERN HIGHLANDS

Route 2 follows the Androscoggin River into Maine from New Hampshire. Just north of this corridor is one of the most interesting

ABOVE: *Umbagog Lake, on the Maine–New Hampshire border, has a wide variety of habitats, including thick forests and ponds, that provide shelter for a diverse population of moose, black bears, loons, and raptors.*

and rugged mountain areas in the Northeast: the **Mahoosuc Range.** Here a well-defined ridgeline trending in a southwest to northeast direction includes three major peaks: Goose Eye Mountain (3,870 feet), Mahoosuc Arm (3,790 feet), and Old Speck (4,180 feet), the third highest mountain in Maine. **Mahoosuc Notch** itself is where the Appalachian Trail, in traversing the range, winds its way around and under immense boulders that have fallen from the cliffs of Mahoosuc Mountain to the northwest. In the shady gloom, snow lingers well into summer, and among people who have hiked the Appalachian Trail end-to-end this section has the reputation of being the single toughest, especially to those encumbered with large packs. The Mahoosucs are owned by the state of Maine (27,000 acres) and the James River Corporation. Access from the south is on the Sunday River Road out of Bethel; from the north by the East B Hill Road between Andover and Upton; and from the west on Success Pond Road.

Hikers can also explore this part of Maine from **Grafton Notch**

194

State Park❖ on Route 26 above Newry. The notch, an alpine glacial valley, is spectacular from the road and includes more than 3,000 acres on both sides of the highway. Several short hikes lead to places of interest, including three cascading waterfalls: Step Falls, Mother Walker Falls, and Screw Auger Falls (named for a twisty logging tool). Over the centuries the rushing waters have worn away the lower layers of rock, forming the only two known natural bridges in Maine.

Distances are great in the interior of Maine, and drivers will find a bit of planning is required to link various natural areas they hope to visit. For example, West Paris is reached by continuing east on Route 2 from Newry, then heading south on routes 232 and 26. Just south of town is **Snow Falls Gorge,** a roadside 100-yard-long gorge where the Little Androscoggin River rushes through sheer granite walls. Rock collectors and gem hounds have made the town something of a rock-hunting center. **Perham's of West Paris❖** maintains four quarries within a ten-mile radius, where for no charge people can hunt for examples of tourmaline, quartz, and the other minerals that have made Oxford County one of the most popular rock-hunting locales in Maine.

Travelers have a choice here; those heading for the coast area can follow Route 26 toward Portland, perhaps stopping in Gray at the **Fish and Wildlife Visitor Center❖,** which is particularly appealing to children. Here, orphaned or injured wildlife that cannot be returned to the wild (black bears, porcupines, skunks, wild turkeys) are given a home; interpretative exhibits, including a pool stocked with big brown trout, acquaint the public with Maine's wildlife resources. Just west of Gray along Route 302 is the famous area of summer resorts and fishing camps on 14-mile-long Sebago Lake. Sebago is thought to be the original home of the landlocked salmon, whose Latin name is *Salmo sebago.*

Those who prefer to head north from the West Paris area can work their way back toward Route 2 using the network of smaller back roads in the area. In Chesterville, south of busy Farmington, is the **Chesterville Wildlife Management Area❖,** which includes a diverse habitat of woods and marsh along Little Norridgewock Stream; canoe access is at the dam site downstream from town. A short distance south of town near Norcross Pond is the Chesterville Esker, a sharp glacial ridge more than 90 feet high.

Route 156 leads north to Weld and the mountains surrounding

195

Mount Blue State Park❖ on Lake Webb. Along the road that winds through the park are colorful displays of wildflowers—trailing arbutus, lady's slippers, violets, dogwood, wild roses, goldenrod, blue flag irises, jack-in-the-pulpits, daisies, and buttercups. Of the summits that ring the lake, probably the most impressive is **Tumbledown Mountain** (3,068 feet), with some of the sheerest cliffs in Maine on its southern

side, the haunt of rock climbers. A remote pond sits on the eastern slope, and the views from the summit ridges are excellent. The oldest and easiest trail up the mountain, Parker's Ridge Trail, leaves from a dirt road off the Byron Notch Road, about 2.7 miles west of Weld Corner; allow at least two hours for the climb up to the summit. The other popular peak here is **Mount Blue** itself (3,187 feet), which, like Chocorua in New Hampshire, resembles a perfect cone.

Northwest of Weld is the Rangeley Lake area, with some of the most beautiful and melodiously named

ABOVE: *With long tail feathers to prop them against trees, yellow-bellied sapsuckers bore for sap and insects, leaving a clear line of holes behind.*
RIGHT: *Once the hunting grounds of the Abenaki, the Rangeley Lakes area was also the province of private sportsmen in the last century. Saddleback Mountain rises to the east.*

lakes in the country: Rangeley, Quimby Pond, Dodge Pond, Kennebago, Loon, Saddleback, Mooselookmeguntic, Cupsuptic, Upper and Lower Richardson, Aziscohos, and the Maine portion of Lake Umbagog. It was this area of lakes and mountains that Maine author Louise Dickinson Rich, who lived beside the Rapid River connecting Lower Richardson with Umbagog, lovingly described in her classic account *We Took to the Woods.* Written in the 1940s, the book is still popular today. Here she describes this unique setting:

"I like to think of the lakes coming down from the North of us like a gigantic staircase to the sea. Kennebago to Rangeley to Cupsuptic, down

196

they drop, level to level, through short, snarling rivers . . . I like to say their names and I wish I could make you see them—long, lovely, lonely stretches of water, shut in by dark hills."

Maine has two large, wild, undeveloped holdings in the Rangeleys. The first is the 22,806-acre **Richardson Lake Unit**❖, located between Upper Richardson Lake and Mooselookmeguntic. Fishing, boating, and—for the brave—swimming are popular here, with camping available at South Arm Campground. Access to the southern portion is by water, with launch sites at Oquossoc, in Rangeley, and at South Arm in Township C (there being so many unimproved, uninhabited townships in interior Maine, many are referred to by letters and/or numbers). Route 16 passes through the northern portion of the unit in Adamstown. Farther to the east is the 6,081-acre **Four Ponds Unit**❖, which includes the Sabbath Day Pond and a campsite at Little Swift River Pond. The Appalachian Trail traverses the length of this unit, with the trailhead off Route 17 in Township D, or Route 4 in Sandy River. Both units, with their mix of pond, bog, and forest, provide perfect habitat for moose.

Eight-mile-long Rangeley Lake, the most northeasterly in the chain and the busiest, has **Rangeley Lake State Park**❖ (691 acres) on its South Shore Drive—a good camping base from which to explore the surrounding country. Two longtime summer residents of the area, Pat and Edward Kfoury, spearheaded a private organization, the Rangeley Lakes Heritage Trust, with other concerned residents and local corporations. They have now acquired some 10,000 acres, which with the state park and other contiguous preserved lands now leave a great part of this area protected and preserved.

Along with much of western Maine, the Rangeley Lake area has its share of mountains, many with exceptional views. Fifteen lakes can be seen from the top of **Mount Aziscohos** (3,125 feet) south of the lake of the same name, although the trails up it, littered with "blowdowns" (trees that have fallen due to old age or storms), are for experienced hikers only. **Saddleback Mountain** (4,120 feet), east of Rangeley off Route 4, is one of the most striking mountains in Maine, with its long northeast-

---

LEFT: *In rapidly moving waters such as those of Moxie Falls, aquatic plants must attach themselves or be lost. Threadlike diatoms cling to rock surfaces by slimy secretions, often making crossings slippery.*

southwest ridge and pronounced saddle separating its several peaks. The Appalachian Trail crosses this mountain as it winds its way northeastward. Along its path is **Mount Abraham** (4,049 feet), with a 5-mile-long ridge that includes eight high peaks and a large area above timberline.

Another hiking center is the Bigelow-Carrabassett-Stratton area on Route 27 just to the north. A statewide referendum passed in 1976 protects more than 40,000 acres along the south shore of sprawling Flagstaff Lake in the **Bigelow Preserve❖,** which includes some of the best mountain terrain in the state. Lowlands forested with conifers, red maple, and American beech support populations of spruce grouse, whose heavy bodies make considerable noise as they fly, and aptly named springtails, insects with six legs and a springlike appendage at the back. Access to the unit is by rough roads off Route 27 in Carrabassett, or by the Long Falls Dam Road from North New Portland. The Bigelow Range runs east-west for more than ten miles and is crossed by the Appalachian Trail. While trails traverse all the major summits in the range, the view from **Avery Peak** (4,088 feet)—with the expanse of mountains and ponds and Flagstaff Lake spreading out on all sides—is perhaps the most notable. The Bigelow Range Trail is a long day hike, with lots of ups and downs, from the trailhead on Route 27 in Stratton to its end near Cranberry Pond, where it joins the Appalachian Trail several miles west of Avery Peak.

This is the area of Maine through which Benedict Arnold's ill-fated expedition to attack Quebec passed in 1775, still considered one of the toughest wilderness marches ever made. Bigelow Mountain is named for a major in Arnold's army, and one of the expedition campsites was on the shore of the original, smaller Flagstaff Lake. From the lake, they took their bateaux up the north branch of the Dead River toward the Chain of Ponds; crossing these with much hardship, they reached the Chaudière River, which took them to the Saint Lawrence in Canada. Route 27 north of Eustis parallels much of Arnold's route, and the state has erected interpretative panels detailing the progress of the expedition.

The Dead River's confluence with the Kennebec on Route 201 is called The Forks. The Kennebec, which has its source in Moosehead Lake to the north, is one of the most historic rivers in America, flowing 150 miles to the Maine coast. This was one of the first rivers on the continent to be extensively explored, with fragmentary reports coming in as

ABOVE: *Called Mspame or "large water" by the Native Americans, Moosehead Lake is the source of the Kennebec River. Because of the lake's size, sudden storms can be quite rough and even dangerous.*

early as 1600. During the nineteenth century and well into the twentieth, log drives filled the water with trees cut in the interior, rafted and boomed down the river to the mills of Skowhegan and Waterville. Smaller pulp logs were floated down the river until 1974. Between The Forks and Salon, the winding Route 201 traces the river, providing travelers with spectacular views and a particularly scenic interlude.

At The Forks, the crossroads where the road for Lake Moxie branches east from Route 201, is the headquarters for whitewater rafting in this area, with one-day and overnight trips on both the lower part of the Dead and the Kennebec. The rapids on Kennebec, rated as high as class IV, include Harris Dam run, which, with 12 miles of fast water, is considered one of the best in the East. A nearby attraction worth seeing is **Moxie Falls❖,** which, with a free fall of more than 60 feet, is one of the most spectacular waterfalls in Maine; reach it via a woods road east of The Forks.

From The Forks, Route 201 heads northwest toward the Jackman–Moose River area, long a favorite of trout and salmon anglers.

201

Its wealth of sporting camps and canoe routes includes the popular 34-mile Bow Trip, which crosses Attean Pond (the granite around the lake is some of the oldest in Maine, formed during the rise of the Appalachian Mountains more than 430 million years ago), portages slightly more than a mile to Holeb Pond, then circles back on the Moose River. The state of Maine's 18,000-acre **Holeb Unit** protects much of this land.

MOOSEHEAD AND THE NORTH

Forty miles long, almost twenty miles wide, and more than a thousand feet above sea level, **Moosehead Lake** has been a landmark for travelers in the Maine woods for the last two centuries. It is one of the largest—and windiest—lakes in the United States to lie wholly within the confines of one state. Thoreau visited it twice, in 1846 and 1857, crossing it in a birch-bark canoe. He described how "off Lily Bay it is a dozen miles wide, but varied and interesting; mountains were seen, farther or near, on all sides but the northeast, their summits now lost in the clouds. . . . After leaving Greenville, you see but three or four houses for the whole length of the lake, and the shore is an unbroken wilderness."

It remains largely wilderness today, with most of the sporting camps and lodges clustered around Greenville and Rockwood on Route 15 and the southwestern shore. Dominating the lake is **Mount Kineo,** a massive lump of rhyolite lava sculpted by a glacier. It forms a peninsula in the lake accessible only via boat from Rockwood on the mainland. Thoreau's guide, Joe Polis, told him the legend that the mountain was once a cow moose; with some imagination one can still make out the moose, albeit a rather angular one. An 800-foot cliff drops sheer to the lake; walking trails skirt the worst of the cliff and permit a relatively easy climb to the top.

Moosehead Lake is the center of a wide variety of outdoor activities. **Lily Bay State Park❖** is right on the water north of Greenville, with camping and two boat-launching sites. The **Moosehead Marine Museum❖** in Greenville is situated by a restored lake steamer that still makes regularly scheduled excursions up the lake. The SS *Katahdin* dates from 1914, the last remnant of an era when steamboats were the luxurious means of transportation up and down the lake. Moose viewing—a popular early-morning and late-evening pastime here—can be done almost anywhere a road passes a boggy area, but local favorites include Lazy Tom Bog north of Greenville and West Shirley Bog south of town.

Little Wilson Falls Gorge south of Greenville contains one of the tallest waterfalls in Maine and can be reached by following the Appalachian Trail. (Pick up the trail at its junction with Route 15 near Monson and hike northeast about five miles.) **Squaw Mountain** (3,196 feet) towers over the country southwest of the lake; its summit, the site of the oldest continuously operated fire tower in the United States (erected in 1905), has extensive views of the lake. The trailhead is on the Scott Paper Company Road, 5.3 miles north of Greenville; there are no blazes, but hikers with good woods instinct can follow the well-worn path.

Borestone Mountain❖, 12 miles north of Monson, lies within a 1,600-acre sanctuary owned by the National Audubon Society. It features a coniferous forest and deciduous trees that haven't been cut since the 1890s, giving an idea of what this forest looked like before the loggers went to work. For more than 20 years in the early part of this century, a private company raised foxes for their pelts here; escapees bred with the local population of red foxes, and today visitors often spot these animals' distinctively colored descendants. The trailhead is past the Canadian Pacific tracks off Elliotsville Road.

Baxter State Park isn't far, but some outstanding natural features are worth visiting in between the Moosehead region and the park, many reached by the Appalachian Trail. Originally, much of the AT in Maine used old logging roads, linking sporting camps and taking the easiest route. Now, after a 20-year effort, many sections of the trail have been rerouted onto the mountain ridgelines, past many beautiful ponds, and away from roads; public land surrounds the trail. One of the real gems of the AT's entire length is **Gulf Hagas❖,** a wilderness gorge along the West Branch of the Pleasant River in the deep, old-growth woods. Travelers approaching from the Moosehead region can take Route 6 to Milo, then Route 11 up to Brownville Junction. Just north of town a road leads west to the site of the restored Katahdin Iron Works, built in 1843 and fueled by charcoal made from the surrounding forest. From the gatehouse (nominal fee charged), drive about 5.5 miles to the Appalachian Trail parking lot. From this point a short walk takes hikers to the West Branch of the Pleasant River, where they must wade across a ford that can be difficult to cross during high water. From the lovely white-pine grove called The Hermitage, it is about one mile along the AT to the beginning of the Gulf Hagas loop trail.

The gorge, a registered national natural landmark, is a deep and narrow slate canyon about 4 miles long where the Pleasant River falls nearly 400 feet, the water running through a splendid series of pools, rapids, chutes, and waterfalls (especially spectacular during the peak runoff in late spring). The 5.2-mile Gulf Hagas Trail, a blue-blazed side trail of the AT system, provides access to all features of the gorge, including beautiful Pugwash Pond.

ABOVE: *While the intensely blue male indigo bunting sings strident couplets from a high perch in the summer, the female tends the nest she builds in the thickets below.*

RIGHT: *When the state balked at the idea of preservation, Governor Percival Baxter personally donated the land to create Baxter State Park; here Katahdin presides over Little Niagara Falls.*

OVERLEAF: *A dazzling collage of color—from red and orange maples to dark green firs and lighter quaking aspen— greets visitors to Baxter State Park in the fall.*

Farther north, in the rugged country south of the West Branch of the Penobscot, is a part of the Appalachian Trail many hikers rank even higher than Gulf Hagas: beautiful **Nahmakanta Lake❖.** The pond, filled with brook trout, is set deep in the forest and surrounded by low mountains. Almost all of the land around the lake belongs to the National Park Service as part of the Appalachian Trail corridor. The land around this corridor belongs to the state of Maine, so the lake is well protected and remains unspoiled. A nearby outstanding natural feature is **Pollywog Gorge.** Also part of the AT corridor lands, it is reached via an easy hike from the gate of the logging road (an extension of the Jo Mary Road) over Pollywog Stream. The rewarding trail follows the AT upstream along the gorge and past Crescent Pond to an intersection with the same logging road, returning over the road to the gate. The gorge has a tragic logging history—numerous river drivers were killed during log drives through the chasm.

Millinocket on Route 11, a town dominated by the Great Northern Paper Company's mills, is the supply center for those venturing into the woods of north-central Maine. West of town is the mile-long **Ripogenus Gorge,** where the West Branch of the Penobscot, one of the state's most historic logging rivers,

roars down from Ripogenus Dam. The lower portion of the gorge is pink granite, the same rock the Katahdin massif to the north is made of. The walls of the lower gorge are vertical, and the nearby road provides vertiginous views of the rushing water below.

About 20 miles southeast of Millinocket on Route 157 is the town of Mattawamkeag, where the **Mattawamkeag Wilderness Park❖** includes more than 15 miles of wilderness hiking trails, some excellent fishing and canoeing on the Mattawamkeag River, and an old-growth forest of more than 1,000 acres. Some trees among the uncut pines, spruce, hemlock, and hardwoods are almost 300 years old.

It is impossible to understand the human interrelationship with the forests of interior Maine without understanding something of the logging industry. The fine **Lumberman's Museum❖** in Patten on Route 159 north of Millinocket displays more than 5,000 items connected with Maine's early lumbering days. The complex of nine buildings includes models of early lumber camps, as well as a blacksmith shop, a lean-to camp, and the cook's "Wangan box," where loggers would buy their tobacco, clothing, and medicine.

BAXTER STATE PARK

The West Branch of the Penobscot skirts the southern boundary of **Baxter State Park❖,** the 201,018-acre expanse of mountains, forest, ponds, and lakes that—with the magnificence of its scenery, its remoteness, and the careful way it is protected—can only be described as Maine's Yellowstone. Formed from land donated to the state by former governor Percival Baxter, the park includes more than 40 mountains, 18 of which are higher than 3,000 feet. The gem of the park is Katahdin, at 5,267 feet the highest, most imposing mountain in Maine, and the northern terminus of the Appalachian Trail. Governor Baxter insisted the land "shall be forever left in its natural wild state, forever be kept as a sanctuary for wild beasts and birds, and forever be used for public

RIGHT: *At Baxter, wildflowers and berries abound; clockwise from top left: Bunchberries, with brilliant red drupes, or fruits, grow in cool woods; yellow marsh marigolds, or cowslips, bloom in the spring; birds eat the scarlet berries of the American mountain ash tree well into the winter; and the yellow fringed orchid thrives in open meadows.*

ABOVE: *An adult bull moose (left), standing seven feet at the shoulder with antlers six feet wide, tangles with a juvenile. Seventeenth-century traveler John Josselyn called the moose a "monster of superfluity."*

forest, public park, and public recreational purposes." Although just what "wild" means has been the subject of much debate, the park today remains remarkably true to Baxter's vision.

The easiest approach is from Millinocket (park headquarters are located on Balsam Drive) via the south entrance at Togue Pond Gate. The Matagamon Gate is the northeastern entrance, reached via Route 159 west of Patten. During the summer, these gates remain open from 6:00 A.M. to 10:00 P.M. (9:00 P.M. at Matagamon), and all vehicles must stop to register. Inside the park, the **Perimeter Road,** dirt and axle-threatening in places, makes nearly a full circle around the park, with short spurs branching off to reach various ponds and campsites. These are narrow roads, and vehicles must meet size restrictions to enter. Camping is allowed only in roadside campgrounds and designated backcountry sites, and advance reservations are necessary, particularly in summer. There are no grocery stores or gasoline pumps in the park, and supplies should be procured before leaving Millinocket.

The park season for overnight use runs from May 15 to October 15, with limited use possible outside this period with permission of the park director; special restrictions apply from December 1 to April 1, particularly as regards climbing. The state is dedicated to preserving Baxter State Park in its pristine condition and has imposed stringent regulations regarding its use. Even more than in other natural areas, prospective visitors are advised to write for the park guidelines and familiarize themselves with them before arriving.

In early summer wildflowers—blue fringed gentians, yellow avens, pink moccasin flowers—carpet the landscape. With more than 130 miles of trails, moose watching is a popular pastime, especially in the summer when the huge mammals wade into ponds to feed on aquatic plants and avoid pesky insect swarms.

The centerpiece of Baxter, of course, is **Katahdin,** whose long summit plateau, rising so abruptly over the surrounding forest, can be seen for miles around. It was first climbed in 1804. Famous among New England hikers—and accorded a healthy respect—is the long serrated ridge known as the **Knife Edge.** Two feet wide in places, it is, in terms of exposure, the most exhilarating stretch of trail in New England. Extending across the summit ridge is a broad tableland nearly four miles long, the sides of which fall 1,000 to 2,000 feet. The **Great Basin** is the spectacular glacial cirque at the bottom of which lies **Chimney Pond;** this is the center of rock climbing on Katahdin, with routes on the cliffs known as The Diamonds ranging up to a difficulty rating of 5.9.

While one need not be a rock climber to scale Katahdin, none of the trails are easy on the lungs, and hikers should be in good shape and well prepared in order to enjoy the mountain to the fullest. The oldest trail and the one that most closely parallels Thoreau's route is the Abolt Trail, which follows the great slide up the southwestern side of the mountain; it is challenging, steep, and filled with scree. The

OVERLEAF: *The Penobscot believed the mountain's sacred spirits would repel all climbers; Thoreau called it a "cloud factory." However described, Katahdin's summit, with its panoramic vista, is an unforgettable place.*

211

Hunt Trail, the route of the Appalachian Trail, also climbs from the southwest, leaving from Katahdin Stream Campground. Many other trails cross the mountain, and hikers can take advantage of them to do complete circuits of the various lesser peaks on the summit.

Katahdin is not the only mountain here, and many of the others can be reached by easier pathways—the park includes more than 175 miles of trails, including routes up **North Brother** (4,143 feet) in the southeastern part of the park and **Double Top** (3,488 feet) off the western side of the Perimeter Road. Self-guided nature trails can also be found at Daicey Pond in the southwest corner of the park, Roaring Brook at the campground of the same name, and the South Branch Campground, near the site of the huge forest fire that decimated much of this area in 1903.

Fishing for wild brook trout can be excellent in the park. **Kidney Pond** in the southwest part of the park has one of the best settings in Maine, with mountains towering over its shores. Nearby a number of smaller ponds, some with brookies of considerable size, can be reached by hiking.

Because of the park's undeveloped state and general lack of roads, opportunities for wildlife viewing abound. Moose are spotted so often they are hardly commented upon. (They are particularly easy to spot at Sandy Stream Pond and the outlet of Nesowadnehunk Lake.) Black bears are often seen feeding on blueberries on the exposed slopes (more than 200 bears live in the park), and white-tailed deer are plentiful.

THE AROOSTOOK REGION
On an ordinary map, the huge expanse of the Maine woods from Baxter Park to the Canadian border appears to be roadless and inaccessible. In fact, almost all of it is crisscrossed by a network of private logging roads, many of which—with special regulations in effect—are open to the public. Access to the roads is managed by North Maine Woods Inc., an organization of landowners partnered with Maine's natural resources agencies, headquartered in Ashland on Route 11. More than 1,000 miles of roads are permanently maintained and several thousand more miles are temporarily maintained in this vast region, which includes two of the most famous wild rivers in New England: the Saint John and the Allagash.

Public access by anglers, birders, canoeists, and hikers is permitted on these roads, but several important regulations should be kept in mind. Visitors must log in and check out at one of the 15 checkpoint registration stations on every visit (one important checkpoint is Six Mile just west of Ashland, the gateway to the Allagash region). Drivers must proceed with caution, watching and pulling over for logging trucks, which have the right of way. In addition, fires and camping are allowed only in authorized areas. Finally, through traffic into Canada is not permitted. Despite all the roads, this is private forest, and there are no gas stations or grocery stores in the region. Still, for the adventurous, these roads permit access to some of the wildest and most beautiful land in the Northeast.

For more than a century now, the Allagash River has been synonymous with world-class canoe runs through the heart of the Maine woods. The **Allagash Wilderness Waterway❖** was established in 1966 to create a protected 92-mile-long corridor of lakes, ponds, rivers, and streams in what otherwise is commercial timberland. Protection was enhanced in 1970 when the Allagash was named the first state-administered component of the National Wild and Scenic River System, and "habitat disturbance" was prohibited within 500 feet of the waterway. Recently, the state of Maine has acquired some large tracts of land along the Allagash, furthering the protection; these include tracts at Chamberlain Lake and Round Pond.

Vehicle access is possible over the North Maine Woods roads from Millinocket, Greenville, Ashland, or Allagash, depending on where canoeists wish to start. Many canoeists join organized trips led by registered Maine guides and other professionals, some of whom gain access to the area via floatplane; group size in all cases is limited to 12 persons. The river and lakes don't usually begin to thaw until late May, and the river becomes canoeable soon thereafter, although the blackflies can be persistent well into summer. Thanks to the lakes and ponds that feed it, the Allagash maintains a high enough water level to be canoeable all summer long. Canoeing the entire route takes from seven to ten days.

The brook trout fishing, while not as good as in the past, due in part to overfishing by ice fishermen and poor regulations, can still be rewarding under the right conditions. The usual canoe trip begins at Telos Landing at the foot of Telos Lake and ends at the village of Allagash at the river's confluence with the upper **Saint John River❖**.

Inland Maine

RIGHT: *Where oil-burning loco-motives once carried pulp-wood, in season hundreds of canoeists per day now ply the spectacular Allagash Wilder-ness Waterway; environmental guidelines protect the area from recreational overuse.*

The Saint John itself is another famous canoe run, with 143 miles of canoeable water from Fifth Saint John Pond to the village of Allagash. However, because water levels drop quickly, this run has to be done in the spring.

Although the Allagash is not a particularly demanding river to canoe, there are class II whitewater sections, and with the distances and windy lakes, it's not the place for an unaccompanied beginner. Watch for historic reminders of the logging industry here, including the remains of a cable tramway built in 1902 to ferry logs from Eagle to Chamberlain lakes, and the locomotives from the abandoned Eagle Lake and Umbazooksus Railroad, built in the 1920s. Telos Dam, on the lake of the same name, is the site of a canal cut through a natural gorge in 1842. By diverting the Allagash headwaters into the Penobscot, it permitted local loggers to float their logs to the south rather than to Canada.

Aroostook County sprawls across most of northern Maine. The famous potato-growing region is centered around the Saint John River near Presque Isle and Houlton along Route 1, but the county also takes in huge areas of forest as wild as any in Maine. The state has three large holdings of wild land here. The **Squa Pan Unit** includes 16,731 acres near Squapan Lake, west of Presque Isle off Routes 163

and 11; **Aroostook State Park❖** on Echo Lake features a fine, eminently hikeable mountain called Quaggy Joe. Even farther to the north, the **Eagle Lake Unit❖** includes 23,287 wild acres, with access off Sly Brook Road, which connects with Route 11 at Soldier Pond and with Route 161 at Fort Kent. Still farther to the west is the **Deboullie Unit❖,** managed by the Maine Bureau of Public Lands. Although somewhat remote, this unit includes all of wild Township 15, Range 9 (here in the north Maine woods, uninhabited townships are given these numerical designations). There are campsites here on the numerous ponds, including Togue Pond, where the brook trout can be most cooperative. Access is via the Saint Francis checkpoint of North Maine Woods on Route 161.

COASTAL MAINE:
THE SHORE AND ISLANDS

Rugged, exhilarating, rockbound—the adjectives used to describe the coast of Maine are so familiar they have become clichés, but remarkably apt ones. This region's distinct combination of land and seascape entrances people with its beauty. Perhaps no other part of New England is so liberally endowed with preserves, refuges, and parks. This is the country's northeastern edge, the first place in the United States the sun touches. Viewed from a rocky peninsula such as Pemaquid Point, the orange disk appears to emerge slowly, then suddenly, from the watery horizon.

A quick glance at a map shows that the coast stretches as much east as north. The old schooner captain speaks of sailing "down east" from Boston to Maine, meaning downwind to the east. The coast is a convoluted one, with countless indentations and wrinkles. It is 281 air miles from Kittery to Calais, but the actual shoreline, if every kink were straightened out, is more than 3,000 miles long. This distance features a great deal of variety: the famous sand beaches of the southwestern coast, including Old Orchard; the rocky midcoast from Portland to Camden, with its hills; the spectacular Mount Desert Island and Acadia; and the lesser-known coast on up to Machias and Eastport, a region of salmon rivers, blueberry barrens, and extreme tides. Then there are the offshore

LEFT: *One of the most beautiful areas of Maine's long, convoluted coast is Mount Desert Island and Acadia National Park. Evergreen-topped cliffs rise above pounding surf; minke whales patrol offshore.*

Calais

NEW BRUNSWICK

1

MOOSEHORN
NWR

1

*Bay of
Fundy*

Dennysville   Eastport   Campobello I
191   *Cobscook
                  Bay*   Lubec
MOOSEHORN
NWR   COBSCOOK
                 BAY SP

95   2

Penobscot River

6

QUODDY
HEAD SP

191

15

Grand Manan I

:AIG BROOK
HATCHERY

*Tunk
Lake*   ×Pineo Ridge   ROQUE
                           BLUFFS
East Orland   SP

:or

1   Cherryfield   187

STANWOOD HOMESTEAD
MUS   Beals   *Englishman Bay*
Ellsworth   3   Steuben   Jonesport
Blue   HULLS COVE   Great Wass I
Hill   VIS CTR   WILD GARDENS   Bois
                  OF ACADIA   ~Bubert I
ne   PETIT MANAN NWR
     INDIAN POINT/
     BLAGDEN PRES
HOLBROOK I   ACADIA
SANCTUARY   Mt Desert Island NP   Petit Manan I
:REN I   Cranberry
                     Isles
CROCKETT
'E WOODS   ISLEFORD
 PRES   HISTORICAL MUS
lhaven   Stonington \ ACADIA
land   NP
       Isle au Haut   Swans
                      Island
    AREY'S ACADIA NP
    NECK
:ST WOODS
'R

15

Blue Hill

Deer Isle

Blue Hill Bay

Frenchman Bay

GULF   OF   MAINE

OCEAN

LANTIC

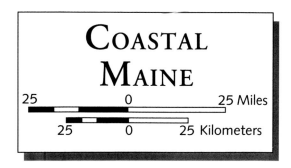

COASTAL
MAINE

| 25 | 0 | 25 Miles |

| 25 | 0 | 25 Kilometers |

ABOVE: *A native of the Pacific Northwest that has naturalized all along the Maine coast, wild blue lupine (*Lupinus polyphyllus) *shares a seaside perch with a patch of daisies near the village of New Harbor.*

islands—hundreds of them, some large and inhabited like Vinalhaven, others completely wild, home to nesting seabirds and sunbathing seals.

Geologists refer to this as a drowned coast. During the last ice age, the weight of a glacier forced New England below its earlier level; as water from the melting ice emptied into the ocean, the sea level rose to flood the low-lying coast up into the larger valleys. Eventually, the land rose to its present level and the sea backed off, but not all the way to its former, preglacial position. The lower valleys remained flooded, and the narrow headlands and bays—and the islands—of the present coast are the scenic result. In certain areas, mostly to the southwest, the flood left a layer of sand over the predominantly clay coast, creating beaches. The beach sand varies in composition, from Popham Beach's pinkish sand with its high percentage of garnet, to Sand Beach's greenish sand, comprised largely of broken shell fragments. Considerable reshaping of the coastline continues today, although now the chief forces are ocean currents, waves, and storms, including the three to five major northeasters the coast can experience in a typical year.

ABOVE: *White-tailed deer prefer young forests and thickets, where leaves are in easy reach. The improved pastures of Swan Island, a wildlife management area, are ideal habitats for these populous mammals.*

The damp evergreen forest so typical of the coast consists chiefly of balsam fir and red spruce, while a thick belt of white spruce—which thrives on even colder, wetter weather—grows along the immediate coastline. The tang of balsam mixed with the iodine smell of the ocean is the characteristic odor of coastal Maine. In cleared fields returning to forest, or the sites of forest fires, deciduous forests have taken hold, with sun-loving species like gray birch, trembling aspen, and bigtooth aspen.

Maine's rugged coast has few sheltered bays, and thus salt marshes are not as common as in southern New England. The ones that exist are located mainly below Portland and dominated by the two familiar marsh grasses: the saltmarsh cordgrass and the shorter saltmeadow cordgrass, also known as "salt hay." More common on this coast are granite headlands swept by tides, with thick, slippery mats of blue-

OVERLEAF: *The coastal trail of Quoddy Head State Park passes through a moist evergreen forest to steep cliffs and a quiet bog. Mushrooms, mosses, liverworts, and lichens line the well-trodden woodland path.*

LEFT: *The Atlantic puffin is reestablishing nesting colonies on the coastal islands of Maine. Its large, colorful bill, with an outer sheath that is shed each fall, can carry more than a dozen fish at a time.*
RIGHT: *Basking on rocks or floating upright in the sea, the harbor seal is one of the state's most familiar marine mammals. When alarmed, it dives and can remain underwater for up to 28 minutes.*

green algae lying along the tidemark, and knotted wrack and bladder rockweed drifted in from offshore; this rockweed is marked by air sacs that make it float high on the water to obtain the maximum sunlight. Rachel Carson, who lived and worked on the Maine coast and knew it intimately, wrote: "When we go down to the low-tide line, we enter a world that is as old as the earth itself—the primeval meeting place of the elements of earth and water, a place of compromise and conflict and eternal change."

One of the habitats most characteristic of the Maine coast is these tidal pools—pockets of seawater left in rocky basins when the tide retreats. This is favored territory for a whole host of species, including pincushionlike sea urchins, acorn barnacles, starfish, periwinkles, and the ubiquitous blue mussel, which anchors itself to the rock by tufts of filaments called byssuses. The tide distributes oxygen to these creatures, removes wastes, scatters eggs, and buffers the extreme temperature variations between summer and winter. Exploring tidal pools can bring many hours of fascination, but walkers—especially along the northeastern part of the coast—should check tide tables and plan their trips accordingly. Another caution: On the way out to the rocks, be-

ware of poison ivy, which grows abundantly a short distance inland.

Anyone who spends much time exploring this area will be struck by the brightly colored floats visible on the ocean a short distance off-shore. These are lobster buoys, the most visible evidence of the industry so closely tied to the Maine coast. The lobster harvest exceeds 25 million tons most years, although with increasing competition, lobster-men have to work ever harder, and it is not unusual for one man or woman to tend upwards of a thousand traps.

The heavily forested Maine coast hosts species similar to those found in the interior forest, including deer, moose, beavers, porcupines, rac-coon, and foxes. It really comes into its own, however, with its birds. Roger Tory Peterson, dean of American ornithologists, lists Mount Desert Island with Acadia National Park as one of the top 12 birding spots in the United States, for good reason; in a crucial spot under the Atlantic Flyway, it is visited by more than 300 species, with more than 140 species actually breeding there, including 22 varieties of warblers. The birdlife elsewhere is just as extraordinary, especially considering that much of it was seriously damaged early in the century when hunting for their meat and eggs nearly exterminated the puffins, eiders, cormorants, gannets, and murres. The formation of the Audubon Society in the late 1800s and the passage of the first bird protection laws helped build populations back up, although some species remain threatened. Atlantic puffins have now been reintroduced to their historic nesting islands in the Gulf of Maine; when they are about ten days old, puffins from Great Island in Newfoundland are transplanted onto nesting sites such as Eastern Egg Rock in Muscongus Bay, installed in artificial sod burrows, and fed fish by hand. Similar efforts have helped restore terns and storm-petrels to their former nesting sites.

North of Acadia, the coast of Maine changes. The bays become wider, more open to the sea; the peninsulas widen as well, with fewer and smaller offshore islands. Washington County, on the coast's northeastern extremity, is more sparsely inhabited and less visited than the popular vacation spots to the southwest. Long stretches of coast remain undeveloped; at regular intervals the last remaining Atlantic salmon fishing rivers in the United States, including the Machias, Dennys, and Narraguagus, come down to the sea. This is a land of blueberry barrens—Maine is the largest blueberry producer of any state in the country, growing 50 percent of the nation's total and 98 percent of the tiny low-bush wild berries. And this part of the coast has the most extreme tidal range in the continental United States, with tides rising and falling from 18 to 27 vertical feet.

One last reminder for anyone driving this coast. U.S. 1, the main highway here, takes the most direct route up the shore but provides few views of the peninsulas and headlands that rise to its east. Back roads are the way to explore these, or better yet, travel by boat. Sea kayaking has become popular here in recent years, and for the less adventurous most large towns have seal- and puffin-watching trips that give views of this dramatic coast from the sea. Bareboat charters (without a professional crew) and organized windjammer cruises are also popular; with the fog, the thousands of rocky islets, and the strong currents, yachting here is for the experienced and prepared only.

This chapter begins with the sandy southern beaches and proceeds

RIGHT: *Songbirds, black bears, and humans all harvest the blueberry barrens in late summer, though not at the same time. Prized throughout the world, the native berries of eastern Maine are tiny and tasty.*

north along the coast past Portland, Casco Bay, and Penobscot Bay. Moving north, the route detours off the coast to Acadia National Park, including Mount Desert Island, Isle au Haut, and the Cranberry Islands. Finally, the route ends at the Canadian border after passing through the blueberry barrens and the rugged uplands and islands of the far northeastern coast.

COAST TO CAMDEN

The southwestern coast of Maine is a gently rolling, sandy plain cut here and there by slow-moving rivers that empty into the sea. **Vaughan Woods,** in the farming country of South Berwick on Route 4, has six miles of hiking trails on the Piscataqua River. Paths wind through an old-growth hemlock forest and past tree species that are at the northernmost extension of their range, including the shagbark hickory. In town is the **Sarah Orne Jewett House**—the home of the noted writer whose collection of stories *The Country of the Pointed Firs,* with its beautiful lyrical descriptions of place, did much to set the Maine coastal landscape and its people firmly in the American literary consciousness.

The southwestern coast is an area of well-known beaches, including Ogunquit and Old Orchard, where the combination of sand and relatively warm ocean water lures tourists from New England and Canada. The region has many quieter, wilder, lesser-known areas as well, including the **Rachel Carson National Wildlife Refuge❖** in Wells. Named for the beloved naturalist whose book *Silent Spring,* with its condemnation of indiscriminate pesticide use, remains a bible of the environmental movement, the refuge consists of ten separate divisions between Portsmouth, New Hampshire, and Portland, Maine, totaling nearly 5,000 acres. In Wells, the one-mile Carson Trail follows the edge between a mature upland forest and the tidal salt marsh the refuge protects. Just south of the refuge office and also encompassing refuge marshlands is the **Wells National Estuarine Research Reserve❖,** with a visitor center at Laudholm Farm. Trails lead across the varied habitat of upland fields, woods, salt marsh, dune, and beach. Birders

LEFT: The snowy egret's "golden slippers," as noted naturalist Roger Tory Peterson calls them, help identify this marsh bird. Its large yellow feet are invaluable to the egret, who shuffles them to stir up food.

will also want to explore the prime salt marsh areas in Wells via Mile Road, Lower Landing Road, and Drakes Island Road, all of which cross the marsh and provide excellent opportunities for sighting great blue herons, egrets, willets, least terns, piping plovers, numerous gulls, sandpipers, common mergansers, loons, eider ducks, buffleheads, harlequin ducks, and Canada geese.

A short distance up the coast is **Kennebunk Plains❖,** off Route 9A in Kennebunk. This coastal sand-plain grassland was managed for years as a commercial blueberry barren and is home to the grasshopper sparrow, a small, very rare, hermitlike sparrow known for its insectlike buzzing sound. The bird needs dry grassland habitats to thrive—the same prime land coveted for development—and its population was down to a dozen breeding pairs in 1987. Then the state of Maine, with the assistance of the Nature Conservancy, acquired this 1,500-acre site, one of the largest sand-plain grasslands left in New England, and today Kennebunk Plains boasts one of the largest grasshopper sparrow breeding populations in New England.

The Saco River, which has its origins on the slopes of the Presidential Range in New Hampshire, empties into the ocean between Biddeford and Saco—a site that was explored as early as 1616. Directly on the coast on Route 208 is **Biddeford Pool,** a saucer-shaped tidal basin entered through a narrow channel and called, in local parlance, a "gut." The **East Point Sanctuary❖** here, a 30-acre preserve maintained by the Maine Audubon Society, has both fine ocean views and quiet walking trails. A short way offshore, accessible only by boat, are two of Maine Audubon's island sanctuaries: **Stage Island** and **Wood Island,** habitat for nesting gulls, egrets, herons, ibis, and eiders. The poison ivy can be a problem here, but Wood Island has a boardwalk for safe exploration. This area is an exception to the prevailing sandy coastline: Biddeford Pool is dominated by a rocky headland, and the East Point Sanctuary is dotted with pebbles and boulders left by the last glacier.

With a diverse landscape of hardwoods, swamps, and dunes, **Ferry Beach State Park❖** in Saco (a crowded beach on weekends) also contains a rare stand of tupelos, or black gum trees, uncommon this far north, which prosper, it is believed, because of the swampy topography and abundant sunlight. The tree's names carry clues to its preferred habitat: *Tupelo* literally means swamp in the language of the

ABOVE: *In 1883 American artist Winslow Homer set up a studio in Maine. "Painted fifteen minutes after sunset—not one minute before," he wrote of* West Point, Prout's Neck, *which he finished in 1889.*

small Ogeechee tribe in Georgia where the species generally grows; *Nyssa sylvatica*, the botanical name for black tupelo, honors a mythological Greek water nymph named Nyssa.

Drive a short distance north on Route 1 and then south on Pine Point Road to reach **Scarborough Marsh Nature Center❖,** which includes more than 3,000 acres of tidal marsh, saltwater creeks, freshwater marsh, and forested uplands. Preserved as a state wildlife management area, it is a prime example of the variety of estuarine habitats found along this stretch of coast. Maine Audubon offers programs at the center during the summer, with naturalists available to answer questions, as well as self-guided walks and canoe tours. Nearby **Prouts Neck,** a rocky promontory jutting into the Atlantic, was the site of the studio of Winslow Homer. This nineteenth-century painter captured much of the coast on his canvases and began the association of artists with Maine that continues to this day, from Rockwell Kent, George Bellows, and Georgia O'Keeffe to the various members of the Wyeth family. The **Prouts Neck Bird Sanctuary❖** there is open to guests of the Black Point Inn.

Portland is both the largest city in Maine and the dividing point between the sandy, level southwestern coast and the rockier midcoast region to the northeast. It is located on Casco Bay, filled with more than 100 islands large and small. Within city limits is Maine Audubon's **Fore River Sanctuary❖.** This 76-acre preserve on the Fore River estuary features hemlock ravines, red oak and white pine uplands, and a portion of the old Cumberland and Oxford Canal, as well as Portland's only waterfall. A two-and-a-half-mile hiking trail traverses the property.

ABOVE: *The red fox was brought from England to be hunted by colonial landowners. Today the red fox of North America is a mixture of the native gray fox and its European relative.*

RIGHT: *Open meadows, dense forests, thickets, and tidal flats form a dynamic coastal habitat that draws thousands of migrating Canada geese to Swan Island each year.*

Casco Bay extends 20 miles to the east of Portland, and many of its islands can be reached by regular ferry service, including the boats of the Casco Bay Lines, founded in 1845 and one of the oldest continuing ferry companies in the United States. On **Eagle Island❖** is the fortresslike home of Arctic explorer Robert E. Peary, which is now maintained by the state of Maine. The house contains many souvenirs from his journeys, and the island has some fine hiking trails. Eagle Island is reached by excursion boat from Cape Elizabeth.

Just north of Portland where the Presumpscot River estuary joins Casco Bay is the **Gilsland Farm Sanctuary❖,** on Old U.S. Route 1 in Falmouth. This 60-acre preserve, the state headquarters of Maine Audubon, features a nature trail through the salt marsh along the river, where numerous shorebirds rest and feed. The headquarters itself includes a library, nature exhibits, and an energy education center.

Freeport on I-95, noted once for its

mackerel fishing and now for its outlet stores, has two natural areas where the crowds and traffic can be left behind. On Upper Mast Landing Road east of the business district **Mast Landing Sanctuary❖**, another Maine Audubon preserve, protects 140 acres of open fields, apple orchards, salt marsh, and forest set around Mill Stream where it empties into the Haraseeket River estuary. This variety of habitat is especially attractive to migrant shorebirds, warblers, and even those species associated with the Maine woods, such as woodcock and ruffed grouse. Nearby **Wolfe's Neck Woods State Park❖** on Wolf Neck Road includes a shady hemlock forest on a rocky peninsula on the ocean side of the Haraseeket.

THE MID COAST

Changes in the terrain, noticeable since Portland, become even more pronounced northeast of Freeport, with deep indentations and headlands forming a series of ragged ins and outs. This is the coast of flooded river valleys and ridges, deep bays, and fingerlike peninsulas left from the last ice age. Between Brunswick and Bath is the happily named Merrymeeting Bay, formed by the junction of five rivers: the Androscoggin, Kennebec, Muddy, Cathance, Abagadusset, and Eastern. Known as a rendezvous for migrating ducks and geese coming down the Atlantic Flyway, the bay is the site of the **Steve Powell Wildlife Management Area❖** (1,753 acres) on Swan Island. The island's mix of forest, pasture, wetland, and tidal flats attracts as many as 5,000 Canada geese during the autumn migration. Situated in the upper part of the bay, it is reached by a Department of Inland Fisheries and Wildlife ferry from Richmond, with advance reservations required.

In Bath, the famous shipbuilding center on the Kennebec, is the **Maine Maritime Museum❖.** Located on the waterfront, the museum is a good place to gain a better understanding of the long interrelationship on this coast between humans and the sea. Route 127 leads from Bath to Georgetown, where the **Josephine Newman Sanctuary❖** takes in 119 acres of salt marsh and woods along the tidal mudflats of Robinhood Cove. Similar to many coastal preserves, this one hosts not only the usual shorebirds but also mammals associated with areas much farther inland, including white-tailed deer and coyotes. Just a few miles southeast, directly on the ocean, **Reid State Park❖** offers one of the finest sand beaches on the Maine coast, Mile Beach, as well

Above: *"I have felt bound by a solemn obligation to do what I could,"* *wrote Rachel Carson of her fight against pesticides. The author-biologist was photographed at work in a Maine tidal flat in the late 1950s.*

as a diverse habitat of dunes, marsh, and ocean ledges. The high knob to the northeast here is **Griffith Head,** a lump of coarse-grained granite deeply eroded by the sea.

Many tourists detour off Route 1 to the next peninsula on the coast, the Boothbay Harbor region. Others, finding this area overcrowded, prefer to explore the Damariscotta region and the Pemaquid peninsula jutting out into the sea. Damariscotta Lake, just inland of town, was for many years the home of nature writer Henry Beston, whose books *Northern Farm* and *Herbs and the Earth* were based on his observations here of the natural year. In *Northern Farm*, Beston writes, "If the opening music of the Northern year begins with a first trumpet call of the return of light, and the return of warmth is the second great flourish from the air, the unsealing of the waters of the earth is certainly the third." *Northern Farm* includes a memorable description of the annual herring run into

ABOVE: *Pemaquid Point Lighthouse rests on ancient bedrock of granite, gneiss, and tilted layers of sedimentary rock. Small stones carried by crashing waves have gouged distinctive ridges in the surrounding cliffs.*

the lake, an event that still takes place late in May in Damariscotta Mills.

Another writer, Rachel Carson, is again commemorated by a small but lovely natural area out on the coast near the lobster port of New Harbor: the **Rachel Carson Salt Pond Preserve**❖ on Route 32, a mile north of the village. This is an excellent place to explore tidal pools, including the quarter-acre salt pond immediately below the small parking area, where Carson collected material for her 1955 book *Edge of the Sea.* At low tide barnacles, blue mussels, hermit and green crabs, periwinkles, and starfish are often in evidence.

The nearby **Pemaquid Point Lighthouse**❖ is one of the most frequently photographed sites on the coast, and the peninsula it sits on is geologically among the most interesting. The sea has carved bizarre and beautiful shapes in the thin-layered bedrock that juts into the waves. Standing on the western side of the point when the tide is low, one hears a sound that is a cross between rolling bowling balls and clicking castanets, created by smooth round boulders rolling back and forth in channels grooved in the bedrock. A small museum details the lives of Maine's lighthouse keepers and their families in the days before the beacons were all automated. Those venturing out on the rocks here should take care. Several people have been swept away in recent years by unpredictable rogue waves.

An excursion boat, the *Hardy III*, makes daily trips during the summer from the wharf in New Harbor out to **Monhegan Island,** the lobstering community and artist colony. Monhegan, a mile long and a half mile wide, fronts the ocean with some of the highest and most dramatic cliffs on the New England coast. Trails lead out to them from the tiny harbor, bypassing the poison ivy that grows here in annoying abundance. John Cabot stopped here as early as 1497, and from that era on the island served as a station where Portuguese, Norse, Basque, Breton, and English fishermen could dry the cod they found offshore. Unlike other lobstermen on the Maine coast, the Monhegan fishermen have since 1909 set out their traps only in winter—a rugged time to be out in a small boat, but a season when the lobsters command the highest prices. Harbor seals can usually be spotted on Duck Rocks just west of the harbor. Scheduled boat service is also available to the island from Boothbay Harbor during the summer and from Port Clyde year-round.

A much larger, more populous island sits at the mouth of Penobscot Bay off Rockland: eight-mile-long **Vinalhaven❖,** known for its granite quarrying and summer colony. The several preserves and protected natural areas here include **Lane's Island Preserve** off Vinalhaven's southern tip, with rolling moorland covered with blueberry bushes and bayberry; **Ambrust Hill Wildlife Reservation❖,** a tranquil spot in a site once quarried for granite; and **Arey's Neck Woods❖,** a spruce woods near a cove and marsh. Vinalhaven is reached by passenger and car ferry from Rockland all year. Closer to the mainland near Lincolnville is secluded, spruce-dotted Warren Island. The only public land here, reachable only by boat from the town of Isleboro, is **Warren Island State Park❖.**

Camden is a resort town on Route 1 along the western shore of Penobscot Bay. The fleet of windjammers docked in the harbor takes passengers on trips along the coast, ranging from half-day excursions to tours lasting a week or more, as do similar fleets based in Rockland. The town's backdrop, forming an unmistakable landmark, is the Camden Hills. It was the vista of these hills that dominated the view from poet Edna St. Vincent Millay's childhood home and which she commemorated in her famous poem "Renascence": "All I could see from where I stood, was three long mountains and a wood..." **Camden Hills State Park❖** (5,500 acres), the largest state park on the Maine coast, preserves these mountains, including Mount Megunticook (1,380 feet), which is the second highest spot on the eastern seaboard after Cadillac Mountain in Acadia. Nearby Mount Battie has a road leading to the summit, with wide views of Penobscot Bay. There are 25 miles of hiking trails here, some following the shoreline of the bay, others heading up the mountains.

ABOVE: *Preferring rocky shores, great cormorants are a common sight on the Maine coast. A dark-colored, able fisher, the cormorant's name comes from the Old French for "raven of the sea."*

RIGHT: *Around each bend in Acadia National Park's craggy coast hides another wonder, another unexpected view—here Little Hunters Bay. Beneath the surface lurk creatures such as the formidable northern lobster.*

OVERLEAF: *At sunset the granite rock atop 1,500-foot Cadillac Mountain glows a brilliant pink. The summit provides panoramic views of Mount Desert as well as island-dotted Frenchman Bay below.*

Just to the west of the park on Megunticook Lake off Route 52 is **Fernald's Neck Preserve❖,** a Nature Conservancy property that protects more than 18,000 feet of shoreline. One of its prime attractions is a bog covered with leatherleaf, sweet gale, and rhodora, which forms a protected nesting site for red-winged blackbirds, woodcocks, and Canada geese.

The meadows just inland from the coast, both along the main artery of Route 1 and off secondary roads, are colored by wildflowers beginning in spring, including the beautiful blue spikes of lupine that reach their peak

in late June and early July. Local children's author and illustrator Barbara Cooney, in her classic *Miss Rumphius*, tells the delightful tale of a woman who goes up and down the Maine coast sowing lupine seed in further-ance of her goal to make the world a prettier place.

The Penobscot River empties into the bay of the same name. Bald ea-gles and osprey are common in this area. One of the handful of Atlantic salmon rivers in Maine to maintain its run of salmon through the bad days of dam building and pollution, it still has the largest run of these fish in the United States. **Craig Brook National Fish Hatchery❖** on Route 1 in East Orland raises smolt to be released in upstream areas, where they begin the long process of growing to maturity, descending the river to the sea, then returning as adults to spawn. A visitor center and a short nature trail here tell the tale.

In the town of Searsport off Route 1 along the Penobscot Bay is the **Penobscot Marine Museum❖,** which is an excellent place to learn about the region's relationship to the sea. Here the visitor can inspect a former ship captain's home and a collection of tools used in ship build-ing. In Bradley, an hour's drive north from the coast on Route 178, is the University of Maine's **Maine Forest and Logging Museum❖,** where an eighteenth-century logging community has been lovingly re-created.

Many travelers, reaching this part of the coast, hurry on to reach Acadia National Park and miss one of the most beautiful peninsulas in Maine. This quiet area, fingered with bays rolling under low hills that frame ocean views, sits between Penobscot Bay to the west and Blue Hill Bay to the east, over which can be seen the mountains of Mount Desert Island. Castine and Blue Hill are the primary towns here, with Deer Isle off the southern tip reached via the bridge over Eggemoggin Reach on Route 15.

In Brooksville on Route 176 is the **Holbrook Island Sanctuary❖,** an undeveloped natural area of upland forest and meadow on the shores of Penobscot Bay. Eight miles of hiking trails here traverse di-versified habitat of deer, black bears, foxes, and beavers. West of Stonington on Deer Isle, the Nature Conservancy's **Crockett Cove Woods Preserve❖** offers a self-guided nature trail through a mix of white pines and oaks, supporting masses of lichen and mosses encour-aged by coastal fog.

Stonington, the deep-water port on the southern end of Deer Isle, is the place from which mail boats leave for the six-mile-long bulk of **Isle au Haut❖.** Called *Ille Haut* by Samuel de Champlain when he discovered it in 1604, the island has been labeled with various spellings of the name ever since. Half the island is part of Acadia National Park (see the following section); with the work involved in getting there and the lack of facilities, this portion of the park is not as heavily visited as the larger portion on Mount Desert Island, 18 miles to the northeast. Duck Harbor Campground offers primitive campsites and serves as a base to explore the island's rich birding terrain and fascinating tidal pools along the rocky shore. The number of visitors allowed on the island at any one time is controlled by the National Park Service; call park headquarters in Bar Harbor for information.

Across a narrow channel from Stonington is **Crotch Island,** site of about the only remaining working granite quarry of the many that once dotted the Maine coast. This quarry was the source of the pink granite that forms the Kennedy memorial in Arlington National Cemetery.

In Ellsworth back on the Maine coast's Route 3, **Birdsacre** at the **Standwood Homestead Museum❖,** home of the ornithologist Cordelia J. Stanwood, has eight trails around four ponds and forms a tranquil 133-acre woodland in an otherwise busy resort town.

MOUNT DESERT ISLAND AND ACADIA NATIONAL PARK

Just ten miles east of Ellsworth across the Route 3 bridge over the Mount Desert Narrows is the most famous portion of the Maine coast: **Mount Desert Island** and **Acadia National Park❖.** Superlatives apply here. Acadia is the only full-scale national park in New England. Its borders embrace the highest point on the East Coast and the largest rock island off it; the place where, for at least part of the year, the rising sun first hits the U.S. mainland; some of the most dramatic glacially sculpted scenery in the entire country; and some of the best birding to be found anywhere in the world.

Visited by Samuel de Champlain in 1604 and named by him *Isles des Monts Déserts* (Isle of Bare Mountains), its landmark summits and capacious bay at Bar Harbor have been recognized and marveled at for almost 400 years. Writer Freeman Tilden tried to sum up what makes Acadia so special: "Mountains that come down to the ocean . . .

granite cliffs alongside which the biggest ship could ride . . . bays dotted with lovely islets clothed in hardwood and hemlock, altogether a sweep of rugged coastline as has no parallel from Florida to the Canadian provinces."

Once the preserve of wealthy "cottagers" who summered here, the park got its start in 1908 when philanthropist George Dorr began acquiring land with the object of protecting it for the public. By 1919 enough had been purchased to form the nucleus of the new national park (originally Sieur de Monts National Monument, then Lafayette National Park), the first in the country east of the Mississippi. Another philanthropist, John D. Rockefeller, Jr., donated more than 10,000 acres to the park, one third of Acadia's total, and 50 miles of the carriage roads he had lovingly constructed around the bays and headlands—still the most popular walking and biking routes in the park.

The best place to begin a visit is at the **Hulls Cove Visitor Center** on Route 3 between the bridge to the island and Bar Harbor. Available here is a whole range of interpretative literature and guides, bird and animal lists, regulations, self-guided taped tours, and a

RIGHT: *Acadia National Park's popular Sand Beach, where the hardy actually swim, is composed of grains of feldspar, quartz, shell fragments, and even a plentiful supply of green sea urchin spines.*

schedule of ranger-led activities. Travelers with limited time usually
drive the 27-mile Park Loop Road through the dark fir forest that pre-
dominates here, drive up Cadillac Mountain, and explore **Sand Beach**
on the eastern shore of the island. Also popular is the **Wild Gardens
of Acadia** near Sieur de Monts Spring, featuring more than 400 species
of plants and flowers native to the park. Hikers with more time will
want to try the 120 miles of trails, including paths up **The Beehive**
(520 feet), **Champlain Mountain** (1,058 feet), and **Cadillac
Mountain,** at 1,530 feet the commanding summit. While these elevations are low, the mountains' location on the coast and their generally
bare summits make for extraordinarily expansive views across
Frenchman Bay and the Atlantic. Acadia's many remote freshwater
ponds are reached by a network of trails. These include the Jordan
Pond Shore Trail, which leaves from a parking area north of Seal
Harbor and leads to a beautiful pond. The two shapely mountains
above the pond's north shore are nicknamed The Bubbles.

248

Mount Desert Island, roughly 16 miles long and 13 miles wide, is divided into east and west sections by the waters of **Somes Sound,** described as the only true fjord on the East Coast. Although less heavily visited than the area around Bar Harbor, the western part of the island and the park has the same spectacular mix of mountains, headlands, forest, and shore. One of the best views for the least amount of effort can be obtained by climbing **Flying Mountain** at the entrance to Somes Sound. From its summit is a breathtaking view of Southwest Harbor, Northeast Harbor, and the islands to the south; the Flying Mountain Trail leaves the east side of the parking area at the Fernald Cove end of the Valley Cove truck road.

The park also protects portions outside Mount Desert Island, including Isle au Haut, Schoodic Peninsula to the east with its shoreline of red granite and black basalt slabs, and the Cranberry Islands just offshore. Access to Isle au Haut is described in the previous section. On the smaller Little Cranberry Island, reachable with its bigger neighbor by ferry from Northeast Harbor, is **Isle Ford Historical Museum,** with displays of island life over the past 200 years.

ABOVE: *The American woodcock is a shy shorebird. During courtship, however, it loses its inhibitions and plummets noisily down from the sky at dusk.*

LEFT: *Spruce, tamarack, and golden sedges combine in a boglike wetland called a fen at Maine's Cobscook Bay State Park—an often overlooked coastal jewel.*

While with just a little effort it is possible to escape the crowds that visit during the school vacation months, visitors wanting the park to themselves should think about coming off-season, in late fall or early spring. In winter, snow and ice add a dimension most visitors never see (on winter weekends, however, the numerous snowmobiles do create a din). When snow conditions are right, the Acadia National Park carriage roads offer outstanding cross-country skiing. Although park campgrounds are closed off-season, accommodations are plentiful in Bar Harbor; during the summer the town is a base for whale watching, windjammer cruises, lobstering trips, sea kayaking, and other outdoor sports.

ABOVE: *Looking more like a squadron of bombers than a flock of shore-birds, these ruddy turnstones are indeed pugnacious and will vigorously*

Peaceful even in summer, the Nature Conservancy's **Indian Point-Blagden Preserve❖** includes the northern half of Mount Desert Island off Indian Point Road. This tall red spruce, white cedar, and balsam fir forest survived the great forest fire that began just a short distance away and devastated much of the island in 1947. It now includes some of the oldest trees on the island and makes a fine birding spot; ruby-crowned kinglets, boreal chickadees, and nesting ospreys are among the 130 species seen here. The rocks along the northwestern shore provide views of seals.

defend their feeding grounds along rocky coasts. They use their wedge-shaped bill to flip shells and stones to search for crustaceans and insects.

THE NORTHEASTERN COAST

The coast changes beyond Acadia, becoming wilder and more remote, the villages smaller and farther apart. Southeast of Steuben off Route 1 is another long peninsula, this one jutting out toward the Atlantic along Dyer Bay. Petit Manan Point is the mainland section of the **Petit Manan National Wildlife Refuge❖** (3,335 acres), which also includes acreage on Bois Bubert Island, treeless Petit Manan Island, and Nash Island with its nesting eider ducks and gulls. Spruce forests, jack pine stands, blueberry barrens, and fresh- and saltwater marshes cover the mainland por-

251

tion of the refuge. The islands are dominated by rocky cliffs, some more than 100 feet high, which provide superior habitat for nesting seabirds, particularly black guillemots and razor-billed auks. Trails lead from the parking area at the tip of the mainland peninsula; the islands can only be visited by boat, a practice discouraged during nesting season.

Just inland of this part of the coast is a wild, seldom-visited land more reminiscent of the deep Maine woods than its typical coastal areas. The **Great Heath**❖ north of Cherryfield is the largest peat bog in Maine; it is bisected by one of Maine's eight precious Atlantic salmon rivers, the Pleasant. Five miles northeast of town in an area of intense blueberry cultivation is **Pineo Ridge**❖, one of the best examples of glacial washboard moraine in the eastern United States. This is the remains of a 25-square-mile delta, now high and dry, where the ocean once lapped against the ice of a retreating glacier. Now the delta is marked by a prominent cliff on the south face where torrents of meltwater carved channels in the delta's surface.

East of Cherryfield off Route 182 are **Donnel Pond**❖ and **Tunk Lake**❖, both fine examples of wild land just inland from the coast. The Maine Bureau of Public Lands has undeveloped, unimproved frontage on both lakes, including long sand beaches and several mountains; **Schoodic Mountain** has fine views of Acadia.

Jonesport, back on the coast along Route 187, is the mainland jumping-off place for the Nature Conservancy's **Great Wass Island Preserve**❖—a 1,540-acre tract that comprises almost all of the southern part of the small town of Beals. The island, accessed by a short bridge across Moosabec Reach, juts farther out to sea than any other land mass in eastern Maine. With the ocean waters of the Gulf of Maine and the Bay of Fundy mixing right offshore, the climate remains cool and humid year-round. This moisture is perfect for several botanical rarities found few other places in Maine, such as the beach-head iris, marsh felwort, and bird's-eye primrose. The island's interior supports one of the state's largest stands of jack pine, a stunted, bonsai-like tree that is at its southern limit in Maine. Also of natural significance on Great Wass are the bogs; these are coastal raised bogs, a type of peat bog more common to the Canadian Maritimes than to Maine. Two other rare plants thrive in the acid, peaty soil, the dragon's mouth orchid and the baked-apple berry, a relative of the raspberry, with a bland flavor that does faintly resemble that of a baked apple. This is also prime seabird habitat, with great rafts of common eiders forming off the granite shore.

Jonesport is also the mainland starting point for organized boat trips to **Machias Seal Island❖**. This small island (20 acres), well out to sea in the Gulf of Maine, is a world-famous birding spot with, among other species, more than 2,000 breeding pairs of Arctic terns, 3,000 puffins, and 150 endangered razorbills. A nature cruise is available from Jonesport, and Maine Audubon offers trips as well.

South of the busy town of Machias, directly on the waters of Englishman Bay, **Roque Bluffs State Park❖** features one of the very few sand beaches on this part of the coast.

Washington County, the northeasternmost county in Maine, is a wild, rugged land characterized by extreme tidal variations, blueberry barrens, and rolling forested uplands. Much of this land is encompassed by the **Moosehorn National Wildlife Refuge❖**, established in 1937 as a refuge for migratory birds, especially the woodcock. The refuge has two units, the southernmost being the 6,665-acre **Edmunds Unit** along the tidal waters of Cobscook Bay near Dennysville on Route 1. This is one of the best areas in the United States to spot the reclusive woodcock and observe its acrobatic courting dance, which takes place at twilight during late spring. While the refuge is not developed for visitors, more than 500 miles of old roads and trails closed to vehicles are open to hiking and cross-country skiing. If refuge visitors call ahead, they can accompany wildlife biologists on waterfowl and woodcock banding operations. Bald eagles also nest here. Adjoining the Edmunds Unit is **Cobscook Bay State Park❖** on Whiting Bay. Be forewarned that the tide here can fluctuate more than 28 feet, and beachcombers should consult tide tables and plan accordingly. The northern part of the Moosehorn NWR is the **Barling Unit** (16,065 acres), with its entrance just south of the junction of U.S. Route 1 and Route 191. Wild, forlorn even, it is one area where solitude comes guaranteed.

The northeasternmost town in Maine, and in the United States, is Lubec. This fishing port on Route 189 is situated on a long neck jutting up into the narrows of Cobscook Bay, as if this remote corner of the country were straining northeastward to be even more isolated. Across the narrow channel separating Maine from New Brunswick is Campobello Island, part of Canada but famed as Franklin Roosevelt's summer retreat, which is open to the public. The easternmost point of land in the United States is in **Quoddy Head State Park❖.** Spruce forests atop high cliffs provide an appropriately dramatic setting for the much-photographed red-and-white-striped West Quoddy Head Lighthouse. Hiking trails lead along the water to a peat bog more typical of the Canadian north than Maine and past excellent views of the high cliffs of New

Brunswick's Grand Manan Island 16 miles out to sea. The channel between Deer Island Point and Dog Island (just northeast of Eastport) holds the **Old Sow Whirlpool❖,** thought by many to be the largest in the world. This area has the most extreme tides on the eastern seaboard—the high tides sometimes rise and fall 27 vertical feet as water from the ocean is squeezed up the narrowing Bay of Fundy to the even narrower channel of Cobscook Bay. Here on the cliffs it is possible to stand and face the sea to the east with, as Thoreau said about a similar ocean overlook, "all America behind you."

ABOVE: *Called "the grey-hound of its tribe" by naturalist A. C. Bent, the graceful roseate tern nests in colonies along the Atlantic coast, where its small numbers are declining.*

RIGHT: *"Shifting, salty, thin," wrote poet Elizabeth Bishop about the fog; the steep cliffs of Gulliver's Hole in Quoddy Head State Park are a fine place to watch, as it "comes closing in."*

FURTHER READING: NORTHERN NEW ENGLAND

CARSON, RACHEL. *The Edge of the Sea*. Boston: Houghton Mifflin, 1955. A beautifully written study of the marine biology of the North Atlantic coast by one of the pioneers of the conservation and environmental movements.

FITZGERALD, BRIAN, AND ROBERT LINDEMANN, EDS. *Day Hiker's Guide to Vermont*, 3rd ed. Waterbury, VT: The Green Mountain Club, 1992. Guide to many of Vermont's short trails suitable for day hiking. Includes directions to trails, maps, and trail distances and descriptions.

FROST, ROBERT. *The Poetry of Robert Frost*. (Edward C. Lathem, ed.) New York: Holt, Rinehart and Winston, 1969. The comprehensive collection of the New England poet's works, which describe the writer's discovery of himself and the natural world around him.

HAWTHORNE, NATHANIEL. *The Great Stone Face and Other Tales of the White Mountains*. Boston: Houghton Mifflin, 1935. The famous nineteenth-century New England writer set his imagination free over the White Mountains of New Hampshire and created these classic stories.

JEWETT, SARAH ORNE. *The Country of the Pointed Firs and Other Stories*. 1896. Reprint, Garden City, NY: Doubleday, 1956. With an introduction by Willa Cather, these sketches of turn-of-the-century New England life lyrically describe the writer's surroundings of Maine "seaside villages, lonely farms, and fisher-folk."

JOHNSON, CHARLES W. *The Nature of Vermont: Introduction and Guide to a New England Environment*. Hanover, NH: University Press of New England, 1980. An engaging and up-to-date natural history of Vermont for the lay reader and professional alike. Illustrated with photographs, drawings, and maps, it provides an excellent overview of Vermont's diverse ecological communities.

KING, BRIAN, ED. *Appalachian Trail Guide to Maine*. Harper's Ferry, WV: Appalachian Trail Conference, 1993. The official handbook to the Maine segment of the trail. Includes detailed descriptions of trails, shelter, water sources, and camping, as well as historical background information. Appalachian Trail Guides can be ordered directly through the Appalachian Trail Conference.

————. *Appalachian Trail Guide to New Hampshire and Vermont*. Harper's Ferry, WV: Appalachian Trail Conference, 1992. The New Hampshire and Vermont version of the official Appalachian Trail handbook, with trail descriptions and maps.

KULIK, STEPHEN, ED. *The Audubon Society Field Guide to the Natural Places of the Northeast: Inland*. New York: Pantheon, 1984. A well-organized guide to adventuring throughout the Northeast. Includes trail distances and descriptions and notes on wildflower viewing, fossil spotting, fishing, mountaineering, and stargazing.

The Maine Atlas and Gazetteer, 17th ed. Freeport, ME: DeLorme, 1994. Highly detailed road maps that highlight particularly scenic routes through back roads and natural areas. Also includes much practical recreation and touring information, including campgrounds, bicycle routes, wildlife areas, terrain, elevations, museums, and historic sites.

New England: Land of Scenic Splendor. Washington, D.C.: National Geographic Society, 1989. The history, culture, and natural beauty of New England's landscape and cities through words and evocative color photographs.

The New Hampshire Atlas and Gazetteer, 9th ed. Freeport, ME: DeLorme, 1988. Highly detailed road maps and recreation information for the state of New Hampshire, in a format similar to the Maine version described above.

PERRY, JOHN, AND JANE GREVERUS PERRY. *The Sierra Club Guide to the Natural Areas of New England*. San Francisco: Sierra Club Books, 1990. Travel guide dedicated to the natural recreation areas of New England. Short descriptions of each area's location, wildlife, and visitor resources are matched with easy-to-read reference symbols for the site's recreational opportunities.

THOREAU, HENRY DAVID. *The Maine Woods*. 1864. Reprint, Princeton, NJ: Princeton University Press, 1972. In this early, impassioned plea for the conservation of our wilderness areas, Thoreau also gave his time-honored personal account of exploration and discovery in the primitive Maine forest of the 1800s.

The Vermont Atlas and Gazetteer, 8th ed. Freeport, ME: DeLorme, 1988. Highly detailed road maps and recreation information for Vermont, in the same series as the Maine and New Hampshire versions listed above.

WETHERELL, W. D. *Upland Stream: Notes on the Fishing Passion*. New York: Little, Brown, 1991. The author's lyric prose ranges over subjects from fly-fishing to natural history to the meaning of things in general as he explores the streams and rivers of Vermont and New Hampshire.

———. *Vermont River*. New York: Lyons & Burford, 1984. In 1990, *Trout* magazine selected this collection of essays as one of the best fishing books of the last 30 years.

GLOSSARY

abscission layer location on a plant where natural separation of flowers, fruit, or leaves occurs

alpine zone region on mountaintops above the timberline where dense, continuous tree growth ceases

anadromous referring to those fish that ascend rivers from the sea in order to breed and can live in both salt and fresh water; such fish include salmon, trout, and shad

biome that part of an ecological community consisting of plant and animal life

bog wetland, formed in glacial kettle holes, common to cool climates of northern North America, Europe, and Asia; its acidic nature produces large quantities of peat moss

boreal relating to the northern biotic area characterized especially by dominance of coniferous trees

brackish referring to salty or briny water, particularly a mixture of fresh and salt water found in estuaries

cirque large, bowl-shaped depression hollowed out in a mountain by glacial movement

climax forest forest community that has reached the hypothetical condition of evolutionary stability in which all successional changes in the community have taken place

coniferous describing the cone-bearing trees of the pine family; usually evergreen

deciduous describing trees that shed leaves seasonally and remain leafless for part of the year

delta flat, low-lying plain that forms at the mouth of a river as the river slows and deposits sediment gathered upstream

esker long, winding rise of gravel and sand that marks the trail where a river once flowed beneath a glacier

estuary region of interaction between ocean water and the end of a river, where tidal action and river flow mix fresh and salt water

fen any low land covered wholly or partly with water

fjord narrow inlet of the sea between cliffs or steep slopes

glacial erratic rock or boulder transported from its original resting place by a glacier

herbaceous referring to a plant having little or no woody tissue and persisting usually for only a single growing season

igneous referring to rock formed by cooled and hardened lava

intertidal referring to the shoreline zone between the highest high and the lowest low tide

kame cone-shaped hill of rock debris deposited by glacial meltwater

kaolin dull, yellowish, clay mineral widely used in pottery and ceramics and as a filler in paper products

kettle hole glacial depression that, when fed by groundwater and precipitation, often evolves into a bog

krummholz (from the German) stunted forest; charateristic of timberline area

lateral moraine hill or ridge of debris (rock, sand, gravel, silt, and clay) deposited along a retreating or advancing glacier's side

littoral of or on a shore, especially a seashore

massif zone of the earth's crust raised or depressed by plate movement and bounded by faults

metamorphic referring to a rock

that has been changed into its present state after being subjected to heat, pressure, or chemical change

monadnock height of land containing more erosion-resistant rock than the surrounding area

oxbow lake that forms where a meandering river overflows and forms a crescent-shaped body of standing water; called an oxbow because its curved shape looks like the U-shaped harness frame that fits around an ox's neck

pluton underground formation of molten lava that cooled before reaching the earth's surface; found both underwater and on land

schist metamorphic rock with a layered appearance; composed of often flaky parallel layers of minerals

scree accumulation of loose stones or rocky debris lying on a slope or at the base of a hill

smolt young salmon or sea trout at a stage of development when it assumes an adult color and is ready to migrate to the sea, usually at two years of age

sphagnum moss that grows in wet, acidic areas; decomposes and compacts to form peat

subclimax forest ecological forest community unable to evolve naturally due to outside factors such as repeated fires or logging

talus accumulated rock debris at the base of a cliff

tarn small, steep-backed mountain lake or pool

terminal moraine final deposit of rock and debris that has formed at a glacier's farthest leading edge, and is left behind as the glacier retreats

tidewater glacier glacier that terminates in the sea, usually at the head of a fjord or inlet

timberline boundary that marks the upper limit of forest growth on a mountain or at high latitudes; also called the tree line

tundra cold region characterized by low level of vegetation; exists as alpine zones of mountain ranges in lower latitudes, or arctic zones of polar areas in the far north

wetland area of land covered or saturated with groundwater; includes swamps, marshes, and bogs

LAND MANAGEMENT RESOURCES

The following public and private organizations are among the important adminis-trators of the preserved and protected areas described in this volume. Brief expla-nations of the various legal and legislative designations of these areas follow.

MANAGING ORGANIZATIONS

Maine Department of Conservation
State agency that administers and maintains all state parks, forests, public lands, and historic sites. Includes Bureau of Parks and Recreation, Maine Forest Service, Maine Geological Survey, and Bureau of Public Lands.

Maine Department of Inland Fisheries and Wildlife
Responsible for conservation and enhancement of state wildlife and fish-eries. Maintains 85,000 acres of wildlife management areas, regulates hunt-ing and fishing licenses, and protects and studies wildlife resources.

National Audubon Society (NAS) Private organization
International nonprofit conservation, lobbying, and educational organiza-tion. Owns a private network of wildlife sanctuaries managed by teams of NAS employees. Strives to protect natural ecosystems through grassroots organization and education.

National Park Service (NPS) Department of the Interior
Regulates the use of national parks, monuments, and preserves. Resources are managed to protect landscape, natural and historic artifacts, and wildlife. Administers historic and national landmarks, national seashores, wild and scenic rivers, and the national trail system.

The Nature Conservancy (TNC) Private organization
International nonprofit organization that owns the largest private system of nature sanctuaries in the world, some 1,300 preserves. Aims to preserve significant and diverse plants, animals, and natural communities. Some areas are managed by other private or public conservation groups, some by the Conservancy itself.

New Hampshire Department of Resources and Economic Development
State agency that administers and maintains all state forest and park prop-erties. Includes Division of Forests and Lands and Division of Parks.

New Hampshire Fish and Game Department
State agency that administers and maintains approximitely 150 wildlife management areas ranging in size from 1 acre to 3,300 acres. Maintains state hunting and fishing areas and licenses and all boat access areas.

Society for the Protection of New Hampshire Forests
Voluntary nonprofit organization dedicated to wise use of the state's natur-al resources. Owns outright and manages 90 permanent properties consist-ing of 23,000 acres of primarily forest land. Maintains land easements on 326 properties consisting of 50,000 acres.

U.S. Fish and Wildlife Service (USFWS) Department of the Interior
Principal federal agency responsible for conserving, protecting, and en-

hancing the country's fish and wildlife and their habitats. Manages national wildlife refuges and fish hatcheries as well as programs for migratory birds and endangered and threatened species.

U.S. Forest Service (USFS) Department of Agriculture
Administers more than 190 million acres in the national forests and national grasslands and is responsible for the management of their resources. Determines how best to combine commercial uses such as grazing, mining, and logging with conservation needs.

University of Vermont Environmental Program
Administers nine natural areas totaling 2,000 acres in size that represent the variety of Vermont's natural landscape. Although primarily utilized for study by faculty and students, areas are frequently open to the public.

Vermont Agency of Natural Resources
Manages Department of Forests, Parks and Recreation, Department of Fish and Wildlife, and Department of Environmental Conservation. Administers, maintains, and protects all state parks, lands, and wildlife areas.

DESIGNATIONS

National Forest
Large acreage managed for the use of forests, watersheds, wildlife, and recreation by the public and private sectors. Managed by USFS.

National Historic Site
Land area, building, or object preserved because of its national historic significance. Managed by NPS.

National Monument
Nationally significant landmark, structure, object, or area of scientific or historic importance. Managed by NPS.

National Natural Landmark
Nationally significant natural area that is a prime example of a biotic community or a particular geologic feature. Managed by NPS.

National Park
Spacious primitive or wilderness area containing scenery and natural wonders so outstanding it is deemed worthy of preservation by the federal government. Managed by NPS.

National Recreation Area
Site established to conserve and develop for recreational purposes an area of scenic, natural, or historic interest. Managed by NPS.

National Wildlife Refuge
Public land set aside for wild animals; protects migratory waterfowl, endangered and threatened species, and native plants. Managed by USFWS.

Wildlife Management Area
Natural area owned, protected, and maintained by the state for public recreational activities, including hunting, fishing, trapping, and cross-country skiing. Managed by individual states.

261

NATURE TRAVEL

The following is a selection of national and local organizations that sponsor nature-related travel activities or can provide specialized regional travel information.

NATIONAL

National Audubon Society
700 Broadway
New York, NY 10003
(212) 979-3000
Offers a wide range of ecological field studies, tours, and cruises throughout the United States

National Wildlife Federation
1400 16th Street NW
Washington, D.C. 20036
(703) 790-4363
Offers training in environmental education for all ages, including wildlife camp and teen adventures and conservation summits involving nature walks, field trips, and classes

The Nature Conservancy
1815 North Lynn Street
Arlington, VA 22209
(703) 841-5300
Offers a variety of excursions based out of regional and state offices. May include hiking, backpacking, canoeing, horseback riding. Contact above number to locate state offices

Sierra Club Outings
730 Polk Street
San Francisco, CA 94109
(415) 923-5630
Offers tours of different lengths for all ages throughout the United States. Outings may include backpacking, hiking, biking, skiing, and water excursions

Smithsonian Study Tours and Seminars
1100 Jefferson Dr. SW
MRC 702
Washington, D.C. 20560
(202) 357-4700
Offers extended tours, cruises, research expeditions, and seminars throughout the United States

REGIONAL

Appalachian Trail Conference
PO Box 807
Harper's Ferry, WV 25425
(304) 535-6331
Nonprofit organization coordinates the preservation and management of the 2,100-mile Appalachian Trail, which includes trails through Maine, New Hampshire, and Vermont. Prepares and distributes trail guidebooks and other information relevant to hiking the trail

Maine Publicity Bureau
PO Box 2300
Hallowell, ME 04347
(207) 623-0363
Publishes and distributes seasonal tour packages and maps. Also fields specific travel questions and can direct travelers to the regional travel offices of chambers of commerce

New Hampshire Office of Travel and Tourism
PO Box 1856
Concord, NH 03302-1856
(603) 271-2665
(800) FUN-inNH (for 168-page New Hampshire recreational guidebook)
Maintains and distributes transportation, recreational, and accommodation information for both natural and historic areas within the state

Vermont Chamber of Commerce
PO Box 37
Montpelier, VT 05601
(802) 223-3443
Publishes and distributes seasonal guidebooks containing information on transportation, recreation, and accommodations. Also answers specific travel queries and can direct travelers to local chambers of commerce that can provide regional information

262

How to Use This Site Guide

The following site information guide will assist you in planning your tour of the natural areas of Vermont, New Hampshire, and Maine. Sites set in **boldface** and followed by the symbol ❖ in the text are here organized alphabetically by state. Each entry is followed by the mailing address (sometimes different from the street address) and phone number of the site's immediate managing office, plus brief notes and a list of facilities and activities available. (A key appears on each page.)

Information on hours of operation, seasonal closings, and fees is usually not listed, as these vary from season to season and year to year. Please also bear in mind that responsibility for the management of some sites may change. Call well in advance to obtain maps, brochures, and pertinent, up-to-date information that will help you plan your northern adventures.

Each site entry in the guide includes the address and phone number of its immediate managing agency. Many of these sites are under the stewardship of a forest or park ranger or supervised from a small nearby office. Hence, in many cases, those sites will be difficult to contact directly, and it is preferable to call the managing agency.

The following umbrella organizations can provide general information for individual natural sites, as well as the area as a whole:

MAINE

Maine Audubon Society
Gilsland Farm
PO 6009
Falmouth, ME 04105
(207) 781-2330

Maine Dept. of Conservation
State House Station 22
Augusta, ME 04333
Bureau of Parks and Recreation:
(207) 287-3821
Bureau of Public Lands:
(207) 287-3061

The Nature Conservancy
14 Maine St., Suite 401
Brunswick, ME 04011
(207) 729-5181

NEW HAMPSHIRE

Audubon Society of New Hampshire
3 Silk Farm Rd.
PO 528B
Concord, NH 03301
(603) 224-9909

The Nature Conservancy
2½ Beacon St., Suite 6
Concord, NH 03301
(603) 224-5853

New Hampshire Dept. of Resources and Economic Development
PO 1856
172 Pembroke Rd.
Concord, NH 03302
Forests: (603) 271-2215
Parks: (603) 271-3254

New Hampshire Fish and Game Department
2 Hazen Dr.
Concord, NH 03301
(603) 271-3421

Society for the Protection of New Hampshire Forests
54 Portsmouth St
Concord, NH 03301
(603) 224-9945

VERMONT

The Nature Conservancy
27 State St.
Montpelier, VT
05602-2934
(802) 229-4425

Vermont Agency of Natural Resources
103 S. Main St.
Waterbury, VT 05671
(802) 241-3636

Vermont Audubon Council
PO 112
South Strafford, VT 05070
(802) 765-4118

MAINE

ACADIA NATIONAL PARK
PO 177, Bar Harbor, ME 04609
(207) 288-3338
Includes Cadillac Mountain, Otter Cliffs,
Sand Beach, Thunder Hole; camping
in official areas only
**BT, BW, C, CK, F, GS, H, I
MT, PA, RA, RC, S, T, TG, XC**

ALLAGASH WILDERNESS WATERWAY
Maine Bureau of Parks and Recreation
State House Station 22, Augusta, ME 04333
(207) 287-3821
Rigorous canoeing; contact Parks and
Recreation to arrange trips
BW, C, CK, F, H, MT, PA, S, T

AMBRUST HILL WILDLIFE RESERVATION
Vinalhaven Town Office
PO 815, Vinalhaven, ME 04863
(207) 863-4471
Day use only **BW, H**

AREY'S NECK WOODS
Vinalhaven Town Office
PO 815
Vinalhaven, ME 04863
(207) 863-4471
Day use only **BW, H, MT, PA, S**

AROOSTOOK STATE PARK
Maine Bureau of Parks and Recreation
87 State Park Rd.
Aroostook, ME 04699
(207) 768-8341 **BT, BW, C, CK, F, GS,
H, I, MT, PA, S, T, XC**

BAXTER STATE PARK
Maine Bureau of Parks and Recreation
64 Balsam Dr.
Millinocket, ME 04462
(207) 723-5140
Reservations required for public-use
cabins; no RVs **BT, BW, C, CK, F, H,
I, L, MT, PA, RC, S, T, TG**

BIGELOW PRESERVE
Maine Bureau of Public Lands
PO 327, Farmington, ME 04938
(207) 778-4111
Includes segment of Appalachian Trail
**BW, C, CK, F, H, MT,
PA, RC, S, T, XC**

BORESTONE MOUNTAIN SANCTUARY
PO 112, Monson, ME 04464
(207) 997-3358
Visitors must register at visitor center;
bring drinking water
BW, GS, H, I, MT, PA, RA, RC, TG, XC

CAMDEN HILLS STATE PARK
Maine Bureau of Parks and Recreation
State House Station 22
Augusta, ME 04333
(207) 236-3109
Camping May 15–October 15, in desig-
nated areas only
BT, BW, C, GS, H, I, MT, PA, T, XC

CHESTERVILLE WILDLIFE MANAGEMENT AREA
1 FW Regional Office
RFD 3, PA 3770
Farmington, ME 04938
(207) 778-3324
Canoe access only; hand carry **CK**

COBSCOOK BAY STATE PARK
RFD PO 51
Dennysville, ME 04628
(207) 726-4412 **BW, C, CK, GS, H,
I, MT, PA, T, XC**

CRAIG BROOK NATIONAL FISH HATCHERY
Hatchery Rd., East Orland, ME 04431
(207) 469-2803 **F, I, MT, PA, S, T**

CROCKETT COVE WOODS PRESERVE
The Nature Conservancy of Maine
Fort Andross
14 Maine St., Ste. 401
Brunswick, ME 04011
(207) 729-5181
Day use only **MT**

DEBOULLIE UNIT
Maine Bureau of Public Lands
Dept. of Conservation
1235 Central Dr.
Presque Isle, ME 04769
(207) 287-3061
Reservation required for public-use cabins
BW, C, CK, F, H, L, MT, S, T

DONNEL POND
Maine Bureau of Public Lands
State House Station 22, Augusta, ME 04333
(207) 287-5936

BT	Bike Trails	**CK**	Canoeing, Kayaking	**F**	Fishing	**HR**	Horseback Riding
BW	Bird-watching	**DS**	Downhill Skiing	**GS**	Gift Shop	**I**	Information Center
C	Camping			**H**	Hiking		

All campsites accessible by foot or boat
only   **BW, C, CK, F, H, MT, PA, S, T**

EAGLE ISLAND
19 Pilot Point Rd.
Cape Elizabeth, ME 04107
(207) 774-6498
Day use only; accessible by boat only,
open May–September
    BW, CK, F, H, I, MT, PA, RA, T, TG

EAGLE LAKE UNIT
Maine Bureau of Public Lands
Dept. of Conservation
1235 Central Dr.
Presque Isle, ME 04769
(207) 287-3061
Boat access only
    C, CK, F, H, L, MT, PA, S, T

EAST POINT SANCTUARY
Maine Audubon Society
PO 6009, Falmouth, ME 04105
(207) 781-2330   **BW, H, MT, XC**

FERNALD'S NECK PRESERVE
The Nature Conservancy of Maine
Fort Andross, 14 Maine St., Ste. 401
Brunswick, ME 04011
(207) 729-5181
Day use only   **BW, F, H, MT**

FERRY BEACH STATE PARK
Maine Bureau of Parks and Recreation
Dept. of Conservation
95 Bayview Rd.
Saco, ME 04072
(207) 283-0067   **BT, BW, H, I, MT,
PA, RA, S, T, XC**

FISH AND WILDLIFE VISITOR CENTER
RR 1, 328 Shaker Rd.
Gray, ME 04039
(207) 287-3303   **I, MT, PA, T**

FOUR PONDS UNIT OF RANGELEY AREA
Maine Bureau of Public Lands
PO 327, Farmington, ME 04938
(207) 778-4111
Includes segment of Appalachian Trail
    BW, C, CK, F, H, MT, S, T, XC

FORE RIVER SANCTUARY
Maine Audubon Society
PO 6009, Falmouth, ME 04105
(207) 781-2330   **BW, H, MT, XC**

GILSLAND FARM SANCTUARY
Maine Audubon Society
PO 6009, Falmouth, ME 04105
(207) 781-2330
    BW, GS, H, I, MT, PA, RA, T, TG, XC

GRAFTON NOTCH STATE PARK
HCR 61, PO 330, Newry, ME 04261
(207) 824-2912
Bring drinking water and rain gear
    F, H, MT, PA, RC, S, T, XC

THE GREAT HEATH
Maine Bureau of Public Lands
State House Station 22
Augusta, ME 04333
(207) 287-5936
Day use only; includes Pleasant River
    BW, CK, F

GREAT WASS ISLAND PRESERVE
The Nature Conservancy of Maine
Fort Andross
14 Maine St., Ste. 401
Brunswick, ME 04011
(207) 729 5181
Day use only, prepare for damp weather
    H, MT

GULF HAGAS
PO 885
Bucksport, ME 04416
(207) 469-1275
    BW, C, F, H, MT, RC, S, XC

HOLBROOK ISLAND SANCTUARY
PO 280,
Brooksville, ME 04617
(207) 326-4012
Day use only, includes Fresh Pond
    BW, CK, H, I, L, MT, PA, RA, S, T, TG, XC

INDIAN POINT–BLAGDEN PRESERVE
The Nature Conservancy of Maine
Fort Andross
14 Maine St., Ste. 401
Brunswick, ME 04011
(207) 729-5181
Day use only   **BW, I, MT**

ISLE AU HAUT
Acadia National Park
PO 177
Bar Harbor, ME 04609
(207) 288-3338
Boat access only
    BW, C, CK, F, H, MT, S, T

L	Lodging	**PA**	Picnic Areas	**RC**	Rock Climbing	**TG**	Tours, Guides
MT	Marked Trails	**RA**	Ranger-led Activities	**S**	Swimming	**XC**	Cross-country Skiing
				T	Toilets		

Site Guide

JOSEPHINE NEWMAN SANCTUARY
Maine Audubon Society
PO 6009, Falmouth, ME 04105
(207) 781-2330
Mosquitoes   **BW, H, MT, XC**

KENNEBUNK PLAINS
The Nature Conservancy of Maine
Fort Andross
14 Maine St., Ste. 401
Brunswick, ME 04011
(207) 729-5181
Day use only; stay on trails to avoid disturbing nesting birds   **BW, F, H, MT, XC**

LILY BAY STATE PARK
HC 76, PO 425
Greenville, ME 04441
(207) 287-3824
          BT, BW, C, CK, F, H, I, MT, PA, S, T

LUMBERMAN'S MUSEUM
PO 300
Patten, ME 04765
(207) 528-2650
Open Memorial Day–Columbus Day;
call for hours   **GS, I, T**

MACHIAS SEAL ISLAND
RR 1, PO 990
Jonesport, ME 04649
(207) 497-5933
Boat access only; restricted access
          BW, T, TG

MAINE FOREST AND LOGGING MUSEUM
University of Maine
5768 South Annex
Orono, ME 04469–5768
(207) 581-2871
          BW, F, H, MT, PA, T, TG, XC

MAINE MARITIME MUSEUM
243 Washington St.
Bath, ME 04530
(207) 443-1316
Small shipyard   **GS, I, PA, T, TG**

MAST LANDING SANCTUARY
Maine Audubon Society
PO 6009
Falmouth, ME 04105
(207) 781-2330
Includes wildlife observation area; historic dam and mill site
          BW, H, MT, PA, RA, T, TG, XC

MATTAWAMKEAG WILDERNESS PARK
PO 5, Mattawamkeag, ME 04459
(207) 736-4881
Seasonal camping in designated areas only
          BW, C, CK, G, H, I MT, PA, RC, S, T, XC

MOOSEHEAD MARINE MUSEUM
PO 1151, Greenville, ME 04441
(207) 695-2716   **GS, T, TG**

MOOSEHORN NATIONAL WILDLIFE REFUGE
U.S. Fish and Wildlife Service
PO 1077, Calais, ME 04619
(207) 454-7161
          BT, BW, CK, F, H, MT, PA, T, XC

MOUNT BLUE STATE PARK
RR 1, PO 610, Weld, ME 04285
(207) 585-2261   **BT, BW, C, CK, F, GS,**
          H, I, MT, PA, RA, S, T, TG, XC

MOXIE FALLS
Maine Bureau of Parks and Recreation
State House Station 22
Augusta, ME 04333
(207) 287-3821   **F, H, MT, PA**

NAHMAKANTA LAKE
Maine Bureau of Public Lands
State House Station 22, Augusta, ME 04333
(207) 287-3061
Permit required for camping
          BW, C, CK, F, H, S, T, XC

OLD SOW WHIRLPOOL
RFD 1, PO 51, Dennysville, ME 04628
(207) 726-4412
Several miles from shore; charter boats
available   **TG**

PEMAQUID POINT LIGHTHOUSE
Bristol Parks Dept.
PO 147, Bristol, ME 04539
(207) 677-2494
Day use only; open Memorial Day–
Labor Day (subject to change)
          BW, GS, H, I, L, T

PENOBSCOT MARINE MUSEUM
Church St.
PO 498, Searsport, ME 04974
(207) 548-2529   **GS, T, TG**

PERHAM'S OF WEST PARIS
PO 280, West Paris, ME 04289
(207) 674-2341   **GS, I**

BT	Bike Trails	**CK**	Canoeing, Kayaking	**F**	Fishing	**HR**	Horseback Riding
BW	Bird-watching	**DS**	Downhill Skiing	**GS**	Gift Shop	**I**	Information Center
C	Camping			**H**	Hiking		

266

**PETIT MANAN NATIONAL
WILDLIFE REFUGE**
PO 279
Milbridge, ME 04658
(207) 546-2124
   Day use only; much of park is accessible by boat only   **BW, H, I, MT, T, XC**

PINEO RIDGE
Maine Bureau of Public Lands
State House Station 22
Augusta, ME 04333
(207) 287-5936
   Day use only   **BW, CK, F**

PROUTS NECK BIRD SANCTUARY
510 Black Point Rd.
Prouts Neck, ME 04074
(207) 883-4126
   Day use only; no public parking; accessible only to residents and guests of Black Point Inn   **BW, L, MT**

QUODDY HEAD STATE PARK
Maine Bureau of Parks and Recreation
State House Station 22
Augusta, ME 04333
(207) 287-3821
   Day use only, open May 15-October 15; includes West Quoddy Head Light Station, Heath Bog, Carrying Place Cove   **BW, F, H, MT, PA, RC, T**

RACHEL CARSON NATIONAL WILDLIFE REFUGE
RR 2, PO 751, Wells, ME 04090
(207) 646-9226
   Certain areas limited   **BW, CK, I, PA, T, XC**

RACHEL CARSON SALT POND PRESERVE
The Nature Conservancy of Maine
Fort Andross
14 Maine St., Ste. 401
Brunswick, ME 04011
(207) 729-5181
   Day use only   **MT**

RANGELEY LAKE STATE PARK
HC 32, PO 5000
Rangeley, ME 04970
(207) 864-3858
   Reservations recommended for campsites; summer only   **BT, BW, C, CK, F, H, MT, PA, RC, S, T**

REID STATE PARK
HC 33, PO 286
Georgetown, ME 04548
(207) 371-2303
   Reservation required for day-use shelter   **BW, CK, F, GS, PA, S, T, XC**

**RICHARDSON LAKE
UNIT OF RANGELEY AREA**
Maine Bureau of Public Lands
PO 327
Farmington, ME 04938
(207) 778-4111
   Campground accessed by boat only   **BW, C, CK, F, H, PA, S, T, XC**

ROQUE BLUFFS STATE PARK
Maine Bureau of Parks and Recreation
State House Station 22
Augusta, ME 04333
(207) 287-3821
   Day use only; bring your own water; includes Simpsons Pond, Rugosa Rose Field   **BW, CK, F, H, PA, RA, S, T**

SAINT JOHN RIVER
Madawaska Chamber of Commerce
378 Main St.
Madawaska, ME 04756
(207) 728-7000
   Acadia landing   **BT, BW, C, CK, F, GS, H, I, PA, S, T, TG, XC**

SCARBOROUGH MARSH NATURE CENTER
Maine Audubon Society
PO 6009, Falmouth, ME 04105
(207) 781-2330
   Mosquitoes; canoe rentals and tours available   **BW, CK, F, GS, H, I, MT, T, TG**

STANDWOOD HOMESTEAD MUSEUM
PO 485 Ellsworth, ME 04605
(207) 667-8460
   Open May–October   **BT, BW, GS, H, I, MT, PA, T**

STEVE POWELL WILDLIFE MANAGEMENT AREA
Maine Dept. of Inland
Fisheries and Wildlife
RFD 1, PO 6378
Waterville, ME 04901
(207) 547-4167
   Reservations required; primitive camp-

L	Lodging	**PA**	Picnic Areas	**RC**	Rock Climbing	**TG**	Tours, Guides
MT	Marked Trails	**RA**	Ranger-led Activities	**S**	Swimming	**XC**	Cross-country Skiing
				T	Toilets		

267

ing only; accessible by boat only; open
May 1–Labor Day
BW, C, CK, H, MT, PA, RA, T, TG

TUNK LAKE
Maine Bureau of Public Lands
State House Station 22
Augusta, ME 04333
(207) 287-5936
All campsites accessible by foot or boat
only   **BW, C, CK, F, H, MT, PA, S, T**

VINALHAVEN
Vinalhaven Town Office, PO 815
Vinalhaven, ME 04863
(207) 863-4471
Day use only   **BW, CK, F, GS, H, I,
L, MT, PA, S, T, TG, XC**

WARREN ISLAND STATE PARK
Maine Bureau of Parks and Recreation
State House Station 22
Augusta, ME 04333
(207) 287-3821
Primitive camping only; accessible by private boat only   **BW, C, CK, F, I, PA, S, T**

**WELLS NATIONAL ESTUARINE
RESEARCH RESERVE**
PO 1007, Wells, ME 04090
(207) 646-1555
BW, CK, GS, H, I, MT, PA, RA, T, TG, XC

WOLFE'S NECK WOODS STATE PARK
Maine Bureau of Parks and Recreation
State House Station 22
Augusta, ME 04333
(207) 287-3821
BW, F, H, I, MT, PA, RA, T, TG

NEW HAMPSHIRE

ALPINE GARDEN
U.S. Forest Service
White Mountain National Forest
PO 638, Laconia, NH 03247
(603) 528-8721
**BT, BW, C, CK, DS, F, H,
HR, I, MT, PA, RC, S, T, XC**

AMOSKEAG FISHWAYS
1000 Elm St., PO 330
Manchester, NH 03105
(603) 626-FISH
Groups; guided tours; wheelchair access
GS, I, T, TG

APPALACHIAN NATIONAL SCENIC TRAIL
Appalachian Trail Conference
New England District, PO 312
Lyme, NH 03768
(603) 795-4935

BEAR BROOK STATE PARK
New Hampshire Dept. of Resources
and Economic Development
Div. of Parks and Recreation
PO 507, Allenstown, NH 03275
(603) 485-9874
Call (603) 485-9869 for campground information   **BW, C, CK, F, H, HR,
I, MT, PA, RA, S, T, XC**

BEAVER BROOK NATURAL AREA
Beaver Brook Natural Association
117 Ridge Rd., Hollis, NH 03049
(603) 465-7787
Pets need to be on a leash; call ahead to
inquire about camping and guided tours
BT, BW, C, F, H, HR, MT, RA, TG, XC

BEDELL BRIDGE HISTORIC SITE
New Hampshire Dept. of Resources
and Economic Development
Div. of Parks and Recreation, PO 1856
Concord, NH 03302
(603) 271-3556   **BW, CK, F, PA**

BRETZFELDER MEMORIAL PARK
Society for the Protection of New
Hampshire Forests, c/o The Rocks Estate
RFD 3, Rte. 302, Bethlehem, NH 03574
(603) 444-6228   **BW, F, H, I, MT,
PA, T, TG, XC**

CARDIGAN LODGE
Appalachian Mountain Club, PO 712
Bristol, NH 03222
(603) 744-8069 (winter)/744-8011(summer)
BW, C, H, L, MT, S, T, XC

CARDIGAN STATE PARK
New Hampshire Dept. of Resources
and Economic Development
Div. of Parks and Recreation, PO 273
West Ossipee, NH 03890
(603) 323-2087   **BW, H, MT, PA, T**

**CHARLES L. PEIRCE WILDLIFE AND
FOREST RESERVATION**
Society for the Protection of
New Hampshire Forests, 54 Portsmouth St.
Concord, NH 03301
(603) 224-9945

BT	Bike Trails	**CK**	Canoeing, Kayaking	**F**	Fishing	**HR**	Horseback Riding
BW	Bird-watching			**GS**	Gift Shop		
C	Camping	**DS**	Downhill Skiing	**H**	Hiking	**I**	Information Center

Map and compass recommended
BW, F, H, MT, XC

CHRISTA MCAULIFFE PLANETARIUM
3 Institute Dr., Concord, NH 03301
(603) 271-STAR　　　　　　**GS, I, T**

CLARK PRESERVE
Chocorua Lake Conservation Foundation
Chocorua, NH 03817　　**BW, H, I, MT, XC**

COLEMAN STATE PARK
New Hampshire Dept. of Resources and
Economic Development
Div. of Parks and Recreation
RR 1, PO 183, Colebrook, NH 03576
(603) 237-4520
　Primitive camping
　　　　BW, C, CK, F, H, PA, XC

CONNECTICUT LAKE STATE FOREST
New Hampshire Dept. of Resources and
Economic Development
Div. of Forests and Lands, PO 1856
Concord, NH 03302-0856
(603) 271-3456　　**BT, BW, H, HR, MT, XC**

COOPER CEDAR WOODS
Society for the Protection of New
Hampshire Forests
54 Portsmouth St.
Concord, NH 03301
(603) 224-9945　　　　**BW, H, MT, XC**

CRAWFORD NOTCH STATE PARK
New Hampshire Dept. of Resources and
Economic Development
Div. of Parks and Recreation
PO 177, Twin Mountain, NH 03595
(603) 374-2272
　　　BT, BW, C, F, GS, H, I, MT, PA, T

DEERING WILDLIFE SANCTUARY
Audubon Society of New Hampshire
Audubon House, 3 Silk Farm Rd.
Concord, NH 03302
(603) 224-9909
　No motorized vehicles　**BW, H, MT, XC**

DIXVILLE NOTCH STATE PARK
New Hampshire Dept. of Resources
and Economic Development
Div. of Parks and Recreation
RFD 2, PO 241
Lancaster, NH 03584
(603) 788-3155　　　**BW, H, MT, PA, T**

ENFIELD WILDLIFE MANAGEMENT AREA
New Hampshire Fish and Game Dept.
2 Hazen Dr., Concord, NH 03301
(603) 271-2461　　　　**BW, CK, F, H**

FOX STATE FOREST
New Hampshire Dept. of Resources and
Economic Development
Division of Forests and Lands, PO 1856
Concord, NH 03302
(603) 271-3456　　**BT, BW, H, HR, MT, XC**

FRANCONIA NOTCH STATE PARK
New Hampshire Dept. of Resources
and Economic Development
Div. of Parks and Recreation
Rte. 3, Franconia, NH 03580
(603) 745-2452
　Includes the Flume, Lafayette Place
　Campground, aerial tramway
　　　BT, BW, C, CK, DS, F, GS, H, I,
　　　MT, PA, RA, RC, S, T, TG, XC

FRANK BOLLES NATURE PRESERVE
The Nature Conservancy
2 ½ Beacon St., Ste. 6
Concord, NH 03301
(603) 224-5853　　　　**BW, H, MT, S, XC**

THE FROST PLACE
Ridge Rd.
Franconia, NH 03580
(603) 823-5510　　　　**GS, MT, T, TG**

GAP MOUNTAIN RESERVATION
Society for the Protection of New
Hampshire Forests
54 Portsmouth St.
Concord, NH 03301
(603) 224-9945
　Camping by permission only
　　　　　　BW, C, H, MT, XC

GILE STATE FOREST
New Hampshire Dept. of Resources
and Economic Development
Div. of Forests and Lands, PO 1856
Concord, NH 03302
(603) 271-3456　　**BT, BW, H, HR, MT, XC**

GRAFTON POND
Society for the Protection of New
Hampshire Forests
54 Portsmouth St.
Concord, NH 03301
(603) 224-9945　　**BW, CK, F, H, PA, S, XC**

L	Lodging	**PA**	Picnic Areas	**RC**	Rock Climbing	**TG**	Tours, Guides
MT	Marked Trails	**RA**	Ranger-led Activities	**S**	Swimming	**XC**	Cross-country Skiing
				T	Toilets		

Site Guide

GREAT BAY NATIONAL ESTUARINE RESERVE
New Hampshire Fish and Game Dept.
Region 3, 225 Main St.
Durham, NH 03824
(603) 868-1095
Please call ahead to make arrangements
BW, CK, F, GS, H, I, MT, RA, T, TG, XC

GREAT BAY NATIONAL WILDLIFE REFUGE
U.S. Fish and Wildlife Service
601 Spaulding Turnpike, Ste. 17
Portsmouth, NH 03801
(603) 431-7511
Please call ahead to make arrangements

HEALD TRACT
Society for the Protection of New Hampshire Forests
54 Portsmouth St.
Concord, NH 03301
(603) 224-9945   **BW, F, H, MT, RA, XC**

HEBRON MARSH WILDLIFE SANCTUARY
Audubon Society of New Hampshire
Audubon House
3 Silk Farm Rd.
Concord, NH 03302
(603) 224-9909
No motorized vehicles
BW, H, MT, RA, XC

HEMENWAY STATE FOREST
New Hampshire Dept. of Resources
and Economic Development
Div. of Forests and Lands, PO 1856
Concord, NH 03302-0856
(603) 271-3456
Includes Big Pines Natural Area
BT, BW, H, HR, MT, XC

HOYT WILDLIFE SANCTUARY
Audubon Society of New Hampshire
Audubon House
3 Silk Farm Rd.
Concord, NH 03302
(603) 224-9909
No motorized vehicles   **BW, H, MT, XC**

JENNINGS FOREST
Society for the Protection of New Hampshire Forests
54 Portsmouth St.
Concord, NH 03301
(603) 224-9945   **BW, H, MT, XC**

JOHN HAY NATIONAL WILDLIFE REFUGE
U.S. Fish and Wildlife Service
c/o Great Meadows
National Wildlife Refuge, Weir Hill Rd.
Sudbury, MA 01776
(508) 443-4661
Also includes the Fells State Historic Site
(603) 271-3254   **BW, H, I, MT, T, XC**

KONA WILDLIFE MANAGEMENT AREA
New Hampshire Fish and Game Dept.
2 Hazen Dr., Concord, NH 03301
(603) 271-2462
No motorized craft; foot access only
BW, CK, F, H, XC

LOST RIVER RESERVATION
Society for the Protection of New Hampshire Forests
Kinsman Notch, Rte. 112
North Woodstock, NH 03262
(603) 745-8031
Fee required
BW, GS, H, I, MT, PA, RA, T, TG

LOVEJOY MARSH WILDLIFE PRESERVE
Audubon Society of New Hampshire
3 Silk Farm Rd., Concord, NH 03302
(603) 224-9909
No motorized vehicles   **BW, H, MT, XC**

MCCABE FOREST
Society for the Protection of New Hampshire Forests
54 Portsmouth St.
Concord, NH 03301
(603) 224-9945
Exceptional wildflowers
BW, F, H, MT, XC

MEETINGHOUSE POND WILDLIFE SANCTUARY
Audubon Society of New Hampshire
Audubon House, 3 Silk Farm Rd.
Concord, NH 03302
(603) 224-9909
No motorized vehicles   **BW, H, MT**

MERRIMACK RIVER OUTDOOR EDUCATION AND CONSERVATION AREA
Society for the Protection of New Hampshire Forests
54 Portsmouth St.
Concord, NH 03301
(603) 224-9945
BW, F, GS, H, I, MT, T, TG, XC

BT Bike Trails	**CK** Canoeing, Kayaking	**F** Fishing	**HR** Horseback Riding
BW Bird-watching		**GS** Gift Shop	
C Camping	**DS** Downhill Skiing	**H** Hiking	**I** Information Center

MILLER STATE PARK
New Hampshire Dept. of Resources and
Economic Development
Div. of Parks and Recreation, 26 Pine St.
Peterborough, NH 03458
(603) 547-3373   **BW, H, I, MT, PA, T**

MONADNOCK STATE PARK
New Hampshire Dept. of Resources and
Economic Development
Div. of Parks and Recreation, PO 181
Jaffrey, NH 03452
(603) 532-8862
  Permission needed for camping
            BW, C, GS, H, I, MT, PA, T, XC

**MOUNT WASHINGTON STATE PARK
VISITOR CENTER**
New Hampshire Dept. of Resources
and Economic Development
Div. of Parks and Recreation, PO D
Gorham, NH 03581
(603) 466-3347
  Includes observatory; access via cog rail-
  way, (800) 922-8825, or auto road, (603)
  466-3988   **BW, GS, I, T**

NORTON POOL NATURAL AREA
The Nature Conservancy
2 ½ Beacon St., Ste. 6
Concord, NH 03301
(603) 224-5853
  Best access by canoe; call (603) 246-
  3331 to confirm rd. access
            BW, CK, H, S, XC

ODIORNE POINT STATE PARK
c/o Seacoast Science Center
PO 674, Rye, NH 03870
(603) 436-8043
  Please call ahead to make group
  arrangements   **BT, BW, CK, GS, H,
            I, MT, PA, RA, S, T, TG, XC**

PARADISE POINT NATURE CENTER
Audubon Society of New Hampshire
North Shore Rd., East Hebron, NH 03232
(603) 744-3516
  Seasonal **BW, GS, H, I, MT, RA, T, TG, XC**

PHILBRICH-CRICENTI BOG
New London Conservation Commission
Town Hall
PO 240, New London, CT 03257
(603) 526-4821
  Boots recommended.   **BW, H, MT**

PILLSBURY STATE PARK
New Hampshire Dept. of Resources
and Economic Development
Div. of Parks and Recreation, Rte. 31
Washington, NH 03280
(603) 863-2860
  Limited camping
            BW, C, CK, F, H, PA, T, XC

PINE PARK
c/o Richard Nordgren
Rope Ferry Rd.
Hanover, NH 03755
(603) 643-5068   **H, MT, XC**

PINE RIVER STATE FOREST
New Hampshire Dept. of Resources and
Economic Development
Div. of Forests and Lands, PO 1856
Concord, NH 03302-0856
(603) 271-3456   **BT, BW, H, HR, MT, XC**

PINKHAM NOTCH VISITOR CENTER
Appalachian Mountain Club, PO 298
Gorham, NH 03581
(603) 466-2727/2725
            **BT, BW, C, CK, DS, F, GS, H,
            I, L, MT, PA, RA, RC, S, T, XC**

PISGAH STATE PARK
New Hampshire Dept. of Resources
and Economic Development
Div. of Forests and Lands, PO 242
Winchester, NH 03470
(603) 239-8153
            BT, BW, CK, F, H, HR, MT, RA, XC

PONDICHERRY WILDLIFE REFUGE
Audubon Society of New Hampshire
Audubon House, 3 Silk Farm Rd.
Concord, NH 03302
(603) 224-9909
  No motorized vehicles   **BW, H, MT**

PONEMAH BOG BOTANICAL PRESERVE
Audubon Society of New Hampshire
Audubon House, 3 Silk Farm Rd.
Concord, NH 03302
(603) 224-9909
  No motorized vehicles   **BW, H, MT**

REED'S MARSH
New Hampshire Fish and Game Dept.
2 Hazen Dr.
Concord, NH 03301
(603) 271-2461   **BW, CK, F, H, XC**

L	Lodging	**PA**	Picnic Areas	**RC**	Rock Climbing	**TG**	Tours, Guides
MT	Marked Trails	**RA**	Ranger-led Activities	**S**	Swimming	**XC**	Cross-country Skiing
				T	Toilets		

271

Site Guide

RHODODENDRON STATE PARK
New Hampshire Dept. of Resources
and Economic Development
Div. of Parks and Recreation
c/o Monadnock State Park, PO 181
Jaffrey, NH 03452
(603) 532-8862 **H, MT, PA, T**

ROLLINS STATE PARK
New Hampshire Dept. of Resources
and Economic Development
Div. of Parks and Recreation
PO 219, Warner, NH 03278
(603) 456-3808/ (603) 271-3254
BW, H, I, MT, PA, T
RUGGLES MINE
PO 314D
Enfield, NH 03748
(603) 448-6911 **GS, PA, T**

SAINT GAUDENS HISTORIC SITE
RR 3, PO 73
Cornish, NH 03745
(603) 675-2175
Insect repellant recommended; includes
Blow-Me-Down Natural Area
BW, GS, H, I, MT, PA, T, XC

SCIENCE CENTER OF NEW HAMPSHIRE AT SQUAM LAKE
PO 173, Holderness, NH 03245
(603) 968-7194
Exhibit Trail open seasonally; please call
ahead to make arrangements
BW, GS, H, I, MT, PA,T

SCOTLAND BROOK SANCTUARY
Audubon Society of New Hampshire
Audubon House
3 Silk Farm Rd.
Concord, NH 03302
(603) 224-9909
No motorized vehicles **BW, H, MT**

SEACOAST SCIENCE CENTER
Audubon Society of New Hampshire
PO 674, Rye, NH 03870
(603) 436-8043 **BT, BW, CK, GS, H, I,
MT, PA, RA, S, T, TG, XC**

SHOALS MARINE LABORATORY
G-14 Stimson Hall, Cornell University
Ithaca, NY 14853
(607) 255-3717
Limited public access; call for
information **BW, TG**

STAMP ACT ISLAND
The Nature Conservancy
2 ½ Beacon St., Ste. 6
Concord, NH 03301
(603) 224-5853
Please call ahead to make arrangements;
bring binoculars **BW, H, MT**

TAMWORTH BLACK SPRUCE POND PRESERVE
Town of Tamworth Conservation Committee
Town Hall, Tamworth, NH 03886
(603) 323-7971 **BW, H, MT**

UMBAGOG LAKE CAMPGROUND
PO 181, Errol, NH 03579
(603) 482-7795
Wilderness campsites reached by boat
only **BW, C, CK, F, S**

URBAN FORESTRY CENTER
45 Elwyn Rd., Portsmouth, NH 03801
(603) 431-6774
Call ahead to arrange for guided tours
BW, H, I, MT, PA, T, TG, XC

WANTASTIQUET MOUNTAIN STATE FOREST
New Hampshire Dept. of Resources and
Economic Development
Div. of Forests and Lands, PO 1856
Concord, NH 03302
(603) 271-3456 **BT, BW, H, HR, MT, XC**

WAPACK NATIONAL WILDLIFE REFUGE
U.S. Fish and Wildlife Service
c/o Great Meadows National Wildlife Refuge
Weir Hill Rd., Sudbury, MA 01776
(508) 443-4661
Contact Friends of the Wapack for map:
PO 115, West Peterborough, NH 03468
BW, H, MT
WEST BRANCH PINE BARRENS
The Nature Conservancy
2 ½ Beacon St., Ste. 6
Concord, NH 03301
(603) 224-5853
No fishing, biking, or horses **BW, H, XC**

WHITE LAKE STATE PARK
New Hampshire Dept. of Resources and
Economic Development
Div. of Parks and Recreation, PO 41
West Ossipee, NH 03890
(603) 323-7350
Camping by permit only
BW, C, CK, F, H, I, MT, PA, RC, S, T

272

BT Bike Trails	**CK** Canoeing, Kayaking	**F** Fishing	**HR** Horseback Riding
BW Bird-watching		**GS** Gift Shop	
C Camping	**DS** Downhill Skiing	**H** Hiking	**I** Information Center

WHITE MOUNTAIN NATIONAL FOREST
U.S. Forest Service, PO 638
Laconia, NH 03247
(603) 528-8721
**BT, BW, C, CK, DS, F, H, HR,
I, MT, PA, RA, RC, S, T, XC**

WINSLOW STATE PARK
New Hampshire Dept. of Resources
and Economic Development
Div. of Parks and Recreation, PO 295
Newbury, NH 03255
(603) 763-2452   **BW, H, PA, T, XC**

VERMONT

AITKEN STATE FOREST
Vermont Dept. of Forests, Parks
and Recreation
RR 2, PO 2161,
Pittsford, VT 05763
(802) 483-2314
Primitive camping only; use not recom-
mended November–May
BW, C, F, H, MT, XC

AMERICAN MUSEUM OF FLY FISHING
PO 42
Manchester, VT 05254
(802) 362-3300   **GS, I, RA, T**

ASCUTNEY STATE PARK
Vermont Dept. of Forests, Parks and
Recreation, RR 1, PO 33
North Springfield, VT 05150
(802) 886-2215
Hang gliding site, summer camping
only; includes Mt. Ascutney Observation
Tower, Cascade Falls, Norcross Quarry
BW, C, GS, H, I, MT, PA, T, XC

**ATHERTON MEADOW WILDLIFE
MANAGEMENT AREA**
Vermont Dept. of Forests, Parks
and Recreation
RR 1, PO 33, North Springfield, VT 05150
(802) 886-2215
Remote and undeveloped; primitive
camping only   **BW, C, H**

BAR HILL NATURE PRESERVE
The Nature Conservancy of Vermont
27 State St., Montpelier, VT 05602
(802) 229-4425
Includes Sterling Nature Trail
BW, H, MT, PA, XC

BATTELL BIOLOGICAL PRESERVE
Town of Middlebury
94 Main St.
Middlebury, VT 05753
(802) 388-4041
Motorized vehicles prohibited; day
use only   **BW, H, I, MT**

BATTEN KILL RIVER
Manchester and the Mountains
Chamber of Commerce, RR 2, PO 3451
Manchester Center, VT 05255
(802) 362-2100
Camping in designated areas only;
no boat traffic before 9:30 A.M. or after
5:00 P.M.; includes West Arlington
Covered Bridge   **BW, C, CK, F,
I, L, S, TG**

BIG DEER CAMPGROUND
Vermont Dept. of Forests, Parks and
Recreation
103 South Main St., 10 South
Waterbury, VT 05671
(802) 241-3670   **BW, C, GS, H, I, MT, T**

**BILL SLADYK WILDLIFE
MANAGEMENT AREA**
Vermont Dept. of Fish and Wildlife
184 Portland St., St. Johnsbury, VT 05819
(802) 748-8787
Day use only   **BW, F, H, XC**

BILLINGS FARM AND MUSEUM
PO 489
Woodstock, VT 05091
(802) 457-2355
Open all week May–October, weekends
only November–December
GS, I, PA, T, TG

**BIRD MOUNTAIN WILDLIFE
MANAGEMENT AREA**
Vermont Dept. of Forests,
Parks and Recreation, RR 2, Box 2161
Pittsford, VT 05763
(802) 483-2314
Day use only, stay off cliffs March
15–August 1; includes Bird Mountain
BW, H, XC

BIRDS OF VERMONT MUSEUM
Sherman Hollow Rd.
Huntington, VT 05462
(802) 434-2167
Closed Tuesdays; open by appointment
only November–April
BW, GS, H, I, MT, T, TG

L	Lodging	**PA**	Picnic Areas	**RC**	Rock Climbing	**TG**	Tours, Guides
MT	Marked Trails	**RA**	Ranger-led Activities	**S**	Swimming	**XC**	Cross-country Skiing
				T	Toilets		

Site Guide

BOMOSEEN STATE PARK
Vermont Dept. of Forests, Parks
and Recreation,
RR 2, PO 2161, Pittsford, VT 05763
(802) 483-2314
Camping in designated areas only,
seasonal; includes West Castleton State
Area, Lake Bomoseen
BW, C, CK, F, GS, H, I, MT, PA, S, T

BRIGHTON STATE PARK
324 North Main St., Barre, VT 05641
(802) 479-3241
Camping in specific areas, call for
reservations **BT, BW, C, CK, F,
H, I, MT, P, RA, S, T, TG**

BURTON ISLAND STATE PARK
Vermont Dept. of Forests,Parks and
Recreation, 103 South Main St., 10 South
Waterbury, VT 05671
(802) 524-6353
Accessible by boat only; camping in
designated areas only; administers
Knight Island and Woods Island
BW, C, CK, F, H,I, MT, PA, RA, S, T, XC

BUTTON BAY STATE PARK
Vermont Dept. of Forests, Parks
and Recreation
103 South Main St., 10 South
Waterbury, VT 05671
(802) 241-3655
Camping in designated areas and in
summertime only **BW, C, CK, F, H,
I, MT, PA, S, T, TG, XC**

BUTTON POINT NATURAL AREA
Vermont Dept. of Forests, Parks
and Recreation
103 South Main St., 10 South
Waterbury, VT 05671
(802) 241-3655
Day use only, open Memorial Day–
Columbus Day
BW, F, H, I, MT, RA, TG, XC

CALVIN COOLIDGE STATE FOREST
Vermont Dept. of Forests, Parks and
Recreation, RR 1, PO 33
North Springfield, VT 05150
(802) 886-2215
For information on western part of for-
est, call (802) 483-2314; includes
Coolidge State Park Campground
BW, C, DS, H, MT, PA, T, XC

CAMELS HUMP STATE FOREST
Vermont Dept. of Forests, Parks and
Recreation, 111 West St.
Essex Junction, VT 05452
(802) 879-6565
Day use only **BW, F, H, I, MT, RA, XC**

CAMPMEETING POINT NATURAL AREA
Vermont Dept. of Forests, Parks and
Recreation, 111 West St.
Essex Junction, VT 05452
(802) 879-6565
Day use only
BW, CK, F, H, I, MT, PA, S, T, XC

CENTENNIAL WOODS
University of Vermont
Environmental Program
153 South Prospect St.
Burlington, VT 05401
(802) 656-4055
Foot traffic only, stay on designated
trails, day use only, no fires or pets; includes Potash Brook **BW, H, MT, XC**

CHAZYAN CORAL REEF
Isle La Motte Historical Society
Isle La Motte, VT 05463
(802) 928-3434
Open summer only, Saturdays and by
appointment; camping in designated
campsites only
BW, C, CK, F, H, HR, L, S, T, XC

CHICKERING BOG
The Nature Conservancy
27 State St.
Montpelier, VT 05602
(802) 229-4425
Passive recreational area **BW, H, MT, XC**

CLARENDON GORGE
WILDLIFE MANAGEMENT AREA
Vermont Dept. of Fish and Wildlife
RR 2, PO 2161, Pittsford, VT 05763
(802) 483-2314
Day use only, not recommended
November–May **F, H, T**

CRAFTSBURY SPORTS
AND LEARNING CENTER
PO 31, Craftsbury Common, VT 05827
(800) 729-7751
Primitive camping, B&B, dorm lodging
**BT, BW, C, CK, F, GS, H, HR,
I, L, MT, PA, RA, S, T, TG, XC**

BT	Bike Trails	CK	Canoeing, Kayaking	F	Fishing	HR	Horseback Riding
BW	Bird-watching	DS	Downhill Skiing	GS	Gift Shop	I	Information Center
C	Camping			H	Hiking		

DEAD CREEK
WILDLIFE MANAGEMENT AREA
Vermont Dept. of Fish and Wildlife
111 West St.
Essex Junction, VT 05452
(802) 878-1564
Primitive camping only
BW, C, CK, F, H, I, MT, XC

DISCOVERY MUSEUM
51 Park St., Essex Junction, VT 05452
(802) 878-8687
Closed Mondays and holidays
BT, BW, GS, I, PA, T, TG

THE DOME
Williams Outing Club
SU Box 1004, Williams College
Williamstown, MA 01267
(413) 597-2317
Primitive camping only; bring water
BW, C, F, H, MT

EAST WOODS NATURAL AREA
University of Vermont
Environmental Program
153 South Prospect St.
Burlington, VT 05401
(802) 656-4055
Foot traffic only; stay on designated
trails; day use only; no fires or pets;
includes Potash Brook **BW, H, MT, XC**

EMERALD LAKE STATE PARK
Vermont Dept. of Fish and Wildlife
RR 2, PO 2161
Pittsford, VT 05763
(802) 483-2314
Camping in designated areas only; open
Memorial Day–Columbus Day
BW, C, CK, F, GS, H, I,
MT, PA, RA, S, T, TG, XC

ETHAN ALLEN HOMESTEAD
Winooski Valley Park District
Burlington, VT 05401
(802) 863-5744
Primitive camping only, permit required
for campers **BW, C, CK, F, GS, H, I,**
L, MT, PA, RA, T, TG, XC

FAIRBANKS MUSEUM AND PLANETARIUM
Main and Prospect St.
St. Johnsbury, VT 05819
(802) 748-2372
Day use only **GS, I, MT, PA, T, TG**

FISHER-SCOTT MEMORIAL
PINES NATURAL AREA
Vermont Dept. of Forests, Parks and
Recreation, RR 2, PO 2161
Pittsford, VT 05763
(802) 483-2314
Day use only **H, MT**

FORT DUMMER STATE PARK
Vermont Dept. of Forests,
Parks and Recreation, RR 1, PO 33
North Springfield, VT 05150
(802) 886-2215
Camping allowed in summer only and
in designated campsites only
BW, C, GS, H, I, MT, PA, T, XC

GIFFORD WOODS STATE PARK
Vermont Dept. of Forests,
Parks and Recreation, Gifford Woods
Killington, VT 05751
(802) 775-5354
Open Memorial Day–Columbus Day; in-
cludes Appalachian Trail
BW, C, H, L, MT, PA, T

GREEN MOUNTAIN NATIONAL FOREST
U.S. Forest Service
Green Mountain and Finger Lakes
National Forest, 231 North Main St.
Rutland, VT 05701
(802) 747-6700
Hunting and fishing licenses required, toi-
lets closed during winter; includes Robert
Frost Wayside, White River Travelway,
White Rocks National Recreation Area and
Big Branch Wilderness
BT, BW, C, CK, DS, F, GS, H,
I, L, MT, PA, RA, RC, S, T, XC

GROTON STATE FOREST
Vermont Dept. of Forests, Parks and
Recreation, 103 South Main St., 10 South
Waterbury, VT 05671, (802) 241-3655
Includes Seyon Fly Fishing Area, Owl's
Head **BT, BW, C, CK, F, GS, H, I,**
L, MT, PA, RA, S, T, TG, XC

GROUT POND RECREATION AREA
U.S. Forest Service
Manchester Ranger District
RR 1, PO 1940, Manchester Center, VT 05255
(802) 362-2307
One public-use cabin available on first-
come first-serve basis; includes Grout Pond
BW, C, CK, F, H, I, L, MT, PA, S, T, XC

L	Lodging	**PA**	Picnic Areas	**RC**	Rock Climbing	**TG**	Tours, Guides
MT	Marked Trails	**RA**	Ranger-led Activities	**S**	Swimming	**XC**	Cross-country Skiing
				T	Toilets		

275

HALF MOON STATE PARK
Vermont Dept. of Fish and Wildlife
RR 2, PO 2161
Pittsford, VT 05763
(802) 483-2314
Roads impassable March–April; camping
in designated areas only
BW, C, CK, F, H, I, MT, S, T

HARRIMAN RESERVOIR
New England Power Company
PO 218, Harriman Station
Readsboro, VT 05350
(802) 423-7700
Day use only; includes Harriman Dam
Spillway **BT, BW, CK, DS,
H, HR, L, MT, PA, RC, S, T, TG, XC**

HEN ISLAND
The Nature Conservancy of Vermont
27 State St.
Montpelier, VT 05602
(802) 229-4425
Tern nesting island; access by boat only
and restricted May–August **BW, F**

HULBERT OUTDOOR EDUCATION CENTER
RR 1, PO 91A
Fairlee, VT 05045
(802) 333-9840
Prior arrangements must be made for all
visits; usually caters to groups; includes
Winslow Ledges, Eagles Bluff, Lake Morey
**BW, C, CK, F, H, I, L,
MT, RA, RC, S, T, TG, XC**
INDIAN BROOK PRESERVE
Town of Essex, 81 Main St.
Essex Junction, VT 05452
(802) 878-1342
Very remote, primitive camping only,
permit required for campers, motorboats
prohibited; includes Scenic Overlook,
Beaver Pond, Indian Brook Reservoir
BW, C, CK, F, H, HR, L, MT, PA, S, XC

JAMAICA STATE PARK
Vermont Dept. of Forests, Parks and
Recreation
103 South Main St.,10 South
Waterbury, VT 05671
(802) 241-3655
Open April 15–October 15; camping in
designated areas only; includes West
River, Hamilton Falls
**BT, BW, C, CK, DS, F,
H, MT, PA, RA, S, T, TG, XC**

KINGSLAND BAY STATE PARK
Vermont Dept. of Forests, Parks and
Recreation
103 South Main St.
10 South
Waterbury, VT 05671
(802) 241-3655
Reservations for pavilion must be
made in advance
BW, CK, F, H, I, MT, PA, S, T, XC

KNIGHT POINT STATE PARK
Vermont Dept. of Forests, Parks and
Recreation
103 South Main St.,
10 South
Waterbury, VT 05671
(802) 372-8389
Day use only
BW, CK, F, H, MT, PA, S, T, XC

LAKE MANSFIELD
Lake Mansfield Trout Club
4400 Nebraska Valley Rd.
Stowe, VT 05672
(802) 253-7565
Open to club members only

**LITTLE OTTER CREEK WILDLIFE
MANAGEMENT AREA**
Vermont Dept. of Fish and Wildlife
111 West St.
Essex Junction, VT 05452
(802) 878-1564
Day use only, accessible by boat only
BW, CK, F
LITTLE RIVER STATE PARK
Vermont Dept. of Forests, Parks and
Recreation
RR 1, PO 1150
Waterbury, VT 05676
(802) 244-7103 (summer)
(802) 479-3241 (winter)
Open Memorial Day–Labor Day, camp-
ing in designated areas only; includes
History Hike, Waterbury Dam
BW, C, CK, F, H, I, MT, RA, S, T, XC

LONE ROCK POINT
Diocesan Center
5 Rock Point Rd.
Burlington, VT 05401
(802) 863-3431
Private property, visitors must call
for permission

BT	Bike Trails	**CK**	Canoeing, Kayaking	**F**	Fishing	**HR**	Horseback Riding
BW	Bird-watching			**GS**	Gift Shop		
C	Camping	**DS**	Downhill Skiing	**H**	Hiking	**I**	Information Center

LONG TRAIL
Green Mountain Club Inc.
RR 1, PO 650, Waterbury Center, VT 05677
(802) 244-7037
Trails open Memorial Day–Columbus Day, foot traffic only, public-use cabins available on a first-come first-serve basis; includes Green Mountains, Camels Hump, Mt. Mansfield
BW, C, F, GS, H, I, L, MT, RA, RC, S, T, TG, XC

LORD'S HILL
Vermont Dept. of Forests, Parks and Recreation
103 South Main St., 10 South
Waterbury, VT 05671
(802) 241-3670
Day use only; no collecting without permit **BW, H, XC**

MAIDSTONE LAKE STATE PARK
Regional Parks Manager
324 North Main St., Barre, VT 05641
(802) 479-4280
Reservations recommended for waterfront campsites **BW, C, CK, F, H, I, MT, PA, RA, S, T, TG, XC**

MAYNARD MILLER BLACK GUM SWAMPS
Town of Vernon
Town Clerk, PO 116
Vernon, VT 05354-0116
(802) 257-0292
Open 8 A.M. to sunset **BW, H, MT, PA, TG**

McDONOUGH POINT NATURAL AREA
Vermont Dept. of Forests, Parks and Recreation
103 South Main St., 10 South
Waterbury, VT 05671
(802) 241-3655 **BW, CK, H, I, MT, PA, T**

MISSISQUOI NATIONAL WILDLIFE REFUGE
Vermont Dept. of Fish and Wildlife
PO 163, Swanton, VT 05488
(802) 868-4781
Day use only; hiking on designated trails only **BW, CK, F, H, I, MT, T, XC**

MOLLY STARK STATE PARK
RR 1, PO 196, Wilmington, VT 05363
(802) 464-5460
No pets allowed; open Memorial Day–Columbus Day, camping in designated areas only; includes Mt. Olga
BW, C, GS, H, I, MT, PA, T

MONTSHIRE MUSEUM OF SCIENCE
PO 770, Norwich, VT 05055
(802) 649-2200
Includes Hazen Trail
BW, GS, H, I, MT, PA, T, TG, XC

MOSS GLEN FALLS STATE NATURAL AREA
U.S. Forest Service
231 North Main St., Rutland, VT 05701
(802) 747-6700
Climbing prohibited; day use only; includes Long Trail
BT, BW, CK, DS, F, GS, H, I, MT, XC

MOUNT MANSFIELD STATE FOREST
Vermont Dept. of Forests, Parks and Recreation, 103 South Main St., 10 South
Waterbury, VT 05671
(802) 241-3678
Road closed Columbus Day–Labor Day; includes Smuggler's Notch, Toll Road (to summit), Little River State Park
BT, BW, C, CK, DS, F, H, HR, MT, PA, RC, S, T, TG, XC

NEBRASKA VALLEY
Vermont Dept. of Forests, Parks and Recreation, 103 South Main St., 10 South
Waterbury, VT 05671, (802) 241-3478
Primitive camping only; includes Lake Mansfield, Long Trail, Catamount Trail
BW, C, H, MT, XC

NORTH HERO STATE PARK
Vermont Dept. of Forests, Parks and Recreation,
103 South Main St., 10 South
Waterbury, VT 05671
(802) 372-8727
Camping in designated areas only
BW, C, CK, F, H, I, PA, S, T, XC

PEACHAM BOG NATURAL AREA
Vermont Dept. of Forests, Parks and Recreation, 103 South Main St., 10 South
Waterbury, VT 05671
(802) 241-3670
Day use only; fragile area; no collecting without permit **BW, H, MT, RA, TG, XC**

POPASQUASH ISLAND
Vermont Institute of Natural Science
RR 2, PO 532, Woodstock, VT 05091
(802) 457-2779
Tern nesting island, access by boat only and restricted May–August **BW, F**

L Lodging	**PA** Picnic Areas	**RC** Rock Climbing	**TG** Tours, Guides
MT Marked Trails	**RA** Ranger-led Activities	**S** Swimming	**XC** Cross-country Skiing
		T Toilets	

REDSTONE QUARRY NATURAL AREA
University of Vermont
Environmental Program
153 South Prospect St.
Burlington, VT 05401
(802) 656-4055
Foot traffic only, stay on designated trails, day use only, no fires or pets; includes Potash Brook **BW, H**

ROBERT FROST WAYSIDE AREA
U.S. Forest Service
Middlebury Ranger District
RD 4
PO 1260
Middlebury, VT 05753
(802) 388-6688
Primitive camping only; includes interpretative area
BW, C, F, H, MT, PA, T, XC

ROCK ISLAND
Vermont Institute of Natural Science
RR 2, PO 532
Woodstock, VT 05091
(802) 878-1564
Tern nesting island, access by boat only and restricted May–August **BW, F**

SAND BAR WILDLIFE MANAGEMENT AREA
Vermont Dept. of Fish and Wildlife
111 West St.
Essex Junction, VT 05452
(802) 878-1564
Wetlands area is closed to public, day use only **BW, H, XC**

SEYON RANCH FLY FISHING AREA
Vermont Div. of Forests, Parks and Recreation
103 South Main St., 10 South
Waterbury, VT 05671
(802) 241-3655
Day use only; includes Spruce Mountain Firetower, Noyes Pond
BW, F, GS, H, I, L, MT, T, XC

SMUGGLER'S NOTCH
Vermont Dept. of Forests, Parks and Recreation
103 South Main St., 10 South
Waterbury, VT 05671
(802) 241-3655
Hiking and camping in designated areas only **BT, BW, C, DS, F, H, I, L, MT, PA, T, TG, XC**

SNAKE MOUNTAIN
Vermont Dept. of Fish and Wildlife
111 West St., Essex Junction, VT 05452
(802) 878-1564
Includes old hotel site; panoramic view
BW, F, H, MT, XC

SOMERSET RESERVOIR
New England Power Company
PO 218, Harriman Station
Readsboro, VT 05350
(802) 423-7700
Primitive camping only, extremely remote
BT, BW, C, CK, DS, F, H, L, MT, PA, RC, S, T, XC

SOUTH BAY WILDLIFE MANAGEMENT AREA
Vermont Dept. of Fish and Wildlife
184 Portland St., St. Johnsbury, VT 05819
(802) 748-8787
Day use only **BW, CK, F, H**

SPECTACLE POND NATURAL AREA
Vermont Dept. of Forests, Parks and Recreation
103 South Main St., 10 South
Waterbury, VT 05671, (802) 241-3665
Motorboats prohibited; camping in designated campsites only
BW, C, CK, F, H, MT, RA, S, TG, XC

SPRINGWEATHER NATURE AREA
Ascutney Mountain Audubon Society
PO Box 191, Springfield, VT 05156
(802) 263-5488
Day use only; tours by prior arrangement; includes North Springfield Lake
BW, H, I, MT, PA, RA, T, TG, XC

STOWE RECREATION PATH
Stowe Area Association
PO Box 1320, Stowe, VT 05672
(802) 24-STOWE
Day use only; recreational equipment available for rent; no motorized vehicles; dogs must be leashed; includes Stowe Community Church, Little River
BT, BW, F, H, I, L, MT, PA, S, T, XC

TEXAS FALLS
U.S. Forest Service, Rochester Ranger District
RD 1, PO 108, Rochester, VT 05767
(802) 767-4261
No swimming; primitive camping only
BW, C, F, H, MT, PA, T, XC

BT	Bike Trails	**CK**	Canoeing, Kayaking	**F**	Fishing
BW	Bird-watching			**GS**	Gift Shop
C	Camping	**DS**	Downhill Skiing	**H**	Hiking

HR	Horseback Riding
I	Information Center

TOWNSHEND STATE PARK
Vermont Dept. of Forests, Parks and
Recreation
RR 1, PO 33, North Springfield, VT 05150
(802) 886-2215
Includes Bald Mountain
BW, C, CK, F, GS, H, I, MT, PA, RA, T, TG

UNION VILLAGE DAM RECREATION AREA
U.S. Army Corps of Engineers
424 Trapelo Rd., Waltham, MA 02254
(802) 295-2855
Day use only; includes
Rogers Woolen Mill   **BW, F, H, I, MT
PA, RA, S, T, TG, XC**

VERMONT MARBLE EXHIBIT
62 Main St., Proctor, VT 05765
(802) 459-3311 ext. 437
Open Monday–Saturday 9–4   **GS, I, T**

VERMONT RAPTOR CENTER
Vermont Institute of Natural Science
Churchill Rd., RR 2, PO 532
Woodstock, VT 05091
(802) 457-2779
Living museum; open 10–4 every day in
summer, closed Sundays in winter
BW, GS, H, I, MT, T, TG

**VICTORY BASIN
WILDLIFE MANAGEMENT AREA**
Vermont Dept. of Fish and Wildlife
184 Portland St.
St. Johnsbury, VT 05819
(802) 748-8787
Day use only   **BW, CK, F, H**

VICTORY BOG
Vermont Dept. of Fish and Wildlife
184 Portland St., St. Johnsbury, VT 05819
(802) 748-8787
Day use only   **BW, CK, F, H**

WENLOCK WILDLIFE MANAGEMENT AREA
Vermont Dept. of Fish and Wildlife
184 Portland St.
St. Johnsbury, VT 05819
(802) 748-8787
Day use only   **BW, CK, F, H**

WEST RUTLAND MARSH
West Rutland Town Hall
Main and Marble St., West Rutland, VT 05777
(802) 438-2263
Day use only; no public parking   **CK, F**

**WILD BRANCH WILDLIFE
MANAGEMENT AREA**
Vermont Dept. of Fish and Wildlife
103 South Main St., 10 South
Waterbury, VT 05671
(802) 479-3241
Roads are poor in spring   **BW, H, XC**

WILGUS STATE PARK
Vermont Dept. of Forests, Parks and
Recreation
RR 1, PO 33, North Springfield, VT 05150
(802) 886-2215
Summer camping only; camping in des-
ignated campsites only; includes
Connecticut River
BW, C, CK, F, GS, H, I, MT, PA, T

WILLOUGHBY STATE FOREST
184 Portland St.
St. Johnsbury, VT 05819
(802) 748-8787
Camp 200 feet from lakeshore and 1,000
feet from public roads
BT, BW, C, CK, F, H, MT, RC, S, XC

WORCESTER RANGE
Vermont Dept. of Forests, Parks and
Recreation
103 South Main St., 10 South
Waterbury, VT 05671
(802) 241-3655
Primitive camping only; very remote;
special permit required for all activities
other than camping; includes Long Trail,
Worcester Mountain, Hunger Mountain
BT, BW, C, F, H, HR, XC

YOUNG ISLAND
Vermont Dept. of Fish and Wildlife
111 West St.
Essex Junction, VT 05452
(802) 878-1564
Bird nesting island   **BW, H**

L	Lodging	**PA**	Picnic Areas	**RC**	Rock Climbing	**TG**	Tours, Guides
MT	Marked Trails	**RA**	Ranger-led Activities	**S**	Swimming	**XC**	Cross-country Skiing
				T	Toilets		

279

INDEX

Numbers in **bold** indicate illustrations; numbers in **bold italics** indicate maps.

Index

ACKNOWLEDGMENTS

The editors gratefully acknowledge the assistance of Tim Allan, Marni Davis, Jane Hoffman, Susan Kirby, Joseph Roman, Amanda Vender, and Patricia Woodruff.

The following consultants also helped in the preparation of this volume: David Field, Society for the Protection of New Hampshire Forests; Richard Ober, University of Maine at Orono; and Dallas D. Rhodes, Professor and Chair of Geology, Whittier College, CA.

CREDITS

All photography by Diane Cook and Len Jenshel except for the following:

HALF–TITLE PAGE: Robert Villani, Merrick, NY
viii, LEFT: Kevin Shields, Camden, ME
ix, LEFT: Len Rue, Jr., Blairstown, NJ
2–3: Phil Schermeister, San Francisco, CA
9: Andrew W. Mellon Fund, National Gallery of Art, Washington, D.C.
14, 24: Robert Villani, Merrick, NY
31: Paul Rezendes, South Royalston, MA
32, LEFT: Dorothy S. Long/New England Wild Flower Society, Framingham, MA
35: Len Rue, Jr., Blairstown, NJ
37: Bates Littlehales, Arlington, VA
41: Randy Ury, Portland, ME
42: Bates Littlehales, Arlington, VA
54: Len Rue, Jr., Blairstown, NJ
55, 61: Leonard Lee Rue III, Blairstown, NJ
68: A. Blake Gardner, Bennington, VT
70–71: William Johnson, Bristol, NH
72: Paul Rezendes, South Royalston, MA
76: Leonard Lee Rue III, Blairstown, NJ
82: The New-York Historical Society
88: Shelburne Museum, Shelburne, VT
92: Bates Littlehales, Arlington, VA
100: John Shaw, Colorado Springs, CO
101: Len Rue, Jr., Blairstown, NJ
112: Kevin Shields, Camden, ME
113: Ping Amranand, Kensington, MD
120: Kevin Shields, Camden, ME
121: Bates Littlehales, Arlington, VA
123: Tom Vezo, Babylon, NY
126: Bates Littlehales, Arlington, VA
129: Randy Ury, Portland, ME
132: Len Rue, Jr., Blairstown, NJ
139: Culver Pictures, Inc., New York, NY
142: Arthur Morris/BIRDS AS ART, Deltona, FL
146: Len Rue, Jr., Blairstown, NJ
152: Dick Hamilton/State of New Hampshire Tourism
154–155: William Johnson, Bristol, NH
156–157: Syd Nisbet, Tryon, NC
158, LEFT: Robert Villani, Merrick, NY
158, RIGHT: Paul Rezendes, South Royalston, MA
161: Bob Grant, Glen, NH

162: Leonard Lee Rue III, Blairstown, NJ
164: William Johnson, Bristol, NH
166: Portsmouth Public Library, Portsmouth, NH
172: Paul Rezendes, South Royalston, MA
175: William Johnson, Bristol, NH
177: Arthur Morris/BIRDS AS ART, Deltona, FL
181: The Smith College Museum of Art, Gift of Mr. and Mrs. Harold D. Hodgkinson
184: Phil Schermeister, San Francisco, CA
188: Culver Pictures, Inc., New York, NY
190–191: Robert Villani, Merrick, NY
192: Leonard Lee Rue III, Blairstown, NJ
193: Bates Littlehales, Arlington, VA
196: Morgan Hebard, Jr., Lincolnville, ME
204: Arthur Morris/BIRDS AS ART, Deltona, FL
206–207: John Wawrzonek, Southborough, MA
209, TOP (both); **BOTTOM LEFT:** John Shaw, Colorado Springs, CO
209: BOTTOM RIGHT: Paul Rezendes, South Royalston, MA
210: Robert Villani, Merrick, NY
212–213, 216–217: Phil Schermeister, San Francisco, CA
222: Kevin Shields, Camden, ME
223: Randy Ury, Portland, ME
226: Tom Vezo, Babylon, NY
227: Leonard Lee Rue III, Blairstown, NJ
229: Randy Ury, Portland, ME
230: Arthur Morris/BIRDS AS ART, Deltona, FL
233: Sterling and Francine Clark Art Institute, Williamstown, MA
234: Paul Rezendes, South Royalston, MA
237: Erich Hartmann/Magnum Photos, Inc., New York, NY
240: Thomas Mark Szelog, Thomaston, ME
249: Kevin Shields, Camden, ME
250–251: Bates Littlehales, Arlington, VA
254, LEFT: Arthur Morris/BIRDS AS ART, Deltona, FL
BACK COVER (COYOTE): Len Rue, Jr.; **(MAPLE TREE):** Len Jenshel; **(LOON):** Paul Rezendes